The Stolen Village

DES EKIN is Assistant Editor with the *Sunday World* in Ireland. As well as researching news analysis and feature articles, he writes a popular column that reaches almost a million readers every weekend. He was born in County Down, Northern Ireland, and spent a decade reporting on the Troubles in Belfast before moving to Dublin, where he now lives with his wife, son and two daughters. He is the author of *The Last Armada: Siege of 100 days: Kinsale 1601*, as well as two crime novels, *Stone Heart* and *Single Obsession*, all published by The O'Brien Press. *The Stolen Village* was shortlisted for the Argosy Irish Non-Fiction Book of the Year Award in 2007 and the Irish Book of the Decade Award in 2010.

The Stolen Village

BALTIMORE AND THE BARBARY PIRATES

Des Ekin

THE O'BRIEN PRESS
DUBLIN

This edition first published 2008 by The O'Brien Press Ltd.
First published 2006 by The O'Brien Press Ltd.
12 Terenure Road East, Rathgar, Dublin 6, Ireland.
Tel: +353 1 4923333; Fax: +353 1 4922777
E-mail: books@obrien.ie
Website: www.obrien.ie
Reprinted 2006 (twice), 2007, 2008 (twice), 2010, 2012, 2013, 2015.

ISBN: 978-1-84717-104-7

10 12 13 11
15 17 18 16

Printed and bound by CPI Group (UK) Ltd, Croydon, CR0 4YY
The paper used in this book is produced using pulp from
managed forests.

For James and Molly Ekin
– with gratitude

Acknowledgements

This book was a labour of love, and researching it was a joy from start to finish. I'd like to thank some of the kind and generous people who helped to make it so.

The staff of the National Library of Ireland, which became my second home for quite some time.

The long-suffering librarians at the Dublin City Council Library in Terenure, who never batted an eyelid when I asked them to track down rare books from all over Ireland and England.

Iris Bedford at Trinity College, Dublin, who gave me access to the university's library.

Particularly warm thanks to Muriel McCarthy, keeper of Archbishop Marsh's Library in Dublin, and her staff, who not only welcomed me into their unique and wondrous treasury of ancient books, but also shared their tea and biscuits with me (well away from the rare books, of course).

My gratitude also to Stuart Gould of the British Library in London and to Kirsty Brown of the UK National Archives in Kew, who each went beyond the call of duty to ensure that rare documents were waiting for me on my ridiculously ambitious one-day research trips from Dublin to London.

Robin Wiltshire, archivist with the Strafford Papers in the Sheffield Library Archives, procured a copy of a rare 1630 map of Baltimore.

Hugh Alexander of the National Archives helped me obtain the rare document recording the captives' arrival in Algiers.

I'm also indebted to Jona Bjorg Gudmundsdottir, archivist at the Westmann Islands Library, who went to enormous trouble to find me material in English relating to Morat's slave raid on the islands.

In Reykjavik, Anna Einarsdottir also offered invaluable suggestions to guide my researches into the Iceland raid.

Thanks to Frederic Messud of the website www.algerie.info.

Many of the key source books from Algiers were in old French. Thanks to Michael Keating for helping me to make sense of some of them.

In all these cases, any mistakes I may have made are my own.

Michael O'Brien and Ide ní Laoghaire of The O'Brien Press shared my enthusiasm for this project and channeled my obsession into something publishable. Emma Byrne's inspired graphic design evoked the flavour and atmosphere of the pirate era. Special thanks to editor Helen Carr for the perceptive insights and wise advice that shaped this book into its present form.

As always, I'd like to thank Colm MacGinty, Michael Brophy and my other real-job bosses at the *Sunday World*, who've consistently encouraged my writing in all its forms, and have generously helped each new project on its way.

Finally, heartfelt thanks to my family. Chris, Sarah and Gráinne were always an inspiration and often a practical help as well. And of course, my wife Sally who supported me, heartened me, offered valuable suggestions ... and never once complained when my spirit wandered off for hours on end, time-travelling to the 1600s to walk among the corsairs and captives in the colourful slave bagnios of old Algiers.

Contents

Preface

Shortly before daybreak on Monday 20 June 1631 a joint force consisting of 230 elite troops of the Turkish Ottoman Empire and pirates from the Barbary coast of North Africa stormed ashore at the little port of Baltimore, West Cork, and spirited almost all the villagers away to a life of slavery in Algiers. The victims were mostly women and children: altogether fifty youngsters 'even those in the cradle' were abducted, along with thirty-four women and nearly two dozen men.

Today the 'Sack of Baltimore' has been virtually forgotten by the world.

Yet it is extraordinary in all sorts of ways.

It would go down in history as the most devastating invasion ever carried out by the forces of the Islamist *jihad* on Britain or Ireland.

In an era when it was commonplace for white traders from England to land on the African coast and to seize black people as slaves, this was one of the comparatively rare occasions when the boot was on the other foot: a slaving mission from Africa landing on English-held territory and seizing *white* slaves.

The invasion was recognised at the time as an unprecedented act of aggression by the Islamist empire. It left King Charles I incandescent with rage and provoked him into a reaction extreme enough to help create a revolution in England.

Yet nothing about this crucial episode in history was quite what it seemed.

Baltimore may have been a remote harbour town in the southwest of Ireland, but its population was made up almost entirely of new English settlers from Cornwall, Somerset and Devon.

And although the attack was part of the endless *jihad* or holy war waged against the Christian nations of northern Europe, the man who led it was not some Turkish general from Constantinople, but a fanatical Dutch renegade with an agenda all of his own.

The story of the raid on Baltimore is a tale of plotting and intrigue, of conspiracy and betrayal, and it involves allegations of corruption in the highest ranks of the King's Navy.

And perhaps most fascinating of all is the theory that the raid may have not been a chance event, but a mission of revenge: a pre-planned act of ethnic cleansing aimed at removing the English newcomers and restoring the village to its original Irish owners.

I first heard about the Sack of Baltimore in the mid-1990s, on a Sunday afternoon radio programme. It was a mere mention in passing, a casual aside to the main topic under discussion. The reference left me intrigued and hungry for more information. But a quick skim through the bookshops and libraries failed to find any books about the invasion, and I was too busy preparing my first novel for publication to embark on any detailed research.

Years passed, but I could not forget the Baltimore episode. It stayed at the back of my mind, niggling me, constantly demanding my attention. Eventually I stopped resisting and decided to find out more.

A few weeks later I was sitting under the magnificent domed ceiling of the National Library of Ireland, feeling awestruck and decidedly uneasy. Placed on the desk in front of me was a stack of aged books and documents which, I'd been informed, were essential reading for anyone who wanted to understand the Baltimore saga. I flicked through them despondently. Some sections were in old Irish script. Others were in Latin.

My spirits slumped. What on earth was I doing here? I was a journalist by trade, not an academic and certainly not a professional historian.

But I persevered. Lifting another weighty tome, I gingerly turned the pages to a document headed *A List Of Baltimore People Who Were Carried Away By The Turk, The*

Within seconds, I was engrossed. At first glance, it was nothing special: just a dull catalogue of over a hundred names. But viewed in context, it transformed into a roll-call of personal tragedy on an almost unimaginable scale. Down through the centuries, every single line, every single name, cried out its own tale of heartbreak and loss.

A Mr William Gunter had been left devastated by the abduction of his wife and all seven sons. John Harris had lost his wife, his mother and three children. Robert Chimor – his wife and four children were torn away from him. Stephen Broadbrook had lost his pregnant wife Joane, his two children and, of course, his unborn third baby.

Entire families had vanished into the gaping maw of the Barbary slave machine: John Ryder and Tom Paine, each with his wife and two children; Corent Croffine with his wife, daughter and three male servants; Richard Lorye with his wife, his sister, and four children. Bessie Flood was captured along with her son; Bessie Peeter escaped, but lost her daughter.

Altogether a total of 107 slaves were stuffed into the hold of the pirate vessel and shipped off to Africa for sale like so many cattle.

The Baltimore List fascinated me. It showed me that these were not dry statistics from a history book. These had been living, breathing human beings – people with good and bad relationships and everyday anxieties, people with hopes and frustrated dreams. These were families very much like my own family. They were ordinary folk who'd been quietly getting by as best they could when, in the calm of a midsummer night, their lives had been shattered forever.

From that moment, I knew there could be no turning back.

I had to tell their story.

First of all, I want to make a hands-up, full disclosure about the limitations of this book. It is the true story of an entire village – well, almost an entire village – that disappeared. Only two or three Baltimore people ever made it home; the remaining survivors of the raid simply made the best of their lot and merged quietly into the fabric of their new African homeland. Some married and had children. Some prospered financially. They became used to life by the Mediterranean, and they seem to have had no great urge to return home, even when the opportunity was offered to them. I found this concept fascinating. However, it does send the narrative plunging off a cliff, stylistically speaking.

As a writer, I faced a dilemma. This is a true-life book. Nothing in it has been made up. I did not want to use fiction or novelisation to complete the Baltimore story.

However, as I carried on my research to greater and greater depths, I began to realise that there really wasn't a problem. The *individual* tales of these stolen villagers may be unknown, but that does not mean that their story is *unknowable*. I could still tell what happened to them without resorting to fiction. I could tell it through the parallel experiences of the other Irish, English and European captives who were sold as slaves in Barbary at around the same time. Through their written recollections, we can get an exceptionally accurate picture of what life must have been like for the Baltimore captives who ended up in the slave galleys, the harems, the souks and the chain gangs.

These accounts fill the gap in the Baltimore saga, but much more that that – their stories are fascinating in their own right. You will read about the enslaved clergyman Rev. Devereux Spratt, who turned down his chance of freedom to remain with his slave congregation in Algiers, and helped mastermind one of the most audacious escapes from Barbary under cover of his prayer meetings. You will read about Irish captive Richard Joyce, who picked up the design for his world-famous Claddagh ring while enslaved to a jeweller in Algiers. You will read about the American war hero James Cathcart from Westmeath in Ireland, who was reduced to stealing meat from the lions while working as a slave in the royal zoo of Algiers, but who rose through the ranks of slaves to become one of the highest ranking civil servants in Barbary. You will also read about another Irish slave who became so well-in with his slavemasters that he lived like a lord, ate like a prince and had slaves of his own.

But most of all, I hope, this is still the story of how the ordinary men, women and children of Baltimore adjusted to an extraordinary situation and forged new lives for themselves under the burning African sun.

They are the real heroes, and this book is dedicated to their memory.

D.E.

A note on the text:
I have modernised spellings for greater accessibility. Anything in quote marks is a faithful quotation from the source. Where I use quotation dashes, it signifies indirect speech: that is, an accurate reflection of what was said, but not a direct quote.

CHAPTER ONE

The Sack Of Baltimore

LIKE black sharks scything through the sea towards their prey, the boats of the Barbary corsairs moved soundlessly across the moonlit surface of Roaring Water Bay.

The oars of their stolen fishing smacks moved in and out in perfect time, the blades wrapped in caulking material to muffle even the smallest splash. It was two hours before dawn, and the element of surprise was crucial.

The corsairs landed on the shingle beach, taking care to prevent the wooden hulls scraping hollowly across the stones, and silently assembled along the shoreline.

Nearby, the villagers of Baltimore slept soundly and peacefully – unaware that a small guerrilla army of more than two hundred men was massing for attack just a few yards away from their homes.

They had no reason to be on the alert. The little

harbour town in the southwest of Co. Cork had been invaded before, a generation ago, but in that case the aggressors had been the Catholic troops of King Philip II of Spain. Peace had been made, and that particular threat had passed.

But these invaders were different.

They would have made a terrifying sight – the Barbary pirates, carrying muskets and iron bars to force open the doorways; and the bare-armed Turkish troops in their bright red waistcoats and plumed caps, armed to the teeth with guns and curved *yatagan* sabres.

These soldiers were the legendary Janissaries – a hand-picked elite, highly trained and skilled in the art of war.

Originally formed as a celibate order of religious warriors, they still retained a monkish, contemplative demeanour off the battlefield. But at full charge, their terrifying appearance and loud, crashing war music could strike fear into the toughest troops in Christendom.

'The famous Janissaries,' one western diplomat wrote home in awe, 'whose approach inspires terror everywhere.'

Tonight, however, their foes would mostly be defenceless mothers and children.

The attack had yet to begin, but the fate of Baltimore was already decided.

Morat Rais, alias Jan Jansen, alias Matthew Rice, alias

Captain John, was one of the most experienced pirate chieftains on the Barbary Coast. A veteran of daring raids on targets as far away as Iceland, he had honed his attack strategy to perfection.

His intelligence information was immaculate too. The corsair chieftain had been well briefed in advance, and had personally carried out a reconnaissance of the village earlier in the evening. He had already been shown the homes where the toughest villagers were likely to show most resistance.

His first objective was the lower part of town, an area known as The Cove, where twenty-six thatched cottages were arranged in three concentric arcs around the curve of the shoreline. The inhabitants were mostly fishing folk – seine-netters and workers who salted the fish at the processing works nearby.

At a nod from their captain, the 230 musketeers began to fan out along The Cove, dividing themselves into twenty-six attack squads: one for each homestead.

The villagers were extraordinarily unlucky. Even at this late stage, a warning would have enabled some of them to scramble out of their beds and dash for safety in the darkness of the surrounding woodland. All that was needed was one barking dog, one fisherman glancing out to check his boat moorings, one nursing mother hearing a footstep in the night. But Baltimore was lost in sleep, and no-one stirred.

The Janissaries took up their positions and drew their

weapons. Expert hands applied flame to twists of oiled rope-yarn and passed them around. As the torches flared into life, Morat gave the signal and all hell broke loose.

The people of Baltimore didn't have a chance. They woke up screaming as their flimsy doors smashed and splintered to pieces under syncopated, expert blows from the iron bars. The incendiaries were thrust into the thatched roofs of the homesteads. Flames leapt high into the June night. Within minutes, Baltimore was ablaze.

As the villagers poured out into the street, coughing, eyes streaming, they were confronted by attackers who seemed more like demons than men – the Janissaries screaming and slashing the air with their curved sabres; the Barbary pirates terrifying their Christian victims with the most vicious threats and obscenities they could think of. The tactics were mainly psychological. Like modern-day commandos storming a siege building, they were aiming for 'the two Cs': confusion in their victims and control for themselves. The razor-sharp *yatagans* rarely touched human flesh. Panic and terror were the real weapons here – the objective was to capture live, healthy slaves and keep casualties to a minimum.

But where they encountered resistance, the Janissaries were utterly ruthless. At one household, a villager called Timothy Curlew put up a brave fight. He was hacked to death on the spot, and his screaming widow was dragged into the street to take her place among the captives who were bound for the slave markets of Algiers.

A second man, John Davis, also made a bold but foolhardy attempt to fight off the invaders. Like Curlew, he was slaughtered instantly as a warning to others.

The nightmare went on and on. At another house, Stephen Broadbrook's heavily pregnant wife and two children were dragged out of bed and herded through the streets like cattle being driven to market.

No-one was spared, not even the elderly and frail. Three old folk were shoved into the stunned, disbelieving line of captives and shunted down to the beach like all the others. At the Gunter home, seven sons were stolen away.

The raid on The Cove was completed with ruthless efficiency. Within a short space of time, a hundred villagers – men, women, old folk, servants, toddlers – were being pushed and shoved down the dirt road towards the beach and manhandled on to the waiting boats.

Morat Rais made sure the first batch of captives was secured, then turned his attention towards the main village of Baltimore.

In his hillside home, William Harris stirred in his sleep. He had an advantage over his fellow villagers in Baltimore – noises from The Cove were hard to hear in the main part of town, but they would drift up clearly to Harris's eyrie.

Like most of the settlers in Baltimore, Harris would have planned to rise early, at around five or six in the morning. Right now, at just after two, he was in the deepest part of his sleep cycle. We don't know how long he lay there, slipping in and out of consciousness, until he realised that the faint shouts and screams drifting up from The Cove were real and not just a nightmare.

Harris jumped up from his bed and stared out into the night. He probably couldn't believe his eyes: flames were leaping high over the houses of The Cove, and the air was acrid with the smoke from the smouldering thatch.

Looking down the road towards the lower part of town, he could see the exotic red uniforms of the invaders. Harris must have blinked and rubbed his eyes at the sight of the turbans, the plumes, the baggy pants and the curved slippers. Incredible as it seemed, there could be no doubt about it – the soldiers were Turks.

William Harris grabbed his musket and fumbled in the darkness to prepare his powder. He was under no illusions about the gun's ability to fight off an army of Janissaries. But if the town were really facing attack, this could be the only warning system they had.

Down at The Cove, Morat Rais played it safe before moving on to the next phase of the attack. He didn't expect serious resistance, but, like every good general, he made a priority of safeguarding his retreat. Sixty of his musketeers – more than a quarter of his entire force – were stationed in ambush at a strategic high point along the path leading back to the beach. If everything went wrong, at least their escape route would be kept open.

Taking 120 to 140 men, he marched up the track to the main village of Baltimore. It wasn't much bigger than The Cove: there were around thirty houses laid out in rows in a neat square formation outside the walls of a sixteenth-century castle, and a further ten homes arranged in an 'L' shape inside the perimeter.

The raiders fanned out around the streets as before, but this time it was different. Forty houses were smashed open, but only ten captives were found. Something, or someone, had alerted the villagers to the danger. Furious, the pirates began ransacking the houses and looting anything of value.

Then Morat Rais heard something that made him stop short and call a halt to the attack. From the hillside above him, he could hear gunfire. Several musket shots were fired, and then the captain heard one of the most unnerving sounds in his world – the tattoo of a military drum.

Morat Rais paused to take stock of the situation. He had been assured that there was no military presence anywhere near the area – the nearest British soldier was in Kinsale, fifty-four miles away. But the pragmatic pirate chieftain had survived in this hazardous trade long enough to know that you never took anything for granted. If there really were soldiers on the hillside, they would have the advantage of altitude as well as familiarity with the territory. Morat assessed the risk, glanced around the deserted houses, and decided they weren't worth the gamble.

Shoving their ten dejected captives ahead of them, the pirates and Janissaries marched back down to the beach to conduct an organised withdrawal.

The Barbary captain had been fooled by one of the oldest tricks in the book. There was no army on the hillside above him: just a few pathetic escapees, dashing upward through the scrub and undergrowth, barely noticing the brambles tearing at their exposed flesh, or their bare toes stubbing on the sharp rocks. They were the lucky ones – at least they were free.

Nearby, William Harris loaded up his gun for another shot into the night sky. A neighbour, alerted by the quick-thinking Harris, stolidly continued to batter out a military tattoo on his drum. With his single musket and a few balls of shot, Harris had succeeded in turning back one of the most formidable fighting forces in the world.

Three days later, his achievement would be recognised with a mention in despatches to the Privy Council in London. But despite his resourceful actions, he had succeeded in saving only a small proportion of the villagers.

Backlit by the hellish orange glow of their blazing homes,

the captives must have felt like abandoning all hope as they were ferried out of their friendly harbour towards the silhouetted hulks of the pirate ships.

The corsairs had seized a pitiable cargo of victims: nearly four-fifths of their captives were women and children. They were forced into two stinking fishing boats that Morat Rais had captured earlier, and, in this almost Stygian atmosphere, there would have been a deafening cacophony of noise: children screaming for their fathers, wives crying for their husbands, old people praying hopelessly for a deliverance that would not come.

But as the journey continued and the panic subsided, there would have been a more muted sound – the eerie keening of dozens of voices whimpering in abject terror.

For nearly everyone in Christian Europe, the worst fate imaginable was to be captured by the Islamic pirates and sold into slavery on the Barbary Coast of North Africa. They had heard all the stories a dozen times: stories of hideously inventive tortures and scientifically concentrated beatings; stories of living deaths at the galley oars; stories of malicious random cruelties and horrific sexual assaults. All these images had been implanted in their heads and for many years had disturbed their sleep. Now, in an almost literal sense, they were living through their worst nightmares.

Nothing like this had ever happened before. In these parts, capture by Barbary slave traders had been a risk faced mainly by those at sea. Never before had such a concentrated force of Turkish troops and North African corsairs had the audacity to stage an actual *invasion* of the King's territory.

With this in mind, some of the captives would have whispered words of comfort to each other. The authorities would never allow this outrage to happen. And wasn't there a Royal Navy man of war – *The Fifth Whelp* – patrolling the coast and ready to pursue the pirates at a moment's notice?

If someone could have told them, as their blazing homes disappeared from view behind the headland, that a mixture of corruption and bungling would keep the Navy warship idle in harbour for several days, they wouldn't have believed it possible.

If they'd been told that 107 of them would be taken all the way to the notorious slave city of Algiers, and abandoned there for more than a decade by the indifferent authorities in London, they would have been thrown into the depths of despair.

However, it's safe to say that not one of those captives could ever have imagined the astonishing way in which their lives were to be changed under the crescent moon.

CHAPTER TWO

The Last Day

Baltimore, the previous morning

THE iron bells of Tullagh Parish Church rang out to herald Baltimore's last day of freedom. They rang out across the village, over the castle walls and the grand houses, and far beyond to the humble fishing cabins at The Cove. Each Sunday, these same bells summoned the people of Baltimore to prayer. Today, although they did not yet know it, more than a hundred parishioners would be hearing them for the very last time.

In her thatched cottage overlooking the beached fishing boats on the strand, mother-of-two Joane Broadbrook awoke to the shrieking of roosters and the impatient lowing of cows heavy with milk. As she emerged from the stupor of sleep, it must gradually have dawned on her that June 19 was no ordinary day. For a start, it was Sunday – and the Sabbath Day was always special in this God-fearing community. It was a day of rest: the only day in the week when they could down tools and relax with family and friends.

Secondly, it was almost Fair Day. Baltimore had the right to hold a village fair on 24 June, the following Friday, and for the entertainment-starved villagers this was a major occasion. The entire place would soon be *en fête*, with brightly-painted stalls and huckster stands, musicians and showmen turning the town into a riot of noise and colour. Like all the children in the village, Joane's own youngsters would already be in a fever of excitement and anticipation.

There was a third reason why 19 June was no ordinary day. It was nearly midsummer. Midsummer meant a lot to people like the Baltimore fishing folk, who lived their lives in harmony with the changing seasons. Despite the name, it actually signified the *start* of the real summer: two precious months of reasonably good weather when crops would ripen and days would be long and pleasant. On a typical June night, there might be only a few hours of true darkness, and this extra light was a wonderful gift to people whose winters were so long, bleak and gloomy.

There were deeper, more primitive reasons why midsummer was important. It was originally a pagan festival, which the church had rechristened the Feast of

St John. But many still believed in the old superstitions. On Midsummer Night, it was widely believed, the mischievous faeries and sprites of the woodlands would emerge from their hiding-places and play tricks on bumbling mortals. Heads would be turned by love or madness, milk cows turned dry, babes stolen away from their mothers.

But none of this would happen until later in the week. Today, on this peaceful June Sunday, they were safe from dark forces who might come in the middle of the night and steal away their children. They could relax.

Joane rose from the bed she shared with her husband Stephen and prepared to face the world. Perhaps her exit was more of a frantic dash for the door, for Joane was already 'great with child' (as the locals would have said) and she and Stephen were looking forward to the arrival of their third baby.

Throwing on their clothes, Joane and her sleepy, protesting children would have carried out the chores that every household needed to perform. Sunday or no Sunday, cows still needed to be milked and livestock had to be fed. Few people escaped these tasks, for most settler families had to augment their meagre income with a vegetable plot and a few farm animals.

All over The Cove, the same scenes were being played out. Not far away, in the Curlew household, Tim Curlew and his wife rose together, unaware that their happy life was to be shattered forever and that this would be the last dawn they would awaken in each other's arms. Before the morning sun would rise again, Tim would be dead – cut down by a Janissary scimitar – and Mrs Curlew would be dragged off to Africa as a widow as well as a slave.

Other couples yawned and stretched: the more affluent ones had beds, but poorer people and servants slept on straw mattresses on the floor. Fires were poked into life and pots put on the range. Although the houses at The Cove were simple one- or two-roomed cottages, it was a source of pride that each had a stone chimney. To the settlers in Ireland, this was what separated civilised people from barbarians.

Doors were flung open and dim, windowless cabins were flooded with the bright, fragile, liquid light of an early summer morning in the southwest of Ireland. The grass was damp with dew. The fresh, salty air was full of rich, organic odours, from the fishy stench of the processing plant and the tang of rotting seaweed, to the earthy smells of the goats and sheep.

Down at the strand, the fishing boats were bobbing happily at their moorings, the nets drying out on the shingle beach.

After milking the cows and raiding the henhouses for eggs, the villagers snatched a quick breakfast of bread, salted fish or porridge before getting ready for church.

At the house John Ryder shared with his wife and two children, Sunday morning scenes were taking place that would have been totally familiar to us today. The two parents would be frantically racing against time to get ready for service, squeezing their reluctant children into stiff and unfamiliar clothes, rummaging around desperately for missing hats or shoes, putting the final touches to the family dinner preparations before putting on their Sunday best.

Nearby at Dermot Meregey's home, the maidservant had her own reasons for anticipation and excitement as she performed her chores and prepared Dermot's two young children for church. It was almost midsummer, and that was the date when servants traditionally received their quarterly pay.

We know little about the Meregeys' maid. The archives don't even give her the dignity of a name, so for the purposes of this book I will call her Anna. She would have been a young girl in her teens or early twenties whose family had hired her out to domestic service out of necessity. Such servants were reunited with their families only a few times a year, and midsummer was one such occasion.

At Corent Croffine's house, there would have been the same electric sense of anticipation. Corent and his wife – who seemed to be unusually prosperous by the standards of the Baltimore settlers – employed three menservants who would have been savouring the imminent prospect of pay and time off.

Corent's grown-up daughter would also have been looking forward to the rituals and traditions of midsummer. On the shortest night, girls like Miss Croffine would gather with the boys of the village around bonfires that would burn late into the night. It was important to jump over the guttering fire at least once, to ensure good fortune and keep evil spirits at bay. Then the single girls would pick flowers and hide them under their pillows in the hope of dreaming about their future life partners. Perhaps it was just as well that these were just superstitions, for the last thing Miss Croffine would have expected to see was a North African husband wearing a bournous.

Who were all these people, and what were they doing in the remote Irish port of Baltimore? Let's start by dispelling three common misconceptions about them.

The first is that they were aggressive colonists, usurpers who had stolen the village from the local Irish by force or underhand means. There *were* many cases in which the English had grabbed Irish land at swordpoint, but this was not one of them. In fact, the settlers were there on a long-term lease, after paying a substantial rental to the local Gaelic chieftain. Legally and morally, they had every right to be there.

The second myth is that they were all recent arrivals – 'blow-ins', to use the Irish term – and as such had no permanent ties here. They had actually been there for nearly three decades and were well into their second generation. They had built homes, cleared stony land

and raised families. Most of the victims of the corsair raid were young parents and children who had never known any other home but Baltimore.

The third canard is that they were members of the English Protestant establishment, sent there to impose the State religion upon the area. (It has been claimed that they were kept in place by London because of their 'solid Anglican values'.) In fact, almost the opposite was the case. The Baltimore villagers would never have seen themselves as pillars of the Church establishment: they viewed themselves as radicals and dissenters. Far from being oppressors, the founders of this community saw themselves as the oppressed – as refugees who had come here to escape the stranglehold of State religion and to find freedom of worship.

The new Baltimore settlement had been created by a family of intellectual freethinkers whose fierce refusal to conform had made them a thorn in the side of the religious and political Establishment in England for generations.

Their patriarch, the Rev. Thomas Crooke (1545-1598), had been one of the leaders of a group of Protestant radicals who wanted to swap the rituals and vestments of high-church Anglicanism for the simpler worship of Calvinism. The precursors of today's Presbyterians, they wanted the Bible made open to everyone, and they wanted the elite hierarchy of bishops replaced by a structure in which 'every man is his own priest'.

The Elizabethans had regarded such ideas as subversive – after all, the Queen was the head of the Church, and so any attack on her bishops was an attack on her. Printers of offending documents were tortured and some extremists executed. The movement was forced underground.

The heartland of the radical movement was Crooke's birthplace of Northamptonshire. Here, seditious sermons were preached urging 'the multitude' to revolt. As a preacher at Gray's Inns in London, Crooke was an eminent theologian and a potential candidate for Archbishop of Canterbury. Yet secretly he was helping to coordinate the radical network. The full extent of his involvement became known only after his death.

The clergyman shrewdly installed his eldest son Thomas as a lawyer at Gray's Inns, putting yet another radical mole at the heart of the London Establishment.

There was no doubt but that the second generation of Crookes shared their father's egalitarian views. Crooke's second son, Samuel, also became a clergyman and had heated, defiant clashes with the Bishops over his refusal to wear the surplice.

The third son, Helkiah, was a prominent doctor and author of a shockingly frank medical textbook. As the first English physician to map the human anatomy, he outraged his superiors by including the sexual organs. Harassed all his days, Helkiah went on to fight a bitter battle with the authorities in a bid to reform the horrific conditions at the Bedlam lunatic asylum.

But it was the eldest son, Thomas Crooke junior, who made the greatest impact. Aged only twenty-eight at his father's death, he used his legacy to help establish a settlement in Ireland where he and his fellow Calvinist sympathisers could be free to worship as they saw fit. Although there was also a strong economic motive – none of the settlers had any objection to making a profit – almost every reference to the new settlement makes it clear that its primary motivation was religious.

His move was in keeping with the spirit of the age. In the same period, other freethinkers were emigrating to Holland and America to establish Puritan or Pilgrim settlements.

Crooke was aged only around thirty when he sailed into the Irish port and began negotiations with the impoverished Gaelic chieftain, Sir Fineen O'Driscoll, whose village had been almost deserted ever since it had been caught up in an unsuccessful Spanish invasion. The proposal was simple: fishermen from the English West Country would lease the port and use advanced Cornish processing techniques to turn it into a vital centre of food production.

The new King, James I, adopted a pragmatic attitude to settlements like Crooke's. However dangerous their ideas, these pioneers helped reinforce the English presence. Baltimore was granted full recognition with borough status and its own MPs. However, the settlers soon found that if they wanted practical help, they would have to look elsewhere. They were on their own.

Thomas Crooke's project got off to a shaky start. He was no saint – far from it – and there were repeated accusations that his settlers were collaborating with the pirates who frequented these remote ports. But a high-level hearing acquitted him of all wrongdoing and encouraged him to continue his work.

As the years progressed, his settlement succeeded beyond all expectations, encouraged by an Irish Anglican hierarchy that shared his Calvinist outlook. By 1624, Thomas was knighted in recognition of his achievement. But life was getting increasingly tough for the colonists. King James's successor, Charles I, was a solid high-church man who had no time for notions of equality. Meanwhile, back in Baltimore, the settlers were being harassed by Irish dissidents and challenged in court by a hostile local lawyer, Walter Coppinger, whose aim was to expel the English and take control of the port himself.

Caught between belligerent Irish resistance in Baltimore and chilly indifference to their plight in London, the settlers were facing the greatest-ever challenge to their survival when their inspirational leader Sir Thomas Crooke died in 1630 at the age of fifty-six.

His son Samuel inherited his father's problems along with his title. Together with his fellow leaders Thomas Bennett and Joseph Carter, he was still trying to steer the colony through this crisis when the Algerines arrived to make it all suddenly irrelevant.

We have no detailed record of that last Sunday morning, but from contemporary records we have a fairly accurate idea of what it must have been like.

Picture the scene. With the preparations over, the families step out of their homes and begin the walk to Tullagh, on the far side of Baltimore town. Everyone is there, for church attendance is not an option in the early 1600s: it is a legal requirement and a moral duty.

A sort of informal procession is formed: the women in bonnets and dresses, the men in tunics and breeches and stovepipe hats. The Broadbrooks, the Meregeys, the Croffines, Tom Payne and his wife and two children … all the well-known families of The Cove, some chatting sociably, others tight-lipped and serious, but all uniting in this walk to worship.

They pass the fish palace, which lies eerily calm and quiet on this Sunday morning. On any other day, this fish processing workshop would be a noisy crucible of bustle and industry. Workers like Tim Curlew and Corent Croffine would be chipping at salt blocks with pickaxes while others would be washing the preserving salt from last month's catch, engulfed in a blizzard of fish-scales that would settle on their clothes like snow.

This palace (the word means 'cellar') is the nerve centre of Baltimore's economy. Here, fresh pilchards are layered with salt in four-foot piles before being stuffed tightly into huge casks. A false lid, slightly smaller than the barrel mouth, is steadily forced down by a weight until it eventually squeezes out valuable oil for lamps. The salted fish is re-casked and shipped off as far as France, Italy and the New World.

The churchgoers continue their walk, thankful that today is not a working day. Many of the men would spend six wearisome days a week at the oars of the fishing boats – an exhausting routine of high speed chase in which they would try to outpace the flashing shoals of pilchards. The routine is complex. A highly-skilled supervisor known as a huer would stand on top of a hill, his hawk-like gaze fixed upon the water. Below in the bay, men would sit in rowing boats, patiently awaiting his signal. When the huer spotted a silver frisson of motion beneath the waves, he would use his entire body as a signalling device, throwing out his arms in exaggerated gestures, almost like a conductor directing an orchestra.

In response, the oars would dip into the water and dozens of arms would strain as they forced their reluctant craft into action. Fishermen like John Ryder and Tom Paine would feel their muscles scream and their backs ache as they fought to encircle the lightning-fast fish while paying out a net of tarred hemp. As the net formed an incomplete circle, helpers would sail into the only exit and splash the water with heavy bats, keeping the pilchards inside until the gap could be sealed.

At busy times, everyone would help in the processing work – women and children included. It is a filthy task, creating an overwhelming stench that visitors would describe as 'intolerable'.

Yet the womenfolk would tolerate it, knowing that their current prosperity is fragile. Those fish shoals, so plentiful today, could suddenly and inexplicably vanish for decades. So they must not complain, even though at times they must secretly yearn to live somewhere else – somewhere not so cold, somewhere not so damp, and somewhere that life does not revolve around cleaning fish.

From The Cove, they walk through a narrow gulley towards the main part of town. Passing the quays on her left, Joane Broadbrook encounters the walled castle of Dún na Séad – The Fort Of The Jewels. This is the most imposing building in the area, a squat and not particularly attractive tower house overlooking the bay. Dunashad Castle once rang to the piratical shouts and laughter of the Great O'Driscolls, the clan of sea rovers who once plundered passing ships; today its halls are silent and respectable.

Around the tower house Joane can see a high double wall, forming a fortified enclosure. Ten houses, their chimneys smoking pleasantly, line the inside of two of the walls. Outside the perimeter, rows of other houses have been built parallel to the castle boundary. There's a neat line of eight homes near the harbour, and another eight directly above the castle. At the highest point of the village, four substantial homes lie in another parallel row.

On the far side of the castle, a row of nine homes lies at right angles to the others, and a few others are dotted around randomly in sites dictated by the rough terrain.

Walking through the centre of town, Joane passes the shops and craftsmen's workshops. A market town like Baltimore would have been well equipped with a wide variety of stores. One contemporary document says that a typical fishing settlement provided employment to 'bakers, brewers, coopers, ship carpenters, smiths, netmakers, ropemakers, pulleymakers, and many other trades'.

As a Royal Borough since 1612, Baltimore has the right to make by-laws, try minor cases in a weekly court, and 'chasten delinquents'. And right in the centre of the castle yard Joane can see the harsh apparatus of justice: the pillory and the whipping post.

Tullagh is a traditional country church, solidly constructed from stone to withstand the battering of the Atlantic winds. It has a tall central steeple topped by a curious weathervane in the shape of an open-mouthed fish.

Joane shuffles in with all the others and takes a seat on one of the bare wooden pews. In a special pew near the front of the sparse, unadorned church sits the Sovereign Mayor of Baltimore, Joseph Carter, and the Crooke family, headed by Sir Samuel Crooke. Other prominent citizens take pride of place in church. There is Thomas Bennett, a member of the settler family who helped found Bandon town. There is William Gunter, described as a 'person of some credit [status]', with the family he loves – his wife and his seven young sons, their heads all in a row and rising in height like a staircase. The Gunters' fine attire and shiny shoes are in marked contrast to the coarse clothes and bare feet of the poorer folk at the back. Joane looks around the Church and nods to everyone she knows: Mrs Bessie Flood with her son; Mrs Bessie Peeter with her daughter; elderly Mrs Alice Heard; Mr and Mrs Evans with their son, cook, and maid; the seven-strong family of Richard Lorye; old Mr Haunkin.

All these people have come into Tullagh Church for the last time, to kneel on the rough wooden floor and pray for deliverance from evil.

CHAPTER THREE

Hunting For Humans

Algiers, some six weeks earlier

THE thunder of cannons echoed and rolled around the ancient walls of Algiers, from the gate of Bab-az-Zoun on the south of the city, all the way to the portal of Bab-el-Oued on the northwest. High on the hilltop, at the apex of the triangle that formed the citadel, the red-mouthed cannons of the Kasbah cracked their sharp salute, and down by the harbour the mighty long-range guns of the main fortress roared a deep-throated response.

Out in the sparkling turquoise bay of Algiers, Morat's two ships replied with a salute from their thirty-six guns of iron and bronze: one volley in honour of the Sultan of the Turkish Ottoman Empire, and one in honour of the Islamic patron saint who protected the city from all harm. One shot for Church, and one shot for State; one shot for God, and one shot for Mammon. It was a fitting summary of a mission that would unite big business and holy war in one highly satisfactory package.

Fired with excitement, crowds spilled out into the narrow streets and down to the waterfront. A corsair was embarking on a major slaving expedition – that in itself was always an occasion for celebration. But since the corsair in this case was the legendary Morat Rais, the entire city would have been determined to give him a particularly noisy and boisterous sendoff.

The noise was deafening. Citizens scrambled up the time-worn stone steps to the city walls to shout and wave as Morat's two ships hoisted sail. The cheers rose, quite literally, to the rooftops, where in hundreds of secluded roof-gardens, the city's cloistered womenfolk gave their traditional cheer – a curious high-pitched, birdlike whooping that would follow Morat's crew for miles out to sea.

Algiers in those days was a polyglot city. Its population of around 100,000 was a stew of different peoples, a multicoloured *tajin* featuring almost every country and culture under the sun. One contemporary observer recorded:

'Portuguese, Flemish, Scots, English, Danes, Irish, Hungarians, Slavs, Spanish, French, Italians; also Syrians, Egyptians, Japanese, Chinese, South

Americans, Ethiopians ... '

This mix would have been reflected in the crowds that thronged the dockside on that spring morning. There would have been Biskra water sellers in their colourful costumes, carrying massive copper tanks on their backs. Jewish brokers in their gowns and coloured shoes. Moorish craftsmen in their white burnous cloaks and embroidered caps. Wealthy Turkish merchants, twirling their luxuriant moustachios; jet-black porters from the Sahara, leading wheezing, overburdened donkeys.

Swaggering Janissary soldiers in their bright red uniforms and baggy pants. And the notorious European expatriates – renegadoes, as they were known – a mish-mash of rogues and outcasts from places as far apart as Seville and Moscow, Iceland and Italy.

Then there were the slaves. Out on The Mole – the massive breakwater of stones created to protect the vital deep-water dock from the wind and tide – the sweating captives may have paused from their backbreaking labour to sneak a glance at the spectacle before being whipped back to work by their overseers.

In the cool of the evening, families liked to stroll along this breakwater to enjoy the fresh sea air. They walked its 900 ft semi-circle without particularly caring that every single foot had cost the lives of more than four Christian slaves. Nearly four thousand had died in the construction process alone. And yes, they were still dying, regularly, as they toiled under the baking sun.

These slaves, dressed in their homemade linen shirts, their right legs shackled with heavy chain, would have seen Morat Rais's departing ships in an entirely different light. They realised that another generation of captives would soon be coming to the chain gang. But would the newcomers be coming to join them … or replace them?

We don't know the precise date Morat Rais set sail for Baltimore. It was probably in early May of 1631 and most likely on a Friday or a Sunday – traditionally considered the luckiest days to begin a mission. Such considerations were important. Before fixing a date, Morat would have spent hours huddled with the local *marabout* or holy man, sifting through books of auguries to ensure good fortune. And before they set foot on the ship, the crew would have sipped from a special fountain whose waters ensured a prosperous voyage.

The noisy sendoff from the citizens was part of the same ritual process – but it was also based on practical self-interest. Almost every free person in the city, from the ruling Pasha right down to the lowliest bath attendant, had a personal stake in the success of missions like this. Algiers in the 1630s was a city with very few resources: its main income, by far, came from the sale, ransom and forced labour of human beings. It was a machine that would grind to a halt without its fuel of human sweat and blood.

A lot of money would be riding on Morat's expedition.

Much of it would have been invested by the State, and much by Morat himself. But the investors would also have included wealthy merchants and syndicates of ordinary citizens. Each of them hoped that Morat would return with a prize ship or two, a rich haul of stolen cargo and hundreds of valuable captives.

With a bit of luck, these slaves would include rich people or aristocrats who could be relied upon to fetch a high ransom, and a high proportion of skilled workers who would sell at a premium on the slave market.

Ideally, Morat's haul would also include a sizeable batch of women. Not just any women, but the pale-skinned, fair-haired northern women who were highly prized as concubines.

The corsairs had no qualms about hunting down and capturing human beings. According to a reliable Spanish observer, Fray Diego de Haedo, they thought no more of it 'than if they went hunting hares or rabbits'.

Their tactics were simple. 'They very deliberately, even at noonday, or indeed just when they please, leap ashore and walk on without the least dread, and advance into the country, ten, twelve or fifteen leagues or more … and infinite numbers of souls – men, women, children and infants at the breast – [are] dragged away to a wretched captivity.'

As Morat's ships sailed out of the harbour – paying homage to the tomb of the patron saint who reputedly controlled the weather – the ship's company would pause and call out to heaven for a safe journey.

'*We leave you with God. May Allah give us good speed!*'

The walls of the city rocked as thousands of voices, representing dozens of countries and cultures, joined as one in the traditional response:

'*May Allah give you a good prize!*'

Two people watched with special interest as Morat's two ships adjusted their sails and shrouds, their crescent-moon flags fluttering green against the Mediterranean sky.

One was the Pasha, the nominal governor of the Regency Of Algiers. The other was Ali Bichnin, General of the Galleys and boss of the *Taifa Rais*, the Guild Of Corsair Captains.

Pasha Hussein was a remarkable survivor in a troubled age. He was currently enjoying his fourth three-year stint as ruler of Algiers – an extraordinary achievement in an era when rulers tended to be deposed or strangled at short notice – and had long since adjusted to the realities of his unusual situation. He enjoyed all the riches and respect due to a man who represented the mighty and powerful 'Sublime Porte', the Court of the Sultanate in Constantinople. But there – as Hussein well knew – the illusion ended. The city was not ruled by faraway Constantinople: it was ruled by the Janissary troops who protected it by land and the corsairs who protected it by sea.

This dated back to 1516 when, just as the Turks were about to lose Algiers to the Spanish, the desperate inhabitants called for help from the notorious Muslim corsair Khayr-al-Din Barbarossa. His pirates swooped in and saved the city for the grateful Sultan, who made him governor and sent out reinforcements of crack Janissary musketeers to act as a permanent garrison.

With each passing decade, the Janissary militia grew more powerful and more independent. It had its own ruling body known as The Hearth Of The Household (*ocak*) and a ruling council called the Divan. Together with the corsairs, who formed a *de facto* navy, they held the real power in a city that prospered on piracy.

Throughout the ensuing decades, the governors sent out from Constantinople were increasingly controlled by the Janissaries. From 1616 onwards, the Pasha was actually selected by the militia and only afterwards approved by the Sultan.

The *Taifa Rais* or captains' guild was a mirror image of the soldiers' council, the Divan. For the past ten years the head of this council had been a fabulously wealthy renegade from Venice.

Ali Bichnin's name was a translation of his Venetian surname, Piccino or Picenino. Like Morat himself, Ali was a genuine convert to the Faith. His successes at the *corso* – the trade of piracy – had provided Bichnin with two sumptuous palaces in town and a villa in the country. He owned at least sixty-five ships and his personal army of slaves numbered several thousand. Foreign delegates quickly realised that, if there were any single leader in Algiers in those confused days, it was Ali Bichnin.

As Ali watched Morat sail away, we can only speculate how much he knew about the true nature of this mission … how much *anyone* knew.

Was this just another routine trip? Or was there another agenda – a secret one, perhaps known only to Morat Rais himself?

Most voyages of this type were vague, opportunistic affairs. But this one may have been different. It may have been targeted against one particular country … perhaps even at one specific village.

Whatever the truth, we know that Morat's motives were complex. The pirate captain harboured a guilty secret which was bound to have influenced him on this voyage.

To find out what it was, we have to go back five years to another strife-torn country, and meet an English undercover agent who was about to have the most extraordinary date with destiny.

CHAPTER FOUR

The Spark And The Powderkeg

Morocco, 1626

FIVE years before these events took place, a bedraggled and bare-legged figure dragged himself wearily across the hills near Fez, his face burning and sweltering under the blast-furnace heat of the North African sun. He wore a tattered Arab robe, and at first glance could have passed for any poor pilgrim returning from Mecca. But despite his fatigue, his eyes were wary and mistrustful, alert to the constant threat of danger.

The pilgrim's name was John Harrison, and in fact he was an English agent, working undercover on a mission of the utmost delicacy and secrecy. England was at war with Spain, and Harrison was trekking across Morocco in a daring bid to acquire a toehold of English territory at a strategic point on the Atlantic coast.

The time was ripe. Morocco was in upheaval, with no universally recognised ruler. Harrison had his eye on one particular target: the city of Sallee, beside the present-day capital of Rabat. What made Sallee so tantalising was that it wasn't ruled by *any* government – at least, none in the conventional sense. Almost uniquely for the time, it was a democratic republic, financed by robbery and enslavement. Sallee was run by pirates.

This statelet was known grandly as The Republic Of Bou Regreg. Within its boundaries, a motley assortment of northern European renegades and international pirates operated in uneasy alliance with the Hornacheros and Andalusians, two groups of Moroccan exiles who'd been forcibly expelled from their homelands in southern Spain. Sallee was, according to one European observer:

' ... an habitation for villains, a den for thieves, a receptacle for pirates, a rendezvous for renegadoes ... and a miserable doleful dungeon for poor captive Christians.'

So when Harrison received a tip-off that some elements within Sallee wanted to pledge their loyalty to England, it was too tempting a prospect to resist.

'So to do Your Majesty's service,' he reported later, 'I undertook a most desperate journey by land from Tetuan to Sallee in a disguised Moorish habit.'

Harrison would have made a prime catch for the Spaniards, who'd offered a thousand ducats – a huge sum – to anyone who captured him. He'd served as English Sheriff in Bermuda before being appointed special envoy to Barbary. A former groom to Prince Henry (King Charles's late brother), he had close contact with the Royals and ready access to the King himself.

With the aid of two friendly sheikhs, the agent finally made it to Sallee. The exiled Moors welcomed him with open arms and introduced him to the pirates who held the real power.

At that stage, Sallee was ruled by a fourteen-strong council headed by an elected official who held the dual role of pirate admiral and president of the republic.

And so it came about that John Harrison, English agent, sat down to negotiate a pact with Morat Rais, the corsair chieftain of Sallee and the future destroyer of Baltimore.

Unlikely as it seems, the two men appear to have hit it off. They'd both been born in Northern Europe and raised as Protestants, but otherwise they were poles apart. Harrison loathed slavery on religious grounds and worked tirelessly to free as many slaves as he could. Between 1625 and 1630, no less than 260 captives were to be released from Barbary through his efforts.

Morat Rais, on the other hand, was burning with the zeal of the convert. Years beforehand, he had dropped the

Christianity of his childhood and wholeheartedly embraced the religion of Islam. He had become a sword of the *jihad*, the holy war, but he was much more than just a foot soldier in this never-ending cold war. Morat Rais was a tactical mastermind, a man who had reached new heights of evil inventiveness in a bid to bring the war to the very doorsteps of the enemies of his new faith. He was part of a new generation of corsairs who were ready to sail far out into the wild Atlantic, to England, to Newfoundland, and even to the icebound fastnesses of northern Scandinavia, to spread panic and terror among the infidel.

The two men would have despised each other in principle, but, curiously, they were bound by a mutual respect.

They were to meet on many occasions over the next four years. We can picture these two charismatic figures talking long into the night in some warm Moroccan courtyard, their voices occasionally raised against the trickle of a water fountain and the chirping of the cicadas as they sip sherbet and perhaps share a water-pipe. Morat Rais is probably 'seated in great pomp on a carpet, with silk cushions, the servants all around him' (as he's described on a later occasion).

We have no record of Morat's appearance, but we know he would have been in his late fifties, his hair possibly turning grey, his northern skin tanned to leather by a life spent at sea. He would have been wearing the standard attire of a prosperous merchant – a silk shirt under an embroidered waistcoat, baggy pants and iron-soled slippers.

We'll never know the details of their conversation, but one thing is clear. By the time their negotiations ended, Harrison had been totally won over.

Reporting to King Charles, he described Morat as 'a Dutch renegado, but a great friend to our nation.'

They were words that would later come back to haunt him.

The man who was to become Morat Rais was born in the Dutch city of Haarlem some time around 1570. His previous name was plain Jan Jansen. History records it in various versions – Jan Jansz, Jan Janse, Jan Janszoon – and, even more confusingly, he had a range of aliases including John Barber and Captain John.

Jan began his career legitimately as a privateer in the Dutch War of Liberation. He proved so expert at this trade that he began seeking out new opportunities on the Barbary Coast. Here, he was delighted to find a war that would never end and a privateering permit that would never expire. The three Barbary states of Tunis, Tripoli and Algiers formed the western front of the Islamic empire, and the triangular city of Algiers, where he was to settle for the next five or six years, was described as a bow pointed at the heart of Christendom.

Exactly how he got there is unclear. Morat himself maintained that the Spanish were holding him prisoner in Lanzarote when the Algerines captured the island and enslaved him. Another contemporary source has a slightly different take: it claims Morat had been 'a merchant in Lanzarote and was there made a slave by the Algiers men that took the island ... soon after his captivity, by renouncing his faith, he obtained freedom.'

The date of his capture is estimated at around 1613; other sources put it at 1618. Whatever the date, plain Jan Jansen was reinvented as Morat Rais – the word 'rais' meaning captain. The same name appears in various versions – Murad Reis, Matthias Rais, Morato Arraez, Morat Ariaz, and Matthew Rice.

Up until the arrival of Jansen and other expert Northern European seamen, the Barbary pirates had specialised in lightning raids in *xebecs* – open galleys rowed by slaves. Morat and his generation introduced larger sailing vessels capable of taking on the open Atlantic. Suddenly, the Barbary hunting grounds had expanded to embrace the entire known world.

Morat spent some time in Algiers as first mate to another renegado corsair, Suleiman Rais – an excellent teacher. When Suleiman died in 1619, Morat moved westward to Sallee, where his career really began to take off.

'In a short time, [Morat] grew in great esteem among them by the many prizes he took, that in time they made him Admiral of their fleet,' says the same contemporary source, 'which charge he held a long time, to their enriching and to the great detriment of Christian merchants.'

We're told that Moulay Ziden, the emperor of Morocco, 'honoured him with one of his women in marriage'. Some sources say she was actually the Emperor's daughter. It didn't seem to bother Morat Rais that his alter ego, Jan Jansen, already had a wife and children back home in Haarlem.

In fact, there were at least three women in Morat's life. The most significant, from a historical point of view, was the lover he never married – a Moorish concubine he'd taken at some stage in the early 1600s. Her name in Dutch was Margrietje, and she gave Morat two fine sons of mixed race. Both Anthony, who was born in 1607, and Abraham, born in 1608, were to emigrate to America, where Anthony Jansen Van Salee went on to become one of the most prominent and controversial citizens of Manhattan and the unlikely patriarch of some of America's most blue-blooded families.

In the strangely advanced society of Sallee, where the most able leaders were chosen by democratic vote, the charismatic Morat Rais rose rapidly to the top. He also became very rich. As admiral, he received a cut of all the profits of the harbour.

Yet he seems to have been a man who bored easily. He refused to give up the pirate life, even though he no longer had any need to do the dirty work personally. In

1622, he travelled north in search of booty and sailed audaciously into the Dutch port of Veere. The Dutch authorities were furious – after all, Morat had spent the past five years raiding their ships. But the United Provinces had just signed a treaty with Morocco, and nobody could risk endangering it.

As Morat cheekily loaded up with provisions from the same merchants he'd been terrorising, a rather pathetic incident took place. His Dutch wife came on board with all her children and begged her runaway husband to come back home. What she thought of her Jan in all his Moroccan finery has never been recorded; nor whether the corsair ever came clean and admitted that he had two other women in Africa. But her tears were wasted, and the poor woman was left to lead her fatherless brood back to their bleak home in Haarlem, as the pirate admiral sailed back to his new home in the sun.

Harrison quickly wrapped up his negotiations with the Spanish Moors. The situation was simple – he wanted the English slaves, and they wanted English guns. It was time to sail back to London with the good news.

There was only one ship available in Sallee, a small and leaky Flemish man o'war. Harrison had her victualled for five months and set off.

The seas around Morocco were infested with enemy ships. But Harrison was not entirely alone. His escort through these troubled waters was to be Morat Rais himself, commanding three warships 'to waft me off the coast for fear of Spaniards.'

But, disastrously, he lost Morat's escort in the darkness. Then, about a week later, alone and unprotected, he ran into three aggressive Spanish vessels.

The Spaniards fired a volley of shots, but Harrison's leaky tub proved surprisingly fast. 'We trusted to our sails,' he said, 'and after they had shot at us, gave us chase, but we were to windward and sailed better.'

The agent was literally running for his life. But suddenly, the incredible happened. The Spaniards turned tail and fled. Harrison, bewildered, sent a lookout to the top of the mainmast and found out why – there were five mysterious ships on the horizon sailing to his rescue.

His benefactor was none other than Morat Rais. The pirate admiral had seized two ships from Hamburg, and their captured crews – including a handful of English sailors – were on their way back to Sallee.

Morat produced the five miserable Englishmen and delivered a goodwill gesture that was to leave a deep and lasting impression on Harrison.

'He released [them] and gave [them] freely to me,' Harrison reported warmly, 'as he hath ever done Englishmen, never doing hurt to any, but good to many.'

Back in England, Harrison's mission was recognised as a

huge success. King Charles himself wrote to Sallee praising Harrison's work and adding: 'Out of respect to us, you have set at liberty many of our subjects, for which we give you thanks.'

Throughout all this, Harrison seems to have deliberately closed his mind to the less desirable activities of his new friend Morat. He saw only Morat the charmer, the diplomat and the Anglophile. And indeed, the shrewd Dutchman had a silken tongue and the ability to be all things to all men. Cultured and intelligent, he had been responsible for negotiating a delicate treaty which gave France favoured status in Sallee. At around the same time, he wrote letters to Holland promising 'to respect and honour my fatherland as long as I draw breath'. And when he professed to Harrison his undying love for England, he was no doubt continuing this diplomatic chameleon act.

In 1630, Morat saved Harrison's life a second time. The English agent's ship was in the harbour at Sallee when a hijacked Spanish warship manned by drunken mutineers sailed right into port and opened fire, killing one of his officers. Harrison fled for the protection of the castle, and the Sallee guns roared back at the invaders.

At that stage Morat Rais appeared on the scene. In an impressive display of courage, he went straight on board the maverick ship and used all his powers of diplomacy to persuade the mutineers to stop shooting.

'In this fight, our master's mate was slain, his head shot

off,' Harrison recorded pragmatically. 'No other hurt done.'

It was later that same year – 1630 – that Morat Rais dropped his bombshell: an astonishing proposal to Harrison that was to change the situation completely.

Morocco was on tenterhooks. The atmosphere was tense; people were jumpy and nervous. Around that time, reported Harrison, 'a strange prognostication' took place. An unfamiliar dog, pure white in colour, appeared on the streets of Sallee. The animal was savage, biting several locals on their legs, but for some reason it fawned on the English. Many of the Moors interpreted this as a sign that they should turn away from their Islamic faith. It was in this highly-charged atmosphere that Morat Rais took Harrison aside and made an offer calculated to make the agent's jaw drop with surprise.

The pirate admiral of Sallee, the hero of the *jihad*, wanted to defect.

—I want you to procure me leave from His Majesty to come and live in England, he told Harrison.

—When?

—I am prepared to go at the first opportunity, Morat said. At least, as soon as I can set out to sea again and capture a good prize from the Spanish or Portuguese.

The corsair admiral must have read Harrison's thoughts.

—I am still a Christian at heart, Morat whispered to the astonished agent. In my younger years of infirmity, I was forced to convert at Algiers. First I was taken prisoner by the Spanish at Lanzarote. Then, when the Turks took the island, I was made their slave. Afterwards, I was compelled to turn to their religion.

Just in case Harrison was in any doubt, he pledged solemnly: 'I would adventure my life to His Majesty's service.'

It is possible that Morat was lying – but by no means certain. Several leading corsairs had sought amnesties from Christian nations. Morat would have been familiar with the case of Henry Mainwaring, an English corsair who had organised a pardon and then enjoyed a comfortable career as an anti-piratical consultant.

The agent, for his part, would have been delighted with this offer. Solemn promises would have been made, commitments entered into. It would have been taken for granted that a man of Morat's stature could not live in England without some sort of suitable position or reward. There was even provision for this sort of event. A previous Lord Deputy of Ireland had recently tried to entice Dutch corsairs to defect and form an elite coastguard fleet.

But soon afterwards, things started to fall apart. The war between England and Spain had ended, and there was a mounting constitutional crisis at home. An alliance with Sallee was no longer a priority. Whatever promises had been made, whatever commitments given to Morat on that heady day in Sallee ... they were all vanishing before Harrison's eyes, like the desert mirages he would have encountered on his trek across Morocco.

Harrison, by now a man obsessed, began paying for his own trips to Sallee. He suffered the final ignominy when he had to take legal action in a bid to get his basic salary.

And what of Morat Rais? There's no record of his reaction to all this. But he had probably realised long ago that he was being betrayed – not directly by his friend John Harrison, but by the double-dealing diplomats in London.

Instead of settling in England, Morat sailed back to his old corsair stomping ground in Algiers. He returned as a force at the peak of his power – a man burning with fury and bristling for action.

It's not hard to guess his state of mind. He had been taken for a fool. Worse, he had even offered to renounce his Islamic faith.

Morat Rais had seldom needed an excuse to attack any Christian nation. But he *could* choose his targets, and it's safe to assume that he had no love whatever for the English.

He would come to English territory, as he'd promised. But it would be on *his* terms, not on theirs.

For less than one year later, Morat would exact a terrible revenge on the King of England by leading the forces of the *jihad* in the greatest Islamist invasion of the royal realm: the Sack Of Baltimore.

Baltimore lies to the extreme south of Ireland – almost as far south as it's possible to go on the mainland. In this part of the country, dry land seems to dissolve into ocean in a slow fade-out: ragged peninsulas gradually turn into islands, outcrops and, finally, lines of jagged, semi-submerged rocks. The random scatterings of land that lie off the ancient barony of Carbery are romantically known as 'Carbery's hundred isles'. At Baltimore, the mainland doesn't end in a full stop, but in a three-dot ellipsis, like an unfinished sentence: Sherkin Island, the island of Cape Clear, and the Fastnet Rock.

The area lies right in the path of one of Europe's most notoriously unpredictable storm zones. If the warm winds carried up by the Gulf Stream collide head-on with an icy blast from the Arctic, the results can be spectacular. But if a storm howls in diagonally from the southeast, the sea reacts in sheer fury – and it becomes all too clear how Roaring Water Bay got its name.

'With hoarse rebuff the swelling seas rebound,' Jonathan Swift wrote in *Carbery Rocks*. 'Not louder sound could shake the guilty world.'

When a storm is roaring like the mighty judgment of God, desperate men will sell their souls for a sheltered port. And Baltimore enjoys the most blessed spot of all. It sits at the mouth of the Ilen River with its back protected by hills. In front of it, Sherkin Island forms an ideal breakwater. From the mainland, a peninsula curves gently outward to embrace a natural sea-haven.

When the Elizabethan general George Carew came here, he found an almost perfect harbour:

' ... a pool about half a league over, where infinite numbers of ships may ride, having small tides, deep water and a good place to careen ships.'

In such a remote area, smuggling has always created a major headache for the authorities. In would come fine wines and brandies, silks and spices, tobacco and salt. Out would go wool, linen, leather goods ... and the occasional fugitive fleeing the hangman's noose.

It was a profitable business, and no-one took more advantage of this trade than the Great O'Driscoll clan. They were a powerful mafia, one of three major sea-roving families who operated a racket of piracy, smuggling and extortion around the Irish coastline. The name still dominates the district: the joke is that you can't throw a stone without hitting an O'Driscoll, and in view of their fierce temperament it wouldn't be the wisest thing to do.

At the height of their power, the O'Driscolls ruled a territory stretching all the way from Kinsale to Kenmare. The Norman invaders squeezed them out of their ancient lands and into a much smaller territory around Baltimore. Here they threw up a ring of strong coastal fortresses –The Fort Of Ships on Sherkin, The Fort Of Gold on Cape Clear, and The Fort Of Jewels in Baltimore.

In its early days, Baltimore ('town of the big house')

was more commonly known as *Dún na Séad*, the Fortress Of Jewels. The reason for this beautiful name has been lost in history. Perhaps it was a romantic description of its setting. Or maybe it was meant literally – there are many tales of buried treasure in these parts. Either way, there is a local superstition that the very name of *Dún na Séad* was responsible for Baltimore's spectacular run of bad luck.

A local writer, J. E. O'Mahony, referred to this myth in 1887: 'The superstitious,' he wrote, 'think that this seductive appellation led to the desperate onslaught that inflicted upon it such dire and prolonged misery.'

Their secure base at Baltimore left the O'Driscolls untouchable for centuries until the merchants of Waterford, outraged over a particularly heartless act of trickery that had robbed them of a cargo of fine wine, struck back with a scorched-earth offensive that razed their two main castles to the ground.

Over the next few decades – this was the mid-1500s – an uneasy peace developed between the two towns, although the ancient grudge continued to fester. The fortresses were rebuilt and new ships were constructed. Like some crusty old salt recovering from a bloody tavern brawl, Baltimore was back on its feet and back in business.

The O'Driscolls elected a new clan leader, a shrewd and intelligent individual who they believed would protect them against future incursions and possibly lead them back to their former glory. In the event, his notorious double dealing was to divide his people and leave Baltimore weak and vulnerable to the pirate invasion. His name was Fineen O'Driscoll ... or, as history would come to know him, Fineen the Rover.

If the O'Driscolls were among the wildest of Irish sea rovers, Fineen was the most celebrated freebooter of all. He would pass into popular myth as the hero of a swashbuckling ballad that begins with a toast (*sláinte*) to his memory:

> *Then, sláinte to Fineen the Rover*
> *Fineen O'Driscoll the free*
> *Tall as the mast of his galleys*
> *And wild as the might of the sea.*

And, indeed, he would have made a striking figure as he stood on a hillside overlooking Roaring Water Bay, his long hair blowing across his face in the fresh Atlantic breeze as he accepted the symbolic white rod, which 'for time out of mind' had marked the transfer of power to the new chieftain. He would have been wearing the traditional apparel of his race: loose brogues of untanned leather, woollen trews, a saffron-coloured *leine*, or shirt, and over it all, billowing in the wind, the distinctive Celtic *brat*, or cloak, fastened across his breast with an antique clasp of bronze or gold.

In this ceremony, Fineen solemnly pledged to protect

his people and to renounce the leadership when asked to do so. Under the *tanistry* laws that shaped Gaelic society, the land and castles were not owned by any one man – the chieftain would merely hold them in trust on behalf of his people.

On that day in 1573, the O'Driscolls had every reason to feast and make merry to honour their new leader. No-one could have foretold that, within the next few decades, their entire world would fall apart, the structure of Gaelic society would be reduced to rubble, and Fineen would become the last Great O'Driscoll chieftain to hold sway over Baltimore.

A new threat was facing the clan. English land-grabbers were moving into the southwest of Ireland and taking over huge tracts of territory, either at gunpoint or with the aid of dodgy legal deeds.

Fineen was a shrewd diplomat and a master of the art of *realpolitik*. He looked at what was happening around him and concluded that collaboration was the only way to survive. Power, English style, was better than no power at all.

As soon as he became chieftain, he asked the English to let him surrender his Gaelic title and have it re-granted to him as a conventional knighthood.

Soon he was on his way to London for a personal audience with the Queen. Elizabeth had always had a predilection for wild privateers and adventurers, and we can easily imagine this tall, weather-beaten sea rover charming the Royal Court with his swashbuckling tales of battle and stolen treasure. He seems to have won a lasting place in the Queen's affections. By the time he returned home, he was *Sir* Fineen O'Driscoll, a knight of the realm and an English landowner like all the rest.

As for the members of his clan ... suddenly, they had no rights at all.

Conor O'Driscoll, Fineen's eldest son and heir, was furious. It was 1601 and the entire country was ablaze with rebellion. Not just some minor skirmish in a hayfield, but a genuine war of independence that had a realistic chance of success. The Gaelic general Hugh O'Neill had risen in revolt in an attempt to oust the English once and for all. He'd met the enemy on the battlefield and had actually defeated them. Now they were marching southwards to Cork to link up with an invasion force from Spain.

It was the moment every rebel had dreamed of, the moment when they could almost taste the sweetness of victory. Baltimore's fortified harbour was crucial to the invasion – it had been described as 'the King of Spain's bridge into England'.

And yet ... his own father was refusing to join the rising. While many of the other chieftains were sharpening their swords in anticipation of battle, the old man was remaining stubbornly loyal to the Crown.

Conor couldn't understand it. He'd always hated the

English and everything they stood for. Throughout his life he had been forced to endure the anger and taunts of his fellow clansmen when Fineen had entered into agreements with the *Sassenach* invaders.

He must have shuddered with humiliation when he recalled how his father had begged the Queen to let him hand over the ancient rights of his clan:

'Fineen O'Driscoll. The suit to surrender all his possessions to the Queen and to hold them by such tenure as shall seem good to her ...'

Now Conor was an active insurgent and one of the key figures in the southern revolt – even the great English general Sir George Carew singled him out for mention as 'a malicious rebel'.

In September 1601, four thousand Spanish troops under Don Juan del Aguila sailed into Cork and despatched a division to take Baltimore castle.

We have no details of the shouted arguments that echoed through the rafters of the Great Hall of the O'Driscolls on those tense autumn nights. All we know is that, in the end, the old man was 'overruled by his son'. At the eleventh hour, after decades of support for English rule, Sir Fineen chose to change sides and offer support to the Spanish invasion.

It was the wrong call. The invasion proved a fiasco. The ensuing battle was an ignominious rout. The Spanish sailed home and, after holding out for as long as he could, Conor O'Driscoll escaped to Spain to plead for further help. Back home, it took all of Fineen's diplomatic skills to bribe and inveigle his way back into the Queen's good books.

Fineen escaped with a Royal Pardon, but the entire business had left him penniless. And when a syndicate of English colonists offered to take out a long lease on Baltimore harbour in order to create a fish processing works, he nearly broke their arms in his haste to sign the deed.

Fineen the Rover had died. Word spread around the coastline of Roaring Water Bay like the whisperings of the sea-grass in the windswept estuary where he had spent his last lonely days. There was a legend that Lough Hyne was haunted by restless spirits whose whispers could be heard in the ceaseless rustle of the grass and trees. If so, there would only have been one sibilant message on that fateful day in 1630: 'The O'Driscoll is dead. The O'Driscoll is dead.'

Fineen had been a giant of a man whose extraordinary career had spanned nearly six decades and had marked the passing of an era. He had been, in turns, a sea rover, a Gaelic warlord, an English knight, and a reluctant rebel. He had taken up arms against Queen Elizabeth … and then charmed the Virgin Queen into letting him keep his head when all around him were losing theirs.

As his life faded away in his ancient island fortress of Cloghan, everyone knew the great age of the Gaelic lords had faded with him.

There had been a seismic power shift, and things would never be the same again.

When the news reached moneylender Sir Walter Coppinger, he did not think of it as the passing of the era of the Gael or the dawning of a new age for the English colonists. He saw it as a business opportunity.

Coppinger was a brilliant but unscrupulous lawyer, and he wanted the town of Baltimore. He wanted it so badly that for the past three decades he had tried every means at his disposal, legal and illegal, to get his hands on the deeds.

Like some patient spider, he had spun a dense legal web around Baltimore – an agreement here, a mortgage there, a rental from someone else – until the right of title to the town had become tied down by a complex network of threads, nearly all of them leading back to Coppinger.

First he had allied himself with disaffected elements of the O'Driscoll clan. Then he'd moved in on the clan chieftain. Fineen, who'd been destitute at that stage, had mortgaged part of the town to Coppinger in return for money he knew he'd never be able to repay. In doing so, the ageing Fineen had ignored the rights of the English fisherfolk who'd settled there on long-term rental.

Coppinger was a proud Cork City Catholic who had been fined for recusancy (that is, for refusing to attend Protestant services). He had no love for the English Protestant settlers and wanted to oust them from the district by fair means or foul.

He'd organised a localised guerrilla war of intimidation and violence against them. But under the charismatic leadership of Thomas Crooke, the newcomers had proved tougher and more resilient than he could ever have imagined. Coppinger responded by tightening his legal web. He began to claim outright ownership of Baltimore and ordered the settlers to leave.

In 1629, a court had given a mixed ruling on the dispute. Yes, Coppinger had a strong legal case. But no, he could not simply evict the English fisherfolk – they'd put too much work into building their homes and improving the village over the years.

A quarter century of scheming had all been in vain. Baltimore was Coppinger's for the taking – but it was useless to him so long as it was occupied by the settlers.

But if they could somehow be made to disappear, the Fort Of The Jewels would be his.

Under the blistering heat of the Spanish sun, the exiled rebels of the O'Driscoll family heard of the old man's death with mixed emotions of grief and release. Grief for the loss of a patriarch; release from the repugnant promises and dirty deals with which the old man had sold out his clan to the English.

Fineen's son Conor had proved a hero of the 1601 rebellion – one of the last to admit defeat after the rising was soundly defeated at Kinsale. As the Spanish turned tail and fled in humiliation, Conor had continued to hold out against the English at Kilcoe Castle, just a few miles away. He never surrendered: he kept up the fight until he was finally forced to abandon all hope and flee.

Kilcoe Castle (centuries later to become the home of actor Jeremy Irons) held out until 1603, when it was the last fortress to fall.

As the English armies swept through the area wreaking vengeance with fire and sword, Conor became one of their most wanted fugitives. They were so incensed when he slipped through their fingers that they reported a rumour – perhaps started by Conor himself – that the 'malicious rebel' had gone down with a Spanish ship that was sunk by the Navy in 1602.

But they were wrong. On 7 July that year, the Green Pimpernel had managed to slip safely out of Ireland through the Kerry port of Ardea, together with his wife and their nine-year-old son, Conor Óg – Sir Fineen's grandson and the second in line to succeed him as chieftain of a territory that had been lost forever.

Conor O'Driscoll became a captain in the Spanish army, but he had never totally given up his personal war against the English. Throughout the first quarter of the century, Fineen's heir was constantly hatching plans for new invasions and battle campaigns that would oust the Saxon invaders, revive the old Gaelic order, and allow him to accept the ancient white rod as lord of the Great O'Driscolls. In 1617, for instance, fifteen years after his exile, he is recorded as still 'engaged in plots' against the hated *Sassenach*.

He was not alone. General Hugh O'Neill, the leader of the last great Gaelic rebellion, was in exile in Rome, and right up until his death in 1616, he'd continued to devise plots that would allow him to return to Ireland at the head of an overwhelming invasion force.

It was not to be. By 1630, it would have become obvious to the O'Driscoll exiles that the Spanish would never invade Ireland again. If the dissident members of the clan wanted to reclaim their ancient home of Baltimore, they could not count on help from other armies.

Other *conventional* armies, that is.

CHAPTER FIVE

The Warrior Monks

I N the 1600s, a mariner sailing away from the coast of Africa would see the great city of Algiers recede in the distance 'looking from afar like a big vessel, all under sail'.

This was a remarkable city in unremarkable surroundings: a triangular iceberg of pure white glittering against the sunblasted North African coastline. Built on the face of a steep hill, protected by giant walls and fronted by a formidable harbour, the city shone dazzling white in the Mediterranean sun. It was a comforting spectacle for friendly ships, but a daunting sight for even the most determined enemy.

Soon Morat had left this 'well-guarded city' well behind him and was negotiating the hazardous passage through the Straits of Gibraltar. Leaving the Mediterranean was a significant symbolic act for a corsair, and – like all Barbary pirates – Morat would have paused to conduct an important religious ceremony.

A seventeenth-century English slave named Joseph Pitts actually witnessed one of these Straits rituals. Pitts, who was serving as a soldier on a corsair vessel, watched the crew make a bundle of small wax candles and cast them into the sea. Next they emptied a pot of oil upon the waves. 'When this is done,' Pitts wrote, 'they all together hold up their hands, begging the Marabout's blessing and a prosperous voyage.'

The rite continued with the slaughter of a sheep. One portion of entrails was cast over the port side and the other to starboard.

Finally, the corsairs wrapped a small sum of money in linen cloth and affixed it to the mast, with an oil lamp to make it glow through the darkness of the night watch.

When the ritual had ended, Morat turned his prow to the north and west. And as he entered the wild and unpredictable Atlantic Ocean, he may have paused for a moment to remember all the pioneering corsairs who had made this same epic journey before him.

Morat was just the latest in a series of remarkable men who had cast off their ties of nationality and religion in a quest for independence, money, power or, in some cases, as an early form of radical protest against the injustices of their age.

Captain John Smith, of Pocahontas fame, had once sailed as a privateer in Morocco. He summed up the early renegado corsairs in two concise sentences:

'*[John] Ward, a poor English sailor, and [Simon] Danser, a Dutchman, made Morocco their marts, when the Moors scarce knew how to sail a ship … [Peter] Easton got so much as made himself a Marquis in Savoy; and Ward lived like a Bashaw in Barbary.*'

It was the Old Dancer, the Devil Captain, who made it all possible. Without the Dutchman Simon Danser, the corsairs might have remained forever as Mediterranean galley rats; they might never have sailed out from Barbary into the wild Atlantic to bring the Islamic *jihad* to the very doorsteps of the Christian nations of the north.

When he taught them how to sail European-style 'round ships', it was a decisive moment in history – equivalent, in its own way, to the moment the first horses were introduced to the Plains Indians of America. The corsairs took a giant leap of evolution. Within a generation, they had built up a navy that could rival any European nation.

Other corsairs followed. Peter Easton, the Somerset farm labourer who terrorised the seas around southern Ireland with his armada of forty corsair ships, amassed a £2 million fortune and ended his days as Marquis of Savoy. Sir Francis Verney was an English nobleman whose career as an Islamic corsair ended when he was captured by a Christian ship and chained to a galley oar. Sir Henry Mainwaring, an Oxford don who sailed as a Barbary pirate, later defected and returned home to become a respectable statesman.

But perhaps the most feared of all the renegado admirals was Issouf Rais, who was born in Kent as plain John Ward. A Navy deserter, he set up his own corsair fleet in Tunis and considered himself 'the sole and only commander of the seas'. When the possibility of a royal pardon arose, he replied scornfully that the King of England would soon be begging for *his* pardon instead.

By 1609, he had amassed 'incredible wealth' and lived in a sumptuous palace of marble and alabaster.

John Ward died peacefully in Tunis in 1623. His career could be summed up in a verse from a popular ballad written to celebrate an extraordinary life:

Go tell the King of England
Go tell him this from me
If he reign king of all the land
I will reign king at sea.

These 'princes of the sea' had transformed the Barbary states into a formidable naval power. By 1623, Algiers alone had a corsair fleet of seventy-five fighting ships and one hundred other craft. In 1634, a visiting priest counted eighty ships. Combined with other corsair capitals, they had amassed a navy equal to anything England or Holland could put up at the time.

What type of ships did Morat sail? The official English account of the Baltimore raid gives only a minimal description. It reads:

'... Captain Matthew Rice [Morat Rais], a Dutch renegado, in a ship of 300 tons, 24 pieces of ordnance, and 200 men, and another ship of 100 tons, 80 men, and 12 iron pieces ...'

At three hundred tons, Morat's flagship wasn't particularly big. She would most likely have been a captured prize vessel, and had probably been made in Holland. Corsairs preferred the Dutch *flyboat* – long, low and sleek, with a shallow draught that gave them access to tricky ports. Morat's corsort, or second ship, was a mere hundred tons.

With twelve cannons bristling from the gunports on either side of his flagship and another half-dozen iron guns on each side of the consort, the Dutch renegado had enough firepower to see off most naval patrols. He also had the edge on speed. Corsair vessels were polished with tallow until they streaked through the sea like sharks – which, in a sense, they were. At the height of a chase, they knew how to tune for maximum speed: everything was securely fastened and the entire crew had to 'sit stock still' to ensure stability.

But ships and guns were only part of the story. Morat's main comfort came from the knowledge that he carried with him the most fearsome, professional and disciplined fighting force in the world – the Janissaries.

Below deck, the Janissaries would be doing what soldiers always do when they set off on a mission – laughing, joking, kidding around as they stowed their gear. The raw recruits – veterans called them 'bulls', or 'rookies' – would be joshed about how they'd perform in a real battle.

Picture them, in the cramped and dampish area between decks. They're wearing baggy cotton trousers, shirts, sleeveless waistcoats and red caftans. Their red turbans sit aside on their sleeping mats. Around their waist is a long red scarf, folded into a belt to hold some of their weapons. Their iron-heeled shoes clunk heavily as they pace across the wooden decking.

Each soldier has been armed with a musket and pistols, but the distinctive Janissary weapon is the *yatagan* – a short, deadly blade shaped in an exotic double curve.

Maybe some of the veterans are sorting and trimming their arrows. The Janissaries continued to use the Turkish bow right up until the 1700s. If one of the greenhorns, the bulls, had the temerity to make a joke about it, the vets would reply that they could fire thirty arrows while a musketeer was reloading.

There might be a bit of friendly rivalry between the various platoons – the *odjak* – whose numbers ranged from twenty to thirty men. These soldiers were overseen by the *chaouch*, or sergeant, and their overall commander was the *agha-bachi*, or captain.

The troops always enjoyed corsair duty – it gave them a chance to earn real money. Even the lowest grunt, the *yoldach*, would get a fixed share of any prize. If he hit lucky he'd get more in a single day than he could hope to earn in a lifetime's career. And if he didn't? No matter – he would still draw a respectable salary of £20 a year, plus the perks of life assurance, a shopping discount and a paid sabbatical.

Above all, in Algerine society even the lowliest *yoldach* was king. Powerful men would scurry out of his way in the narrow streets, for no-one dare touch a Janissary, on pain of death.

Originally, the Janissaries were celibate – a holy order of monkish warriors. But they were now permitted to marry, and the children they fathered with North African women had created a new class of citizen – *koulouglis* – who were becoming steadily more numerous and influential in Algiers.

The Janissary militia had started life in Constantinople as a kind of foreign legion whose members were trained from childhood. The idea was that their lack of local ties would make them personally loyal to the Turkish emperor. But while it was still nominally under the control of Constantinople, it had grown in size and power until its officers could regularly challenge the emperor's authority. By the 1600s, according to one French diplomat, there were 16,000 to 22,000 militia troops in Algiers and the province was 'entirely in the hands of the officers of the [Janissary] Militia' with the Sultan forced to tolerate the situation.

The Janissaries felt they had every reason to be elitist. They were the result of an extraordinary selection process – the 'tribute of children', which was levied by the Sultan upon the Christian populations he'd defeated. In the late 1400s a grand vizier had advised the emperor: '[L]et them choose the fairest and strongest of the Christian boys to become your soldiers.'

And so it came to be. Torn from their distressed parents, these youngsters were raised in the religion of Islam. The very best were chosen as warriors and subjected to years of rigorous training in which they were:

'... accustomed to privation of food, drink and comfortable clothing, and to hard labour. They are exercised in shooting with the bow and arquebus ...

'[T]hey are placed in cloister-like barracks ... Here not only the younger continue to obey the elders in silence and submission, but all are governed with such strictness that no one is permitted to spend the night abroad ...'

A Fleming diplomat, Ogier Ghiselin de Busbecq, wrote a vivid description of the Janissaries:

'The dress of these men consists of a robe reaching down to the ankles, while, to cover their heads, they employ a cowl which, by their account, was originally a cloak sleeve, part of which contains the head, while the remainder hangs down and flaps against the neck ...

'[T]hey would stand respectfully with their arms

crossed, and their eyes bent on the ground, looking more like monks than warriors ... if I had not been told beforehand that they were Janissaries, I should, without hesitation, have taken them for members of some order of Turkish monks ...Yet these are the famous Janissaries, whose approach inspires terror everywhere.'

De Busbecq was awestruck by the stoicism of the corps. He praised their 'readiness to endure hardships, union, order, discipline, thrift and watchfulness ... what a contrast to our men!'

As Morat's crack troopers settled in for their long journey north, they may have recalled their original mission statement, as voiced by a celebrated *dervish* during their first passing-out ceremony more than a century beforehand.

Ceremonially stretching the sleeve of his gown over the head of the leading soldier, the dervish had intoned:

'Let them be called *Yeni-Ceri* [new-style soldiers]. May their countenances be ever bright; their hand victorious; their swords keen; may their spear always hang over the heads of their enemies; and wheresoever they go, may they return with a white face.'

Morat knew he could trust the Janissaries. But could he trust the renegados who sailed with him?

As he stood on the deck that day, he may have anxiously scanned the faces of the European turncoats who formed the core of his crew. Algiers was full of enemy agents. Any one of his men could have cut a deal to betray him.

What the corsair captain did not know was that his mission had already been compromised.

The authorities in London had already received a secret letter warning them that the corsairs were on their way. It even specified the precise area that the Algerines were about to attack.

The letter was written by an English earl who was in every way a match for Morat Rais in shrewdness, cunning and in ruthless ambition. And he was determined, by any means, to stop him.

CHAPTER SIX

The Wind Dog

Baltimore, early 1631

EVEN on the calmest day, seamen in Baltimore are careful to look out for the wind dog. The wind dog means trouble, especially when the surface of Roaring Water Bay is as flat as a slab of polished grey marble. Before they set out from harbour, they'll check the horizon. If they see a shimmering mirage, a sort of half rainbow floating slightly over the sea, they know the wind is already rising and that it'll soon develop into a stiff breeze. So a skipper will always check for that telltale half rainbow, a phenomenon known locally as the wind dog. It is a warning, and, like all warnings, you ignore it at your peril.

The Great Earl's pen scratched urgently across the parchment.

Richard Boyle, Great Earl Of Cork and joint administrator of Ireland, had just received a reliable intelligence report that the Islamist forces of the Turkish empire were about to launch a huge invasion through one of the ports of south-western Ireland and was passing on the alert to his friend Lord Dorchester, the Secretary Of State in London. 'Such nests,' Boyle warned colourfully, 'should not be left unguarded for Turks to lay eggs in.'

It was February 19, 1631 in the new calendar – that is, four months before the raid on Baltimore – and Boyle had just written one of the most eerily prophetic documents of all time.

Although he turned out to be wrong about the specific targets (he mentioned the two obvious ones, Cork and Kinsale) he was right about the timing and the general area. His intelligence was spot-on.

It was access to crucial information like this which had propelled Richard Boyle from obscurity as a humble legal clerk to his present elevated position. At the age of sixty-four, he owned half of the south-western province of Munster, and he had recently achieved the ultimate in political power when he was appointed as one of the two ruling Lord Justices of Ireland.

Boyle himself was a prime target for pirates. He even knew the price that the corsairs had placed upon his own head: £4,200, or £390,000 in today's money. Just two years beforehand he had been sailing to England with his wife and two daughters when a heavily-armed pirate ship had given chase. The family had narrowly avoided capture, but a second vessel containing their servants was captured and enslaved. After that close call, Boyle had planted highly-placed spies in the pirates' camp. The move paid off: only a few months earlier, he had received word of a corsair plot to kidnap his son and future son-in-law as they sailed from Wales. The earl despatched a sailboat manned by a single expert mariner who was able to warn his relatives with only hours to spare.

Now the Earl had received another tip-off – and he was convinced that a small harbour town in West Cork could hold the key to protecting the entire coastline.

Boyle was so convinced of this port's strategic value that he had a special map drawn up. '[Y]our Lordship may observe,' he wrote to Dorchester, 'how the town and harbour lyeth, and how narrow the entry of the harbour mouth is, and how easily and fit it is to be fortified and secured ... for I have received new intelligence that the Turks are preparing to land infest those maritime ports of Munster ...'. Dorchester's failure to act on the warning, and to fortify this harbour, effectively sealed the fate of 107 innocent people.

For, by a cruel irony of history, the harbour Boyle had selected to *save* the nation from Islamist invasion was Baltimore.

CHAPTER SEVEN

'All Was Terror
And Dismay'

Atlantic Ocean, early June 1631

SOMEWHERE between Gibraltar and the British Isles, Morat seized his first prize ship, and the raw bulls among his Janissary troops had their first taste of action.

The admiral spotted a French vessel – just one of hundreds of merchantmen who plied these waters – and moved in for the kill.

From contemporary accounts of similar attacks, we can build up a reasonably accurate picture of what happened that day. The predators would have kept a low profile, waiting for a suitable victim to sail past. 'A little before day, they take in all their sails and lie a-hull until they can make out what ships are about them,' explained the reformed corsair Henry Mainwaring.

A typical tactic, he said, was to convince the victim that the corsair ship was just another plodding merchantman. The corsairs would drag empty casks to slow themselves and would often fly a false flag.

An English merchant who wrote his memoirs under the initials of 'T.S.' told in 1670 how two mystery ships began tailing his vessel. 'We became jealous of their intentions and to prepare for our defence,' T.S. wrote, 'The guns were charged and everyone had his place appointed to him. We were caught between hope and fear.'

The pursuers displayed a friendly French flag, but T.S.'s captain stuck to his course. As the two sleek craft closed in, they revealed the 'bloody colours' of Algerine corsairs. The victims tried to flee, but were overtaken and enslaved.

In 1793, an American sailor named John Foss spotted a vessel flying an English flag. The deck was empty but for one man in English clothing. But suddenly:

'[W]e heard a most terrible shouting, clapping of hands, huzza-ing, et cetera, and saw a great number of men rise with their heads above the gunwhale, dressed in the Turkish habit ... about 100 of the pirates jumped on board, all armed, some with scimitars and pistols, others with pikes, spears, lances [and] knives.'

Morat would have remained wary and vigilant as he closed in on his French prey. He knew only too well that two could play at the false flag game.

Only five years beforehand, Morat had been on a routine expedition off the coast of Holland when his fleet of three ships had chanced upon an easy target: a Dutch merchantman with only a few men on deck. Fifty of Morat's men swarmed on board to take her over.

Then it happened, right out of the blue. The Dutch flag disappeared from the mast and was replaced by Spanish colours. Dozens of armed troops sprang out of their hideouts and leaped into action.

Too late, the truth dawned on the corsairs. They had fallen into a trap: suckered by rival privateers who'd used the same tired old trick Morat himself had used so many times in the past.

The Barbary men didn't have a chance. Before long the decks were littered with their dead and wounded. Morat lost one of his three ships and barely managed to escape with the other two. They became separated in atrocious weather conditions. One fled for safety into the Maas River and the other retreated to Amsterdam port.

It was the dead of winter and bitterly cold, but not nearly as cold as the welcome they received from the Dutch authorities. The former Jan Jansen was seeking help from the very nation he'd betrayed. Armed soldiers, unmoved by the cries of the wounded and dying, patrolled the quays to ensure no-one left the ship.

The memory of that dreadful winter still haunted Morat Rais. All around him, his men were dying, and he was not permitted even to dispose of their bodies. Instead, he had to hack holes in the ice of the river and push the corpses through. Of the three proud ships Morat had taken to Europe, only one managed to limp home to Africa.

In capturing this French ship, Morat may have used an alternative tactic. It was common for corsairs to close in on their victims by hailing them and entering into 'friendly discourse'.

In 1681 an Englishman named Francis Brooks was sailing past Tangier when a passing ship hailed and asked their port of origin. 'We said from Marseilles. We enquired the same of her, who answered, from Algiers. So he bid our master hoist out his boat.'

This was a typical pirate ploy: rather than risk boarding a ship, the pirates would instruct the ship's officers to row across to *them*.

Brooks's master refused point blank, and the corsairs attacked. '[T]hey entered aboard us all at once, firing their pistols, and cut and wounded us with their cutlasses.'

The English slave Joseph Pitts has left a vivid account of a typical attack in the 1600s. Pitts, from Exeter, was only fourteen when Dutch renegade corsairs targeted his ship.

His captain calculated that the faster pirate vessel would overtake them within two hours, so he simply hauled up sail and waited.

As the corsairs drew near, Pitts was terrified to see a band of 'monstrous, ravening creatures' come into view.

Pitts recalled: 'The very first words they spoke and the first things they did, was beating us with ropes, saying, "Into the boat, you English dogs!"'

A young Flemish soldier named Emanuel d'Aranda was on board an English ship in 1640 when three suspect vessels closed in. When one of the corsair sailors stood up on deck and dramatically unfolded the green crescent of Algiers, d'Aranda knew his days as a free man were numbered.

'A company of ten or twelve Turkish soldiers, eager to pillage and plunder, stormed on board under the command of a captain, who was the first to set foot on our ship,' recalled d'Aranda. 'He was English by birth, but a renegade, and asked me – since I stood on the deck at the time – what nationality I was, and whether I was a merchant.

'I replied, I am a Dunkirker and a soldier by profession. Upon which he replied in Flemish: "Patience, brother, it is the fortune of war; today for you, and tomorrow for me."'

A Tuscan poet, Filippo Pananti, memorably described the panic that swept through his vessel when it encountered Algerine corsairs near Sardinia.

'All was terror and dismay,' he recalled later. 'It seemed to petrify every person ... some were for destroying themselves on board; others proposed jumping into the sea.'

This initial panic was followed by a doom-laden fatalism. 'A deep and mournful silence' descended as sailors and passengers stood listlessly around the deck awaiting their fate. In despair, the master actually began steering *towards* the Algerines.

Pananti was later to learn that this behaviour had convinced the superstitious corsairs that they were destined to be slaves. 'Seeing [us] approach rather than get away, they thought us enchanted ... dragged along by the dark spirit of our inevitable ruin'.

Several agonising hours passed. 'On the barbarians getting near us, we could easily distinguish their horrid yells; and innumerable turbans soon appeared along their decks. It was now that the last ray of hope abandoned the least terrified amongst us.'

The corsairs closed in:

'The shouts of the barbarians are heard close to us. They appear on deck in swarms, with haggard looks, and naked scimitars, prepared for boarding.'

'*No pauro! No pauro!*' shouted the corsair troops. 'Don't be afraid.'

Waving their *yatagans* menacingly, they ferried half their prisoners across to the pirate flagship, where a human passageway opened up between the cheering ranks of captors.

Running this gauntlet could be a painful experience, since it was tradition for each pirate crewman to pinch and pull at every captive in turn, thus claiming a stake in his value.

When this ordeal was over, the prisoners were searched for valuables. Some were literally shaken down: held upside down and shaken until everything fell out.

(One French aristocrat achieved fame by swallowing twenty heavy gold coins to conceal them from the corsairs. He got them back later.)

Next, the corsairs would demand their prisoners' clothes and shoes. Some were re-issued with threadbare garments that crawled with lice. Others, like John Foss, were left in their underwear.

At that stage, Morat Rais would have ordered the new slaves to be brought to his quarters for inspection.

'As we entered the cabin we saw the commander of the pirates, sitting on a mat on the cabin floor,' Foss recalled.

'[He] asked us many questions concerning the vessel, and cargo, and the places of our nativity …

'He then informed us that … we were his prisoners and must immediately experience the most abject slavery on our arrival in Algiers.'

The rais told them to get to work on deck. 'We told him we had no clothes,' Foss wrote. '[H]e answered in very abusive words that … he would teach us to work naked, and ordered us immediately to our duty.'

The corsair captain who enslaved Filippo Pananti treated his prisoners with slightly more decorum. 'We were interrogated in brief and haughty terms,' he wrote, 'but neither insult nor rudeness was offered.'

With elaborate politeness, the *Rais* asked them for their money and valuables and stored them separately in a small box.

'This is for you, and this is for you,' the Rais promised solemnly.

However, the cynical poet was not taken in. '*This is for you, this is for you* … but perhaps in his heart: *All this is for me!*'

Meanwhile, the corsairs were pillaging the captured vessel.

'[They] broke open all the trunks and chests,' Foss recalled, '…and plundered all our bedding, clothing, books, charts, quadrants and every movable article.'

The haul was piled on deck for an instant auction. 'All is brought to the mainmast and sold,' states an official English report of 1675, 'and the money is kept and joined to the rest.'

Having stripped their prize vessel, the pirates had to decide whether she was worth keeping. In this case, the answer was no.

And so Morat Rais pulled the plug on his captured vessel and continued his voyage, leaving the steel grey

Atlantic waters to close over the French ship as though she had never existed.

CHAPTER EIGHT

Desperate Men,
Shameless Women

Kinsale, County Cork, June 1631

As Morat Rais sailed ever closer to his target, only one force stood in his way: the English Navy. But in June 1631, the two naval officers responsible for protecting the villagers of Baltimore were in no position to help anyone. They were already at war ... with each other.

As the commander of the naval gunship *The Fifth Whelp*, Captain Francis Hooke was supposed to patrol the coast for pirates. However, throughout that fateful spring he was locked in bitter contention with the Admiral of the King's Ships in Ireland, Sir Thomas Button.

Hooke was stewing with frustration. Ever since his arrival at Kinsale in April, he had been living from hand to mouth. Warrants for supplies arrived sporadically, if at all. The proud captain had been reduced to wheedling for goods on credit and was now in a classic debt trap. New supply-notes went to pay off old debts – and the crew remained hungry.

They were a sorry bunch even at the best of times. Hooke glanced contemptuously at his motley crew of drunks and cutthroats. Even the ship's master was intoxicated so regularly that he was 'a disgrace to the ship'. The sixty crewmen had not been paid for eight months and were in no mood to fight anyone except themselves and their army counterparts on shore. The drummer, Richard Tanner, and fourteen of his cronies had killed an army lieutenant during a vicious brawl at Ballyhack. But although convicted of murder, they had been allowed to remain on duty. 'We cannot diminish the crew by so much,' was the pragmatic explanation of the Lords Justices.

Life in the Navy had never been easy. Many of the men had been been press-ganged into service and their pay was miserably low – half as much as a merchant sailor's. One eyewitness reported that a Naval patrol on the Irish coast consisted of a hundred men who looked like 'ragged beggars' and shared fewer than forty shirts.

Hooke was required to put to sea for several weeks at a time. But as he later explained to the Admiralty:

'Since the fourth of May, [my] crew have only been provisioned for a fortnight when they plied out to sea, but are … forced to come in again for want of supplies. They live from hand to mouth [while] the Turks are committing depredations, sinking French and English ships and taking crews captive.'

It was a ludicrous situation, made even more frustrating by the fact that no expense had been spared on constructing *The Fifth Whelp* a mere three years ago. The Duke of Buckingham had invested £7,000 on a fleet of ten sophisticated warships – *The Lion's Whelps* – which were designed to equal the pirates in speed and firepower.

Even in port, *The Fifth Whelp* would have made an impressive sight: a fast, lightweight three-master with square-rigged sails and a series of 32 foot oars ('sweeps') modelled on the oars of a pirate galley. A ship of the sixth rank, she was 75 feet long overall, displaced 186 tons, and could carry a crew of seventy men. Originally designed to carry ten cannons, *The Fifth Whelp* was now fitted with fourteen, ranging from brass sakers firing 6lb shot to giant culverins firing 18lb. However, the weight of the four additional guns had seriously affected her sailing ability. When the *Whelp* had taken part in the siege of La Rochelle, even more guns had been added and the 'lion' had sailed like a pig. The extra cannon had to be confined, uselessly, in the hold.

The *Whelps* were not lucky ships. None would survive for very long. The previous October, *The Seventh Whelp* had met a sudden and inglorious end when a dim-witted crewman had inspected the gunpowder hold while holding a naked candle. In the resultant explosion, sixty men died.

And now this debacle.

Hooke was convinced he was the victim of official corruption, and his anger was to spill out in a series of letters to the Admiralty.

He told how Button had made a deal with a corrupt meat wholesaler and supplied *TheFifth Whelp* with rancid meat that stank to high heaven. The starving crewmen ate it anyway and spent days retching with food poisoning.

'[Hooke] complains again of Sir Thomas Button's corruption,' said one official report. 'Sir Thomas spent the money given to him by the Government, and left the butcher and the baker unpaid.'

Unfortunately for Francis Hooke, the man he was accusing of corruption was a war veteran, an intrepid arctic explorer, and a national hero. Sir Thomas Button, then aged around fifty-six, had enjoyed a long and glorious military career. Born in Glamorgan, he'd joined the Navy in his mid-teens and had served in the epic Siege of Kinsale.

His bravery was legendary. On one occasion, he had

taunted an enemy by rowing a tiny boat back and forward under heavy fire, purely to encourage his men. He had also been commended for courage under fire during an attack on Algiers. (Button had been vice-admiral of the English invasion fleet, and if his mission to capture Algiers had succeeded, there would have been no raid on Baltimore.)

As an explorer, he had joined Henry Hudson on his quest to find the Northwest Passage. Later, Button had discovered the western shore of Hudson Bay (which for a brief period was named 'Button Bay'). In 1614 he was made admiral of the fleet in Ireland with instructions to subdue the pirate menace.

He'd been in the job for seventeen years now, and succeeded so well that it was difficult to conceive the scale of the problem he'd faced at the beginning. During the first two decades of the 1600s these waters had been plagued by pirate commanders – mostly renegade Dutchmen and Englishmen – who had organised themselves into a formidable seaborne empire known as the 'confederacy of the sea'. They sailed in vast armadas and regarded themselves, not as criminals, but as admirals and even princes. For instance, one of the pirate leaders, a Captain Jennings, appeared in Ireland with a fleet of eleven ships and 1,000 men, and was expecting another ten ships which would almost double his force. Four other captains – Blomley, Thompson, Saxbridge and Bonyton – held the entire south coast of Ireland in terror. At one stage they had 'robbed a hundred fishing ships, and sent them empty home'.

Even the President of Munster, Lord Danvers, had been trapped in a pirate blockade of Cork and candidly admitted he was too afraid to venture out to sea. The furious Danvers reported that the pirates 'would not leave the gates of hell unripped open in the hopes of gain.'

Algerine corsair admiral Peter Easton was a frequent visitor to the area around Baltimore, as were John Ward from Tunis and his 'admiral' Richard Bishop from Sallee.

Bishop set up a northern base just across the bay from Baltimore at the rocky and treacherous harbour of Leamcon. At one point the pirate fleet in Leamcon alone consisted of nine ships with 250 guns and four hundred men. Many had wives and children in the district. The local vicar was a pirate collaborator and on Sherkin Island, pirates even served as jurors.

The corsairs were protected by Sir William Hull, the leader of the Leamcon settlement, who rose to the position of Vice-Admiral of Munster even though he was described by his own superiors as 'an encourager and countenancer of pirates'.

Hull was particularly friendly with Claes Campian, a Dutch corsair admiral who regularly pillaged ships returning from the East Indies. At one stage, the goods from one of Campian's prize ships were sold off at Leamcon. The inventory included pepper; wax; a hundred Barbary hides; camphor; fourteen rolls of tobacco; bed coverings; and 'three elephant's teeth'. Another pirate ship was recorded as unloading 'hides, iron, earthen dishes, black-coloured woods ... gilt leather, silk, velvet, tobacco ...' and (once again) the puzzlingly ubiquitous elephant's teeth.

At the height of the crisis, in 1611, the English authorities stated bluntly that the pirates who plagued their ships had two main bases: Barbary and the Irish west coast. Barbary was beyond redemption, but 'there is no reason why the latter, being part of His Majesty's Kingdom, should not be kept free from such unjustifiable correspondence.'

All sorts of desperate proposals were considered to deal with the pirate plague. Some extremists wanted all the local ports razed and the islands cleared of their populations.

On the other extreme, there were plans to buy off the outlaws with estates in America.

In 1624, one Lord Deputy of Ireland came up with a plan to turn the Algerine corsairs into a semi-official naval unit employed to quell uprisings in Ireland. '[B]eing birds of prey that have ever been trained up in rapine, an excellent use will be made of their forces and abilities,' Sir Henry Cary wrote coldly.

Cary was convinced it would appeal particularly to 'the Dutch pirates' in Barbary, and appears to have actually contacted them with the offer. Although he probably had Claes Campian in mind, Cary may have also offered the amnesty to another leading Dutch corsair – Jan Jansen, alias Morat Rais. It is intriguing to speculate whether this prompted Morat's subsequent offer to defect.

And how had Baltimore been affected by all these piratical shenanigans? Profoundly, it turns out.

In stark contrast to the Baltimore of 1631 – a hive of legitimate industry – the Baltimore of the early 1600s was a rollicking, raffish pirates' den. It had always been a centre of local freebooting under the O'Driscolls, but this was different. Southwest Ireland became a magnet for huge numbers of English pirates who'd been pushed out of their homeland when James I announced a crackdown on privateering.

Since piracy had never been made illegal in Ireland, the footloose freebooters of Devon and Cornwall began to hang around Roaring Water Bay, like Hell's Angels at a holiday resort. The area became increasingly lawless and disreputable. Between 1603 and the early 1620s, towns like Leamcon and Baltimore were every bit as wild as Port Royal or Tortuga Bay were in their heyday: risky to live in and downright dangerous to visit.

Criminals, whores, fencers and kidnappers hung around seedy 'alehouses' where many an innocent man could fall asleep in the arms of a friendly girl and, somehow, wake up next day on board a pirate ship far from home.

This was the fate of one Roger Notting, a London poulterer. He came to Baltimore in 1609 to visit a relative, but fell in with some friendly seamen and was invited on board their ship. Plied with liquor, the unfortunate Notting woke up next morning to see, through hangover-ridden eyes, the coast of County Cork receding far into the distance.

In 1610, King James was warned of the 'continual relief that pirates have received from time to time in western parts of this Province, in Baltimore, Inisherkin [Sherkin Island] and divers other ports ...'

It was reported to the King that 'desperate and dishonest men' had come to the area to work hand in glove with the pirates.

They'd quickly been joined by 'shameless and adulterous women', to the great annoyance of the law-abiding citizens who constantly complained of 'drunkenness, whoredom and brawls'.

Prostitutes came to the area from all over the British Isles. The ex-pirate Henry Mainwaring, reported that there was 'a good store of English, Scottish and Irish wenches' who were strong attractors for 'the common sort'.

A document of 1607 tells how the crew of one pirate captain, Richard Robinson, offloaded a huge cargo of exotic spices in Baltimore, and then blew all the money 'in a most riotous manner'. Another report complained that English money was rarely seen in the region – the only acceptable currencies were pieces of eight and

Barbary ducats!

A Spanish ship rumoured to have £6,000 worth of gold was captured by pirates and beached at Baltimore. When the Spanish complained, Lord Danvers hotly denied that the coast he controlled had become 'like the Barbary, common and free for all pirates'.

The authorities were particularly infuriated by the ease with which the pirates were able to stock up on food, drink and spares. Baltimore, located near a crucial sea junction, had become the seafaring equivalent of a motorway service station.

But did the locals do this voluntarily? Or were they acting under duress? At least one official document claims the Baltimore villagers had held out against the overwhelming force of pirates for as long as possible before capitulating.

But other officials complained of local suppliers being motivated by gain, 'taking excessively of [the pirates] for such victuals as they sell them.'

According to Mainwaring, the corsairs would storm ashore and 'steal' cattle with much shouting and gunfire, but would quietly compensate the farmers later.

Sir Thomas Crooke, who founded the English settlement at Baltimore, was himself accused of victualling the pirates and entertaining them. On one occasion, his back yard became a temporary abattoir where two hundred cattle were slaughtered for sale to the pirates.

Yet it would be wrong to suggest that the entire population of Baltimore was in league with the pirates. There were recorded cases in which raiding parties of corsairs burned down houses and forced farmers to hand over goods at gunpoint. In fact, it was exactly such a case that landed Sir Thomas Crooke in serious trouble. He had demanded and received compensation from the pirates after they'd burned down a local homestead. This ambiguous exchange of cash resulted in a charge of collaboration against Crooke, who was later 'freed of all imputation'.

Some modern commentators have judged the people of Baltimore harshly for giving in to the pirates' demands. But we should bear three points in mind. The first is that there was no clear dividing line between piracy and honest maritime trade as there is today. The second point is that they were living in a corrupt age: some of the highest authorities were up to their neck in piratical trade. And thirdly, they could call upon no-one – not even the King's Navy – to protect them.

An episode in 1608 illustrates the practicalities of the situation. A Navy captain named Williams tried to capture a pirate ship in Baltimore but was overwhelmed. According to the official account, his crew 'made merry with the pirates and received gifts from them.'

As one sympathetic official explained: 'They were in no position to do otherwise.'

The Privy Council did not agree. 'If it is true that ... he

received from them 19-20 chests of sugar and four chests of coral, it is a sign of too much familiarity.'

This, then, was the daunting scenario that Thomas Button had faced when he became admiral of the fleet in Ireland seventeen years beforehand. But it seems he was up to the task: he tackled the crisis with energy and gusto. He captured a Captain Fleming, who was 'hanged in chains at Youghal.' He defeated a pirate called Captain Austins after an eleven-hour battle in Oysterhaven. And on one frustrating occasion at Lough Foyle, he'd come within an ace of capturing Captain Walsingham, one of Morat's corsair colleagues.

Button was assisted by the Dutch Navy, whose ships sailed into the creeks and inlets of Ireland to root out their tormentors. By the mid 1620s, the tide had turned against the outlaws. Baltimore had settled down and was making big money from commercial fishing. One by one, the pirate 'princes' moved on to fresh territories in the New World, preparing the trail for their notorious successors – the buccaneers of America. It was the end of one era in piracy … and the beginning of another.

Now, in 1631, Button could begin to relax. The carpings of some provincial navy captain would not have bothered him too much. He could never have dreamed that the victualling of *The Fifth Whelp* would become a crucial factor in the corsairs' greatest ever success against the English: the Sack of Baltimore.

CHAPTER NINE

The Turning Of Edward Fawlett

St George's Channel, 17 June 1631

BY the time Morat Rais reached English waters, he had taken and sunk a second French ship and had boosted his crew with twenty-nine captive sailors – seventeen French, nine Portuguese and three others. Off Land's End, he encountered the first of two men who were fated to assist him in the destruction of Baltimore.

It was just a routine voyage for Edward Fawlett, master of a 60-ton merchantman from Dartmouth in Devon. He was crossing St George's Channel, a waterway that swarmed with similar merchant ships. Hundreds of vessels trekked wearily back and forth between England and Ireland, carrying unromantic cargoes and shivering, seasick passengers.

He probably didn't pay much attention to the corsair craft as she hove into view. Morat's round ship, so novel and exotic to African eyes, was almost boringly commonplace here. She merged perfectly into the background.

The moment the corsairs swooped on Fawlett's ship, the lives of the ten Devonmen were turned upside down. They were no longer free men, with their homes just a short distance away and their wives or families waiting to greet them on their return. They had become hostages of the Ottoman Empire and they were doomed to a life of slavery in Africa.

What seems so incredible about Fawlett's experience, and that of so many others, was that the Barbary corsairs were able to operate with such impunity in these waters. All this took place a mere sixty miles from Cornwall, and sixty miles in the other direction from the well-guarded Waterford coast. Fawlett's men could probably still see the hills of their homeland on the horizon.

A fascinating document from the 1620s shows just how active the Barbary corsairs were in the channel at that time – and it also depicts vividly the sort of traumatic experience that Fawlett and his men would have endured at the hands of the pirates.

This document is the nearest thing we have to a Barbary ship's log in northern waters, although it was actually a transcript of an affidavit from a captured seaman.

On May 8, 1623, Hugh Baker, a sailor from Co. Cork, was seized by an infamous Barbary corsair named John Nutt at the very mouth of his home harbour of Youghal. During his week's confinement aboard Nutt's ship, Baker witnessed a series of corsair attacks on English ships.

Nutt was an Englishman – he still kept a wife and three children in Apsham – but for the past three years he'd operated as a corsair, regularly sailing from Barbary to terrorise English shipping.

After capturing Baker, Nutt attacked a bark owned by Captain Morgan Phillipps from Padstow. Phillipps, who was on his way to Dungarvan in Waterford, tried to make a run for it. The corsairs gave chase. Three cannon shots rang out from the corsair ship before Phillips was forced to yield, right at the entrance to Dungarvan port. He had almost made it to freedom.

The ensuing description gives a good idea of the sort of scenes that would have taken place aboard Edward Fawlett's boat when it was seized by Morat Rais.

First the pirates pillaged Phillipps's bark and seized £50. Not content with that, they searched the captain and found another 26 shillings in his pocket.

'And they took Phillipps's boat, and a barrel of wine, and a fat ox, and killed him presently, some 40 or 50 yards of fine canvas, five or six rugs, and some linen and woollen Irish cloth, and two suits of clothes, with a gown and cloak which Phillipps swore, weeping then, that they were worth £20.'

There were also several passengers, including a dozen unfortunate women who were raped by the pirates. In describing such horror, Baker's testimony is deadpan and shows how appallingly routine and commonplace such attacks were in those waters. The list goes on:

'12 of this month, [Nutt] took a Loner of Cornwall and took from him a hogshead and barrel of beer and some wood.

'13', a bark of Apsham … took beer and butter.

'15', took a bark of Foye near the Land's End and bound for Kinsale, with fifty passengers on her, or thereabouts, whereof Captain Tucker was one, and from him the pirate took forty pieces and rifled all the passengers, and took from them plate, rings, jewels and money, as much as came to £300 or £400.'

So, in the course of about one working week, a single Barbary corsair in a 160-ton ship had seized five vessels, around a hundred English subjects, and cash and goods to the value of approximately £500 – that is, over £60,000 in today's money.

When Morat's men attacked Fawlett, they behaved in much the same way – rifling the merchantman for valuables, seizing the ten captives and then dismantling the ship for spare parts. According to the official account:

'They took therewith her masts, cordage and other necessaries …'

And when the entire ship had been stripped, they sent it, bubbling and belching, to the bottom of the sea.

After that, they turned their attention to Edward Fawlett. He had something that the corsairs prized more than spares, more than the finest cargos, even more than gold. He had knowledge.

Soon afterwards, Captain Edward Fawlett went over to the dark side.

For some reason, the Dartmouth captain decided to switch allegiances and to support the Barbary slavers. He was not half-hearted about it. From this point on, Edward Fawlett would be an active – even proactive – participant. He had detailed knowledge of the ports of southern Ireland, and he did not hesitate to volunteer all this information to Morat. It is fair to say that the raid in Baltimore could not have succeeded without him.

Local knowledge was vital to a Barbary corsair. In almost every raid, the pirates used a guide or pilot from the area to ensure that they did not do something stupid like lose direction or run aground on a hidden sandbank. Sometimes these guides were brought with them from Algiers, but they preferred to use locals whose memory was fresh and whose information was up to date.

So why did Fawlett choose to co-operate with his country's enemies? One obvious possibility is that he was coerced.

Many of the Barbary corsairs routinely used torture on

their victims. When they sacked a ship, they could never be completely certain that they had found everything. There might be a purse of ducats secreted in the hold; there might be rich passengers posing as seamen. They needed this situation clarified, and quickly.

They would usually begin with one of the ship's officers and then follow up with one of the crewmen or passengers. Even if the first victim held out, the grisly demonstration would be enough to make the second person blurt out everything he knew.

There was no great ceremony about it, and no need for specialist equipment: the corsairs simply used everyday seafaring objects. A length of wood could be used as a bastinado, or punishment baton, to beat the soles of the feet. A slow-burning match from the gunners could be inserted between the fingers. Basic caulking materials such as oakum and pitch tar could be applied to human skin and set alight.

One of the favourite techniques, possibly because it was fastest and most dramatic, involved a length of thin cord. Every seaman worth his salt had mastered the basic skill of whipping cord around a mast and twisting it to extreme tightness. When the same process was applied to a human head, the results would be quite literally eyepopping.

So was Fawlett tortured into revealing his secrets? It's possible, but unlikely. If he'd held out on Morat Rais, even for a short while, he would have been doomed to a life of slavery in Algiers, alongside all the others. Instead, Fawlett was destined to be released after the raid on Baltimore. It's more likely that he guaranteed his freedom by cutting a deal. Or perhaps the entire encounter was a pre-arranged rendezvous and Fawlett had been an accomplice from the very start. Who knows?

What we know for certain is that, after talking to Fawlett, Morat Rais left Land's End and set a direct course for Cork. He seems to have been in quite a hurry to get there: he made the considerable distance within thirty-six hours or so. By the morning of June 19 – just fourteen hours before the start of the raid – he had reached the prominent Cork landmark of the Old Head of Kinsale.

It was ten o'clock on a Sunday morning, and only fifty miles lay between Morat Rais and Baltimore.

Still blissfully unaware of the impending danger, the churchgoers of Baltimore spilled out of the cold church and into the bright June sunshine, determined to enjoy their treasured day off.

However, this leisure time was not guaranteed: even the strict ban on Sabbath work could be conveniently forgotten if the pilchards were running. (At St Ives in Cornwall the pilchard fishermen would run straight out of Sunday service to the harbour in a mad dash when the fish were shoaling.)

John Ryder, Joane and Stephen Broadbrook, Bessie

Flood and her son would have dallied, exchanging gossip with other villagers before making their way back to The Cove. Then – and it was still only late morning – the villagers sat down with relatives to enjoy a long and satisfying dinner.

At the Broadbrook home, Stephen and Joane and the children would sit on stools around a bare table, eating from platters made of wood or pewter and (youngsters included) drinking ale.

At John Ryder's house, it would be the same story. Perhaps they had invited guests: each of them would have brought along his own dinner knife, a sort of universal broad dagger used for cutting and slicing the meat, which was transferred to the mouth with fingers. Forks were almost never used.

Meanwhile, the better-off townsfolk like William Gunter and Thomas Bennett may have eaten out at the inn or alehouse. A fairly standard menu of the time cost sixpence and consisted of: 'good bread and drink, beef and mutton, boiled or roasted, or else veal … upon fish day … good bread and drink, salt fish or salmon, ling, egg and butter.'

It was washed down with fine claret at 6d a quart.

After their prolonged meal – it could last three hours – the ubiquitous tobacco pipes were lit and the conversation would almost certainly have touched on the political crisis in London. Two years beforehand, King Charles had adjourned Parliament indefinitely and had been exercising his divine right to rule alone and to tax and imprison his subjects as he saw fit. Nobody knew how long this stalemate could continue.

Yet overall, there was a sense of optimism. A year ago, the long war with Spain had finally ended, and England was once more at peace. Despite the ever-present tension, Ireland, too, had been uncharacteristically free of serious strife. 'I have known Ireland for forty-three years,' the Earl of Cork had written just a few months earlier, 'and never saw it so quiet ... contentment is, in fact, general.'

Only a few hours' sailing-time away, at the Old Head of Kinsale, Morat Rais was swooping on a fourth vessel. This one was only a minnow: a little 12-ton fishing boat from Dungarvan in Waterford. As the giant corsair ship towered over him, skipper John Hackett surrendered along with his five-strong crew, and the boat was 'manned by Turks and renegadoes'.

The Old Head Of Kinsale, 256 feet high and three miles from land, has always been a major landmark for sailors. It's no surprise that there was a second Dungarvan boat in the same area – another 12-ton fishing boat skippered by a man named Thomas Carew. This time, Morat didn't scupper the captured boats. He had other plans for them – and for their skippers, Hackett and Carew.

At this point a mist of doubt descends over the story.

Up until now, the key elements of Morat's voyage have been pretty clear: he had looted and scuppered two French ships; he'd taken a third ship from Fawlett off Land's End; and he'd captured the two Waterford boats between 10 am and 11 am on Sunday, June 19. That much is irrefutable. But at this stage, the facts become clouded by ambiguity.

For the crucial events that followed, we have only the later evidence of Edward Fawlett and John Hackett, both turncoats who were testifying to save their lives. The official account of the raid gives their version of events in this curiously worded section:

'Then the said Captain [Morat] demanded Hackett to pilot him into Kinsale. But Hackett answered that the place was too hot for them, for besides the fort, there were there the King's ships; whereupon they altered their purpose, and Hackett brought them to Baltimore ... '

The report makes it clear that 'these things we received by the confession of Hackett and Fawlett afterwards'.

There are those (this author among them) who find it hard to believe that an admiral of Morat's experience was ignorant about Kinsale's status as a well guarded garrison town until he was informed by Hackett. For decades, this port had been one of the main defence points on a coastline that the Barbary corsairs regarded as their second home.

Besides, the wording is ambiguous. Did Hackett

proactively *suggest* that the corsairs target Baltimore? Or did the corsairs decide and then ask Hackett to guide them there? The former notion has always been the popular version, with Hackett being held responsible for Baltimore's ordeal. But that is not what the official account says; and once again, it's difficult to believe that a great corsair admiral should effectively take his orders from a humble fisherman.

But let's get back to facts. The only certainty we have here is that the corsairs headed west towards Baltimore, with Hackett acting as their willing pilot and guide.

Why did John Hackett choose to help the corsairs? He had no shortage of motives. The first and most obvious is that, by going west, he was keeping the corsairs well away from his own hometown to the east. Secondly, there was no love lost between Waterford and Baltimore – they'd had an ancient and bitter grudge dating back to the days when the O'Driscolls plundered passing Waterford ships at will. And thirdly, Baltimore was populated by English Protestants, while Hackett himself was a native Irishman and a Roman Catholic.

It had not been a good year for Roman Catholics in Ireland. Religious persecution had resumed after a short period of tolerance that had followed the coronation of Charles I six years previously. Charles, who was strongly influenced by his French Catholic wife, Henrietta Maria, had promised the Catholic aristocrats in Ireland a series of relaxations in the law ('The Graces') in return for a payment of £120,000.

Although these reforms were never actually implemented, there was a honeymoon period during which the repressed Irish Catholics began openly celebrating Mass and setting up religious houses – seventeen within four months in Dublin alone.

For the Protestants, it was all too much too soon. When an influential report warned that the reforms would destroy the Plantation, the authorities slapped a ban on the new Catholic institutions.

On the day after Christmas, 1629, English soldiers stormed a Franciscan church in Dublin during Mass. Fighting their way through a 3000-strong mob, they arrested the friars and razed the church to the ground.

Now, in 1631, tension was mounting once more. That spring, sixteen nuns were evicted from their convent in Dublin's College Green. In Cork, communities of friars were rooted out and expelled.

By the summer of 1631, a cloud of bitterness and mistrust hung heavily in the air, with Catholics feeling betrayed and Protestants feeling besieged. The loyalty of the Catholic aristocrats was strained to breaking point. There were whisperings forecasting yet another rebellion.

And it was against this turbulent backdrop that John Hackett, a Catholic, guided the fighting forces of Islam towards the Protestant English community at Baltimore.

Just a few sea-leagues away in Roaring Water Bay, the villagers were still enjoying their lazy Sunday. For children like the Broadbrook and Meregey youngsters, Sunday had its own special attractions. Younger children were free to play games such as bladder football or handball, or to practise archery. The older boys, like the Gunter lads, did what teenage boys have always done: tried to get girls. Despite the best efforts of strict parents, pregnancy among unmarried girls was frequent enough to be a cause for concern. In a similar Co. Cork town (Youghal) the authorities had actually passed a by-law against sex:

'Lewd and incontinent persons do ... through their flatteries and wicked practices, labour and endeavour to abuse and overthrow young and silly virgin maids, to the great grief and discontent of the parents, and to the said maid's often utter undoing ... whosoever from henceforth so abuses and deflowers any such maiden virgin shall forfeit: ... Mayor's daughter, £40; Alderman's daughter, £30; Bailiff's daughter, £20; Freeman's daughter, £10.'

And so it went on, this languid June Sunday, as afternoon turned to evening. In his 1844 poem *The Sack Of Baltimore*, Thomas Davis conjures up a poignant picture of the village settling innocently into twilight in the shadow of nearby Mount Gabriel, with the fishing boats ('hookers') lying safely on the shore:

The summer's sun is falling soft on Carbery's hundred isles
The summer's sun is gleaming still through Gabriel's rough
defiles
Old Innisherkin's crumbled fane looks like a moulting bird
And in a calm and sleepy swell the ocean tide is heard.
The hookers lie upon the beach; the children cease their play
The gossips leave the little inn; the households kneel to pray
And full of love, and peace, and rest – its daily labour o'er –
Upon that cosy creek there lay the town of Baltimore.

Sunsets in the Carbery area could indeed be spectacular, as the Victorian writer Daniel Donovan describes: 'At sunset the scene is one which can never be forgotten – the sun sinking to rest in a flood of aureate light – a monarch decked in all the regalia of royalty, encircled by golden-fringed clouds, brilliantly coloured …'

The Broadbrooks and the Ryders were probably too busy to notice. At this stage in the day, they would be settling the livestock and getting ready for evening prayer and bed. With a working day beginning at five or six, most people wanted to be asleep by ten.

And so, long after sunset, when the dark silhouettes of two strange vessels bristling with a total of thirty-six guns were spotted sailing past the neighbouring port of Castlehaven, nobody even gave them a second glance.

CHAPTER TEN

The Dreadful Hour

AN extraordinary combination of good fortune and fair winds brought Morat the final few miles to Baltimore. His two ships were spotted sailing past the nearby port of Castlehaven just after sunset. 'They were seen but not known [to be pirates],' says the official account of the raid, somewhat despondently. Had they been identified, a rider could easily have reached Baltimore in time to warn the village.

Even the weather was on Morat's side. He must have sailed the five miles from Castlehaven (modern day Castletownsend) to Baltimore in just about an hour, which meant a brisk and favourable wind. By ten o'clock that night, the craggy silhouette of Sherkin Island was looming ahead of his bowsprit. He had reached the very mouth of Baltimore harbour.

Even with today's technology, it takes a practised

seaman to negotiate these difficult waters at night. John Hackett proved his skills by guiding them safely to a good mooring point 'about a musket shot from the shore'.

The official account pinpoints their anchorage as 'the eastern end of the north of the harbour'. Sailors have identified this point as the entrance to the Eastern Hole, east of the Whale Rock: a cautious choice, since it was concealed by a rocky outcrop and out of view of the main port.

Morat's anchorage was at the seaward base of a narrow triangular inlet with its two sides bounded by treacherous rocks and cliffs.

The corsair admiral decided to carry out a full reconnaissance before committing himself to an attack. He volunteered to lead this dangerous mission himself, with the aid of Captain Fawlett and ten hand-picked musketeers.

Morat selected a small boat and, with typical attention to detail, instructed his men to wrap oakum – a heavy caulking material – around their oars to deaden the sound of splashes.

Fawlett proved his worth. He seems to have had an intimate knowledge of the village, right down to the occupancy of individual homes.

'Fawlett piloted them along the shore,' says the official account, 'and showed them how the town did stand, relating unto them where the most able men had their abode.'

There are differing accounts of this reconnaissance trip. One version of the document says they conducted surveillance from a small boat just off the shore. Another version claims that the spies 'walked around the town'.

This would have been an act of breathtaking audacity, but would be no surprise with a man like Morat. And what an image – the great corsair admiral walking around the very streets of the town he was about to despoil, perhaps pulling a cloak around him to hide his Moorish garb, perhaps ducking into a darkened doorway at the sound of the approaching footsteps of some late-night revellers.

The reconnaissance took quite a long time – five glasses in seafaring terms, or more than two hours. Eventually the anxious watchers on board the flagship heard the muted splash of oars and saw Morat's little boat re-emerge from the gloom. Climbing back on board, the corsair admiral seemed remarkably upbeat and optimistic.

'We are in a good place,' he told his crew using *Sabir*, the peculiar dialect of the Barbary corsairs, 'and shall make a *boon viaggio*.'

Having decided to raid, they began discussing tactics:

'Then they consulted what time of night was fittest for their intended exploit, and concluded a little before day to be the most convenient season.'

During midsummer, 'a little before day' means three o'clock at the latest. In selecting this time, the corsairs were displaying a remarkable awareness of circadian rhythms. The human body is at its lowest point around two hours before waking, a period known as 'the zombie zone'. Many modern interrogators choose 5 am to question their victims: senses are dulled and resistance is least likely. The fisherfolk of Baltimore, who were due to rise around five, would have been in this same weakened state at 3 am.

It was customary for a corsair captain to give a short speech of exhortation to his troops before an attack. We know that Morat did this – he is said to have 'cheered up the company' – but of his speech, only the fragment quoted above has survived.

Traditionally, these speeches combined two elements – religious duty and personal gain.

'Dread not death,' a corsair captain would typically exhort his warriors, 'since you left your homes in search of wealth and renown, and to render service to our beautiful Prophet.'

Meanwhile, the Janissary commander would be steeling his own troops for conflict.

'My falcons!' he might shout. 'Keep at it boldly! If the most High God wishes it and gives us his help, we will not come home empty-handed.'

And with that, or something quite like that, the raid on Baltimore began.

At exactly 0200 hours, the ship's boats were lowered into the water alongside the two captured fishing boats.

Two hundred and thirty musketeers were crammed into these few small craft, and – leaving a skeleton crew to guard the two ships – the oarsmen began their long, gruelling row around the two headlands that separated them from The Cove.

Their adrenalin was pumping as they emerged from the cover of the outcrop. It was at this stage that they were at their most vulnerable. They were hidden from the view of their comrades manning the big iron guns on the ships. And crammed tightly into the small boats, they were in no position to return fire effectively should a cannon open fire from the shore.

But the sleeping village was as silent as the grave. With nothing more than the occasional muffled splash to betray their presence, the corsair convoy crept stealthily along the surface of the bay. Hackett, in the foremost boat, guided them through the tricky harbour entrance, with its infamous hidden rock that was to bring disaster to a merchant ship many years later. They steered starboard around a second craggy outcrop and entered the tiny, sheltered bay.

The Cove was dense with fishing craft, either bobbing at anchor or moored directly to the beach. The invaders had to be careful to avoid getting entangled in mooring ropes or – much worse – colliding with an empty boat and creating the sort of loud, hollow thud that would have roused everyone in the vicinity. However, they made it safely through this treacherous maze and, with a dull scrape of wood against gravel, finally made landfall on the shingle beach.

The Janissaries crept ashore and filed into position. At last these warriors were in their element. For weeks they had languished on board ship, battling nothing stronger than boredom. Now their hour had come. They grasped their muskets firmly, lit their torches of tarred oakum, and sent up a prayer to heaven before leaping into action with a yell that would have awakened the dead.

A stifled gasp! A dreamy noise, 'The roof is in a flame!'
From out their beds, and to their doors, rush maid and sire and dame.
And meet, upon the threshold stone, the gleaming sabres fall,
And over each black and bearded face the white and crimson shawl.
The yell of 'Allah' breaks above the prayer and shriek and roar
Oh, blessed God! The Algerine is Lord of Baltimore.

Allowing for some creative licence, those lines from poet Thomas Davis accurately convey the panic and terror of the raid.

We know from other accounts that the Janissaries always used noise to psych out their victims – and this was centuries before the Americans spooked the Vietcong with Wagner, or used deafening rock music to soften up Noriega in Panama. Deprived of amplification, the Janissaries used percussion – clapping their hands, banging on drums or striking the hulls of boats – while roaring fearsome threats and exhortations.

Joane and Stephen Broadbrook were startled out of their sleep by the hellish racket and the ominous background crackle of burning thatch. Black smoke drifted through their door and the dark interior of their cabin was alight with the baleful orange glare of a village in flames. Grabbing their frightened children, they burst outside to be confronted by a scene straight out of Dante's *Inferno*.

All around them, their neighbours were screaming in sheer terror at the sight of the Janissaries on full war footing. None of these untravelled fisherfolk would ever have seen anything like the Turkish warriors with their flashing scimitars; their swirling, flowing robes with distinctive cowls; the torchlight glistening on the sweat of bare arms which they contemptuously left unprotected by armour. 'Storm them, my brave ones!' some of the Janissaries would have been yelling, while others responded with shouts of 'Allah! Allah!'

The European pirates were more conventionally dressed, but they countered their 'Christian' appearance with colourful blasphemies and invocations to the Devil – a powerful psychological weapon against devout churchgoing folk.

All around The Cove, doors were flung open and the villagers emerged, coughing, eyes streaming. Through the dense smoke, Joane could see all the people who'd prayed with her in church only a few hours beforehand:

John Ryder, Tom Paine, the Croffines, the Meregeys and Anna their maid, all in varying states of panic and disarray, and each facing an instant decision: to fight, to flee, or to surrender.

It is a cruel irony that the best time to escape a hostage-taking raid is in the confusion of the first few moments (after that, the chances of a successful escape reduce progressively) yet it is precisely in those first few adrenalin-fuelled seconds that the mind is least able to judge the risks involved. At this same volatile stage, the raiders are equally unpredictable and liable to overreact.

Any hostage raid creates a searing crucible of psychological emotions, and there is a basic pattern of human response that has not altered in the last four centuries.

The modern US Marine Corps has produced a book called *An Individual's Guide For Understanding And Surviving Terrorism* which provides an invaluable insight into the pattern of Morat's 1631 raid.

'During the initial moment of capture,' says the *Guide*, 'you must make an instant decision – escape or surrender. Even though it is the most dangerous time of a hostage ordeal, you must remain calm.

'Do not make any sudden movement that may rattle an already anxious gunman. Abductors are tense: adrenaline is flowing. Terrorists themselves feel vulnerable until they are convinced they have established firm control over their hostages. Unintentional violence can be committed with the slightest provocation …

'Escape attempts should be made only after careful consideration of the risk of violence, chance of success, and possible detrimental effects on hostages remaining behind.'

In The Cove, some of the villagers opted to flee in a desperate attempt to summon help from the main town of Baltimore. Joane's husband Stephen must have been among them. He can't be blamed for this, since Joane herself was incapable of running, and this was his best chance to save her.

Brave Tim Curlew and John Davys opted to fight, despite the overwhelming odds. Both men were ruthlessly cut down in front of their horrified families.

But the vast majority of the villagers had little choice. With an average of nine musketeers outside each house, it was suicide to fight back.

'If you eliminate escape as an option,' advises the Marine Corps document, 'avoid physical resistance. Assure your captors of your intention to co-operate fully. Remember, hostage takers usually want you alive.'

This was equally true in 1631. Morat's basic aim was to keep as many people alive as possible. Every corpse on the ground meant less pay for everyone.

It is interesting, incidentally, to compare the tactics of Morat's troops with those used by modern siege-busting forces such as the SAS. The desired effect is to put people in fear of their lives without actually killing them. Whether this end is achieved by the monstrous yells and flaming torches of the Janissaries, or by the smoke bombs and flash detonators of the modern SAS, the result is the same.

We'll never know the precise thoughts that ran through the minds of the terrified Baltimore captives. If any of the victims ever wrote a first-person account of the raid, it has long since disappeared.

However, throughout history, many others have gone through similar ordeals. And in this brief section, I'd like to examine some parallel experiences that could give us some insight into the emotions that raced through the heads of the Baltimore women that dreadful night.

Mary Rowlandson was a clergyman's wife whose village in Massachussetts was raided just thirty-five years after Baltimore. Although the two raids obviously differed in many ways, the traumatic experience was the same.

'Now is the dreadful hour come,' wrote Rowlandson, describing how their houses were set ablaze in exactly the same way. 'Now might we hear mothers and children crying out for themselves, and to one another, "Lord, what shall we do?" ...

'But out we must go, the fire increasing, and coming along behind us, roaring...'

Confronted by sudden violence, human reactions can fly wildly across the emotional spectrum, from fight and flight to pointless self-sacrifice. Rowlandson's sister, for instance, screamed at the intruders to let her die, and was immediately granted her wish.

But Mary's survival instinct was too strong. 'I had often before this said [that] I should choose rather to be killed by them than taken alive,' she wrote, 'but when it came to the trial my mind changed.'

The mind can play strange tricks in the first few moments of an attack, as evidenced by the experiences of Fanny Loviot, a Frenchwoman captured at sea by pirates in 1852.

'It must have been midnight,' Loviot recalled, 'or perhaps a little later, when I awoke, believing myself to be the victim of a horrible nightmare. I seemed to hear a chorus of frightful cries [and] found my cabin filled with a strange red light ... the savage yells grew every instant louder ... I could not speak – I had no voice, and the words died away on my lips.'

This dreamlike, or nightmarish, sensation is a classic symptom. The unthinkable has happened: if we dwell on it, it will affect our chances of survival. So we detach ourselves from reality. We watch events unfold from a distance. We are not involved. It is all a dream.

'Denial is a primitive and very common defence mechanism,' says the Marine Corps *Guide*. 'To survive an incident that the mind cannot handle, it reacts as though the incident is not happening. Hostages commonly respond: "This can't be happening to me!" or "This must be a bad dream!" Denial is one stage of coping with an impossible turn of events.'

This phenomenon, known to troops as 'capture shock' can last between two days and several weeks.

Emanuel d'Aranda, the Flemish writer captured by Algerine corsairs just nine years after Baltimore, describes the feeling perfectly: 'I felt as though I were in a dream in which those around me were strange phantoms inducing fear, wonder and curiosity.'

Fifty of the Baltimore captives were children, ranging from teenagers to babies. How did they react to the trauma? Again, we can get some insight from parallel experiences. Minnie Carrigan, a child of German immigrants to Minnesota, was just seven years old when she was abducted in a hostage raid in 1862.

'While my mother was being murdered I stood about ten feet away from her, paralysed with fear and horror, unable to move,' she wrote later.

'Suddenly I regained my self-control and, believing that I would be the next victim, I started up and ran wildly in an indefinite direction.'

Minnie's narrative gives us one of the most vivid depictions of the surreal, dreamlike world into which hostages retreat. Amid the chaos and death, the only thing the newly-orphaned little girl could think about was picking flowers.

'The birds were singing in the trees above them and the sun shone just as bright as ever. There was not a cloud in the sky. I have often wondered how there could be so much suffering on earth on such a perfect August day.'

On that balmy midsummer night Joane Broadbrook, John Ryder, Bessie Flood and the other captives were no doubt experiencing the same sense of unreality as they were herded like cattle past the burning rubble of their former homes towards the quayside.

Anna the maidservant frantically looked around for her master, Dermot Meregey – but they had been separated in the chaos, leaving her with the youngsters. Only a few hours ago, Anna had been a carefree young woman looking forward to the midsummer festivities. But fate had other plans, and now she was headed for Africa as the *de facto* foster mother of two little children.

As the captives stepped into the stinking fishing boats, it probably would not have occurred to any of them that they might never set foot on European soil again.

By the time the raid on The Cove was over, the corsairs had 'carried with them, young and old, out of their beds, to the number of 100 persons'. A hundred slaves were worth perhaps £2,500 on the slave market – that is, over £230,000 in today's terms. It was a respectable haul, but Morat wanted more. He fixed his sights on the main village of Baltimore.

CHAPTER ELEVEN

A Wretched Captivity

Many towns, villages and farms [are] sacked; and infinite numbers of souls – men, women, children and infants at the breast – dragged away into a wretched captivity ...
They retreat leisurely, with eyes full of laughter and content, to their vessels.

—*Fray Diego de Haedo, Spanish missionary to Algiers.*

MORAT was spooked by the eerie silence from the main village above. There had been no response whatever from the castle fortress. And this silence remains a mystery, even today. How could the townspeople have slept through the noise and the screams and the crackling flames?

This must have worried the admiral: it could mean he was being led into a trap. Corsair lore was full of such stories: of raids on sleepy villages cut short when cavalry troops thundered over hilltops; of quiet woodlands hiding columns of soldiers who would spring out to cut off the pirates' retreat.

Wary of the danger, Morat divided his troops into three contingents. An attack squad of 140 Janissaries would accompany him to the main town, while sixty marksmen would line the hillside overlooking the road to safeguard their retreat. The remainder were left at The Cove to guard the hostages.

The road to the main village was a narrow, winding track fringed by dense woodland. Morat picked John Hackett, the Waterford skipper, to guide him on this dangerous journey: a curious choice, since Edward Fawlett had earlier proved his intimate familiarity with the town. Perhaps it was important that Fawlett should not be recognised. Hackett, on the other hand, seemed to relish the task. Many witnesses were later to identify him leading the raiders, his head held high. He was to pay dearly for his moment of glory.

The Janissaries burst out into the open ground at Baltimore and fanned out around the houses. Within minutes, they had the castle and village under their control.

But this time it was a different story. According to the

official report:

'[T]hey assaulted the said town, where they in like manner surprised ten English inhabitants ... breaking open forty houses and rifling of thirty-seven.'

They would have proceeded further, says the document, if William Harris had not wakened and sounded the alarm:

'[W]ith divers shots in defence of himself, [Harris] wakened the rest of his neighbours who, beating the drum in the upper part of town, caused [Morat] with the rest of his company presently to retreat.'

Morat, already unnerved by the silence, must have interpreted the gunfire and the martial drumbeat as confirmation of his worst fears. He ordered his troops to back off.

The greatest Islamist invasion of the British-Irish Isles was over.

What would have happened if William Harris had not frightened off the corsairs? What greater horrors might have been inflicted upon the villagers if the raid had continued unhindered?

We don't need to speculate. We know.

We know because, only four years earlier in 1627, Morat Rais had led five ships in a raid on remote Heimaey Island in Iceland. On that occasion there had been no interruption. Morat had shown no moral scruples ... and absolutely no mercy. He had given his crew carte blanche to kill and maim; to rape helpless women and girls; to dismember infants; to desecrate a church, and cold-bloodedly slaughter a priest at prayer.

Morat's expedition had sailed all the way from Morocco to the lands of the midnight sun. They split up and launched individual attacks around Iceland before a trio of vessels set their sights on the Westmann Islands.

On Monday, July 16, three hundred of Morat's troops stormed ashore at Raeningjatangay in the volcanic island of Heimaey. The corsairs had already snatched 110 people from Grindavik on the mainland, so the islanders were prepared for the onslaught. A fort called Skans had been built to guard the sea approach to the main town. But instead, Morat landed at an almost-inaccessible cove to the south and marched across.

At first their behaviour paralleled the story of the Baltimore raid: the three hundred corsair troops rampaged through the main town, burning and looting everything in sight.

But left uninterrupted, Morat's men settled down to a long, unhurried orgy of rape, mutilation and murder which seems to have been motivated by nothing more than sadistic sport.

The invaders split into three assault units. Shouting and waving red flags, they ran amok around the entire island. A few pathetic runaways tried to escape along the cliffs: the musketeers picked them off as though they were shooting birds. Around a hundred islanders shivered in a hidden cave in the western shore. The invaders hunted them out and dragged them back.

One account tells of the corsairs cutting people in half and callously snapping the necks of infants.

'Anyone unable to keep up with their pace ... was cut down, and in their madness for blood these villains then chopped and hacked the bodies into small pieces with the greatest of enjoyment and lust for blood,' wrote one eyewitness, Klaus Eyjulfsson.

Flames leaped high over the island church. The corsairs slaughtered one of the priests, Jon Thorsteinsson, as he knelt in prayer. The other, Ólafur Eigilsson, was hurled to the ground and beaten.

Morat's men herded their captives into a harbour warehouse and ordered the most saleable slaves to board the ship. Then the corsairs closed the warehouse doors and torched the building, ignoring the screams of those left inside.

When Morat sailed away from Heimaey on Thursday, he had 242 islanders on board – almost exactly half the island's population. His captives included the wife and children of the slain priest Jon Thorsteinsson, and a married woman of exceptional beauty named Gudridur (Gudda) who will feature later in this story.

The corsairs left behind them thirty-six to forty corpses – that is, one islander in every twelve – and sailed into Algiers with around four hundred slaves from all over Iceland.

Morat's raid left a dark stain on Iceland's history. As late as 1898, a visitor reported that the Heimaey islanders talked of the seventeenth-century atrocities almost daily. Even today, elderly folk still tell how, as children, they were given escape plans to follow should the dreaded corsairs ever reappear.

Accounts of other corsair raids reveal the same pattern. Following the capture of the town, there would be a triumphalist orgy of burning, looting, raping and religious desecration. The Barbary corsairs were seventeenth-century punk rockers: they liked to scandalise, and they loved the shock value of despoiling churches. They'd tear down crucifixes and trample communion wafers underfoot.

When pirates led by the English pirate John Gentleman raided Iceland, an annalist recorded: 'They placed muskets before the priests of the people with laughter and ridicule ... the church bells they seized and fastened to the mast of their ship.'

Dozens of people would escape the first raids, but the corsairs would march deep into the countryside and relentlessly round them up. Haedo, the Spanish cleric, reported that the Algerine corsairs would typically 'advance into the country ten, twelve or fifteen leagues or more'.

Once the fugitives had all been captured, the corsairs would often use horrific forms of torture in a bid to force them to reveal hidden cash ... whether they knew of any or not.

This, then, was the horrific scenario that William Harris had prevented with his single musket.

It was still dark on the early morning of June 20 when Thomas Bennett – one of the founding fathers of the Baltimore colony – opened his door to a breathless, wild-eyed group of fugitives. Stephen Broadbrook and several others had somehow escaped the early raid on The Cove and had dashed through the night to Bennett's house in the hope of intercepting the pirates before they could leave Roaring Water Bay.

Bennett considered his options. The naval base at Kinsale was fifty-four miles away. There was only one ray of hope, so ludicrously impractical that it seemed realistic only to desperate men. At Castlehaven, five miles to the east, a sizeable ship lay at anchor. This vessel, commanded by a Mr Pawlett, could set sail immediately and rescue the captives.

Bennett must have known the idea would never have worked. Even *The Fifth Whelp* with all its naval officers and guns would have been no match for Morat's army. What hope would there be for Pawlett's merchant ship?

Nevertheless, he lit a candle, sat down at his desk, and wrote a letter in the pre-dawn darkness. He wrote, not directly to Pawlett, but to his influential friend James Salmon, begging him to 'use his best endeavours to persuade Mr Pawlett ... to haste to the rescue of the foresaid captives.'

Salmon, another founding father of the Baltimore colony now living at Castlehaven, had made a fortune by buying cloth from questionable sources, and had since risen to become a commanding figure in local politics. If anyone could persuade Pawlett to undertake such a suicidal mission, Salmon could.

As the sun rose to reveal the devastation of his village, Baltimore Mayor Joseph Carter decided his first priority was to alert the neighbouring ports. Unable to find any paper, he ripped out an irregular scrap four-and-a-half inches by eight and scrawled out a rushed warning to William Hull, his counterpart in Leamcon.

This letter displays all the hallmarks of a man in profound shock. Carter's profound apology for failing to find the correct stationery is a classic example of a mind trying to cope with the unthinkable by concentrating on the trivial. He handed it to his fastest messenger, one of a breed of native Irish runners whose remarkable ability to run long distances through dense woodland and bog earned them the unique right to wear the traditional *glib*, a thick forelock of hair that fell over their faces.

June 20, 1631.

Baltimore, this present Monday morning.

Right Worshipful Sir.

This my letter to let you understand that this last night, a little before day, came two Turk men of war of about 300 tons, and another of about 150, with a loose boat to set their men ashore, and they have carried away of our townspeople, men, women and children, one hundred and eleven, and two more are slain; the ships are at present going westward.

I thought presently to give your Worship intelligence, and have sent a messenger apurpose, and I pray to give him content for his pains, and I am doubtful that they will put in about Leamcon or Crookhaven. I pray give intelligence westward. This with my service remembered.

I rest, etc.

Joseph Carter

(desiring excuse, having no paper.)

It was broad daylight by the time the last of the miserable Baltimore captives were dragged on board the two pirate vessels. Birds sang lustily in the woodlands, adding to the sense of unreality.

Safe on board ship, the corsairs made a tally of their human haul. Altogether, 109 captives had been stolen away from Baltimore. Two elderly people, a Mr Osburne and a Mrs Alice Heard, were released almost immediately because they were too infirm to survive the journey.

This left 107: twenty-three men, thirty-four women (including three 'daughters' and five maidservants), and fifty youngsters of whom twelve were classified as 'sons' or 'boys' and thirty-eight were described as 'children'. In the terminology of the time, a 'child' was female.

Nearly all the names in the official list of captives are as English as roast beef: Ryder, Hunt, Roberts, Watts, and so on. For this reason it has often been assumed that there were no Irish among them – but this may not necessarily be true. It would be surprising if some locals did not figure among the many nameless maids, cooks and servants. Frustratingly few of the thirty women captives are identified by name – they are simply someone's 'wife' or 'daughter'.

The slavers now had a grand total of 154 captives on board: the 107 from Baltimore, plus seventeen men from the French ships; nine Englishmen from Dartmouth; nine Dungarvan men; and a further dozen of other nationalities.

Morat had one final act to perform. He gratefully released Fawlett and Hackett, together with a second unnamed Dungarvan fisherman, as a reward for their collaboration.

What happened next was curious. According to the official account, they lingered on at Baltimore until 'three or four o'clock in the afternoon'.

This directly contradicts Carter's letter, dated 'Monday morning' and stating unambiguously that 'the ships are at present going to the westward'.

So according to Carter the ships had left by Monday morning. And there is further evidence to back him up. One letter from the Lords Justices states that 'the invaders stayed only a few hours'. Since Morat arrived at 10 pm on Sunday, a 4 pm departure the next day could hardly be described as 'only a few hours'.

Even the official account – the *same* one that gives the departure time as between 3 and 4 pm – says the invaders did not stay 'longer than they could bring in their anchors and hoist sail' before leaving.

If the 4 pm version is correct, the corsairs may simply have been waiting for a fair wind. Or perhaps they were waiting to establish communication with the relatives of their victims. Barbary corsairs often organised instant ransoms of captives just after a raid. (When the Albanian corsair Murad raided Lanzarote he remained in harbour and began selling the slaves he'd taken only a few hours earlier. The island's Governor paid up and had his wife and daughter returned to him on the spot.)

However, in this case there was to be no second chance. The weeping captives would have heard the familiar noise of departure – the sails being loosened, the yards being braced, and finally the ominous turning of the windlass that lifted the anchor and severed their last link with home.

'Those peculiar, long-drawn sounds which denote that the crew are heaving the windlass began,' wrote one veteran of sailing ships, 'and in a few moments we were under way. The noise of the water thrown from the bows began to be heard, the vessel leaned over from the damp breeze and rolled with the heavy groundswell, and we had actually begun our long, long journey.'

CHAPTER TWELVE

Manifesting The Calamities

'THERE is something in the first grey streaks stretching along the eastern horizon and throwing an indistinct light upon the face of the deep, which combines with the boundlessness and unknown depth of the sea around you, and gives one a feeling of loneliness, of dread, and of melancholy foreboding, which nothing else in nature can give.'

Richard Henry Dana, the American writer, describes a novice seaman's first bleak dawn aboard a sailing ship. It is probably a good physical description of the Baltimore captives' first morning at sea as they began their long journey to slavery; but, more importantly, it would also be a fairly accurate depiction of their emotional state.

Coincidentally, 'loneliness, profound sense of loss, abandonment and despair' is the phrase used in the modern US Navy training document 'Captivity: The Extreme Circumstance' to describe the feelings commonly experienced by hostages soon after their capture.

For captives like Joane Broadbrook, the initial dreamlike detachment would wear off in a few days to be replaced by hopelessness and a bleak, aching despondency.

'Hostage is a crucifying aloneness,' observed Brian Keenan, the Irish teacher who was held as a hostage in Beirut for over four years in the 1980s. 'It is a silent, screaming slide into the bowels of ultimate despair.'

Even the most devoutly religious can suffer a major crisis of faith.

The Rev. Devereux Spratt, a twenty-one-year-old Anglican clergyman based in Ireland, had only recently been ordained when corsairs captured him off the Cork coast in 1641:

'[B]efore we were out of sight of land,' he wrote, 'we were all taken by an Algiers pirate, who put the men in chains and stocks.

'This thing was so grievous that I began to question Providence and accused God of injustice in his dealings with me, until the Lord made it appear otherwise by his ensuing mercies.'

Filipo Pananti, the Italian poet, was equally engulfed by despair. 'Pent up in this filthy Algerian ship,' he wrote, 'every object combined to make us weary of life.'

In their mental and spiritual anguish, hostages tend to search for spurious explanations for their bad fortune. A typical reaction is to imagine fate is punishing them for some previous wrongdoing.

Fanny Loviot, the Frenchwoman captured by pirates, said her feelings of desolation were so intense that they made her fear for her own sanity:

'Being so wretched, what more had I to fear? What were death to one whose sufferings had already touched the bounds of human endurance? … I questioned my past life; I searched all the corners of my memory; I asked myself what I had done to merit this great trial.'

However, in most cases, denial and despair will eventually give way to pragmatism. The US Marine Corps' *Guide For Surviving Terrorism* explains the process: 'As time passes, most hostages gradually accept their situation, and find hope in the thought that their fate is not fixed. They begin to view their situation as temporary, and they believe they will be rescued soon. This gradual shift from denial to hope for rescue reflects a growing acceptance of the situation.'

On this first grey dawn on June 21, most of the Baltimore captives would not yet have reached this liberating stage. To use Keenan's phrase, they would still have been sliding into the bowels of despair.

Once again, let's get a brief insight into their emotions through the words of others who suffered similar fates. For instance, the feelings of the newly-widowed Mrs Timothy Curlew would probably have been summed up by the words of the seventeenth-century Massachusetts captive Mary Rowlandson:

'[M]y thoughts ran upon my losses and sad bereaved condition. All was gone, my husband gone ... my children gone, my relations and friends gone, our house and home ... all was gone except my life ...'

For the Meregey children, robbed of their parents, the uncertainty would have been even worse. Like Mary Jemison, a fifteen-year-old girl from Northern Ireland who was captured in a raid in Pennsylvania in 1758, they would have felt a sense of dread that kept them from sleep. 'The night was spent in gloomy forebodings,' Mary wrote. 'What the result of our captivity would be, it was out of our power to determine, or even imagine.'

Or like Minnie Carrigan, who was captured at the age of seven, they might have slept fitfully, only to be plunged into despair on awakening. 'I could not think where we were, but all at once the horrible scene of the day before came back to me,' Minnie recalled. '... If the earth would have opened then and swallowed me I would have been thankful.'

The morning sun rose on a transformed Baltimore, a devastated shell of burned-out homes and shattered dreams. Wisps of smoke still drifted from the ashes of the houses. The boats lay idle and the fish palace was deserted, its silver treasures left to rot and add to the stench of the smouldering timber.

Most survivors of the raid had long since fled. Only the

bravest and the most grief-stricken wandered around amid the rubble, looking for mementoes of their loved ones.

The bloodstained bodies of Timothy Curlew and John Davis were lifted from the ground and laid out for burial.

The two elderly folk, old Mr Osburne and Alice Heard, were found wandering around The Cove in a distressed state. Only then did a true picture emerge of Hackett's and Fawlett's crucial roles in the attack. Grim-faced officials ordered that the two traitors be hunted down and interrogated.

All along the coast, panic spread like a plague. No-one knew whether this was just an isolated incident or the prelude to a full-scale invasion. The seaports emptied and the inland roads were thick with fleeing refugees.

Joane Broadbrook awoke to find herself in a floating, heaving prison of wood. Home for the female captives and their children was a cramped area of the 'tween decks level, segregated from the crew's sleeping quarters only by temporary curtains made of sailcloth. Much of this space was taken up by the ship's structure and its spares. Amid this jumble of debris, more than seven dozen bodies would have to find room to lie down as best they could.

The chaotic scene would have been even worse than that described by the seaman Richard Henry Dana:

'The steerage in which I lived was filled with coils of

rigging, spare sails, old junk and ship stores, which had not been stowed away ... The sea, too, had risen, the vessel was rolling heavily, and everything was pitched about in grand confusion.'

Cleanliness and hygiene were not high priorities on board any ship in that era. The semi-darkness, the constant damp, the myriad of unreachable nooks and crannies, all combined to provide an ideal environment for rats, cockroaches and fleas. Everyone, crew and captives alike, crawled with lice.

Joane's experience would probably have paralleled that of Fanny Loviot, who was also held prisoner below deck on a pirate vessel: 'The insects which infested our dungeon tormented me incessantly, and my feet were blistered all over from their bites. The rats, also, which at first had fled before the sound of our voices, were now grown but too friendly, and ran over us in broad daylight, as we were lying on the floor.'

Filipo Pananti, the Tuscan captive, found conditions so horrific that he daily expected an outbreak of plague. He was disgusted at 'this filthy Algerian ship' and added: 'This motley crew were all either affected with some corroding humour or swarming with vermin.'

Meanwhile, in Castlehaven, James Salmon was moving heaven and earth to help his neighbours in Baltimore. First he tried to persuade Pawlett to set sail. But the merchant captain quite sensibly refused the invitation to a one-way ticket for the Algiers slave market. The official report says that even Salmon's weighty – and perhaps threatening – influence 'could not prevail'.

Now there was only one route left. Salmon dashed off a letter to Captain Hooke of *The Fifth Whelp* in Kinsale, urging him to give chase.

Salmon was a man of the world – he knew all about naval corruption. Convinced that Hooke could not be relied upon, he instructed his messenger not to linger in Kinsale, but to continue to faraway Mallow to plead directly with Munster President Sir William St Leger, who happened to be an implacable enemy of the Earl of Cork.

Back in Baltimore, Sir Samuel Crooke was writing to the Mayor at the naval base of Kinsale 'manifesting the calamities ... and praying him to hasten the Captain of the King's Ship [Hooke] to their rescue.'

All hopes now rested with the Navy, but it was in such disarray that it could hardly help itself.

As Morat's ships ploughed southeastward through increasingly heavy seas, Anna the maid would be doing her best to comfort her two young charges. Seasickness would have been a major problem, particularly among the younger children. As the seas rolled, the squalor resulting from uncontrolled nausea among dozens of children in a confined space would have been horrendous.

Everyone's clothes rapidly became mouldy, and remained that way. Wooden ships were always unpleasantly damp, even in dry weather. In common with Richard Dana, Joane would have found that:

'Our clothes were all wet through, and the only change was from wet to more wet ... everything was wet and uncomfortable, black and dirty, heaving and pitching.'

This was very much a man's world, with no provision made for female needs. Sailors simply urinated over the side of the ship or used 'seats of easement' with large holes poised over the waves. The female captives would have been required to make do with communal buckets, creating a nauseous filth and stench.

And this was to be their home for the next forty days.

Next morning, Sir William Hull of Leamcon dashed off a letter to the Earl of Cork, Richard Boyle. 'The [Algerine] ships were plying on and off near Mizen Head' Hull wrote, inaccurately. 'They have been there for eight or nine days, but were not known to be Turks.'

The boss of the lucrative Leamcon fishing business made no mention of the captured women and children but pointed out testily: 'They took two excellent pilots with them from Baltimore.'

Although he was one of the richest men in the area, Hull proved niggardly with help. 'I would lend two sakers [cannon] and shot to Baltimore and Crookhaven, but there is a complete lack of powder,' he grumbled. 'I hope we may have more from the King's store.'

The following day, Wednesday, June 22, Munster president St Leger wrote to Boyle urging him to send the naval ship in hot pursuit, but pointing out the practical difficulty that *The Fifth Whelp* could not set sail without supplies. St Leger requested 'that the King's ship may forthwith be provisioned to go to fight them'.

By Thursday, *The Fifth Whelp* was still stuck in Kinsale, and Captain Hooke was desperately defending his position to the impatient authorities.

'We are still victualling here from day to day,' he pointed out, adding hopefully: 'About the last of the month, we shall have three weeks' victuals and be able to go to sea. We had not been paid for ten months. We cannot go to meet the Turks (who took ten men at least from Kinsale) until we are victualled. I wish I could victual my own ship.'

The official account of the raid sums up the final scenes in what, by now, had degenerated into a fiasco:

'[T]he Lord President ... presently sent out his commands to the Sovereign of Kinsale and Captain Hooke, to set forth with the king's ship, and to hasten her to the service, who came accordingly *within four days*.' [my italics].

Morat had sailed on Monday; Hooke did not even leave port until around Friday. What happened next came as no surprise to anyone:

'But the Turks, having not continued in the harbour longer than they could bring in their anchors and hoist sail, were gotten out of view, and the King's ship followed after them but could never get sight of them.'

The last hopes had faded. Nothing, now, could save the Baltimore captives. Nothing stood between them and the slave markets of Barbary.

CHAPTER THIRTEEN

A Bed Of Thorns

The Baltimore women may have suffered horrendous deprivations on board ship – but for their menfolk, conditions were even worse.

John Ryder, Tom Paine and the rest of the male captives would have been thrown into stinking, dripping lockers where they were fettered in chains or wooden stocks.

James Leander Cathcart, born in Co. Westmeath in Ireland, was captured by the corsair Yusuf Rais in 1785. He wrote: 'It is impossible to describe the horror of our situation ... forty-two men shut up in a dark room in the hold of a Barbary cruiser...filthy in extreme, destitute of every nourishment and nearly suffocated ...'

John Foss, enslaved by Algerine corsairs in 1793, recalled how he was confined in the sail room: 'We were obliged to creep in on our hands and knees and stow ourselves upon the sails ...

'[L]ice, bugs and fleas [were there] in such quantity that it seemed we were completely covered.'

And the poet Filippo Pananti described how he and his fellow captives were 'packed like herrings' in the anchor chain locker:

'[It] had infinitely more the appearance of a sepulchre than a place destined for living beings. There it was necessary to extend our wearied limbs over blocks, cables and other ship's tackling, which made ours a bed of thorns indeed!

'In this suffocating state, the bitterest reflections presented themselves in our sleepless imaginations.'

On his first morning, Pananti was taken for a 'promenade' on deck, where the crew gathered to stare at the captives.

Once the ships were far out to sea, John Ryder and the other skilled mariners from Roaring Water Bay would have been freed to work on deck, provided they stayed well away from the helm. On a sailing ship, even the worst weather was preferable to the squalor beneath them, as Richard Dana testified:

'[T]he confusion of everything below, and that inexpressible sickening smell caused by the shaking up of the bilge-water in the hold, made the steerage but an indifferent refuge from the cold, wet decks.'

At least they had freedom to move around. And as they swung heavy tools and spars within a few feet of their captors, John and the other Baltimore men must inevitably have toyed with the thought of mutiny ... and escape.

🐚 🐚 🐚

Escape from a corsair ship was difficult, but not impossible. Eight years earlier, a Hugh Baker from Youghal had escaped from corsair John Nutt's ship while on his way to a life of slavery in Barbary.

Nutt's crew had grown rich on their plunders and, according to Baker, 'play[ed] continually for Barbary gold'. Baker and another captive waited for their opportunity and:

'... perceiving the pirate and his company to be drunk, cut the sea-boat which was fastened to the man-of-war ... and so came in her to Kinsale.'

In 1621, a Captain John Rawlins was seized near Penzance by a corsair captain whose entire crew comprised of renegadoes . Rawlins managed to re-convert them all and sail home as master of his captor's vessel.

In 1663 an English Quaker captain named Thomas Lurting staged a similar reversal of fortune by instructing his captured men to obey all orders so enthusiastically that his Algerine captors became careless. During a rainstorm, the corsairs all took shelter in the cabins. Lurting's men simply locked them in and took command. Magnanimously, he released the corsair crew near Algiers and they 'parted in great love'. The corsairs even tried to persuade him to come ashore for supper. Lurting declined – he was virtuous, but he wasn't stupid.

Not all shipboard escapes had such happy endings. The fourteen-year-old slave Joseph Pitts was kept shackled in a grim locker where he and his shipmates became 'almost weary of our lives'.

Hope came when someone smuggled in a pincer to loosen their chains. They managed to obtain two swords and planned a full-scale mutiny. However, the corsairs rumbled the plot and selected one man at random for punishment. Pitts describes what happened:

'[He] was forthwith laid down on the deck … one man sitting on his legs and another at his head, and in this posture, the captain, with a great rope, gave him about 100 blows on his buttocks.'

For their part, the Baltimore men were constantly supervised by two hundred crack troops and had little chance of escape. Their only sensible option was to hang on grimly … and concentrate on staying alive.

For the Baltimore womenfolk like Joane and Anna, there was another terror involved in captivity … and this fear was often justified.

European renegado corsairs were notorious for raping and violating women prisoners. There had been an infamous case in Ireland in May 1623, when Barbary corsair John Nutt captured a bark outside Dungarvan. The twelve to fourteen women on board were all raped by the crew. Mrs Jones, the wife of a Cork saddler, received Nutt's special attention. According to the same Hugh Baker's deposition:

'Captain Nutt took [Mrs Jones] for himself into his cabin, and there had her a week before [my] departure from him, and there he left her.'

(Sometimes the corsairs took on more than they could handle when they assaulted women. The fearsome Irish pirate queen Gráinne O'Malley was once attacked by Algerine pirates as she lay breastfeeding her child in her cabin. She flew up on deck in a rage and appeared in the thick of the fray, wild-haired and screaming. Having routed the invaders, she returned with grim satisfaction to nursing her baby.)

However, there is no evidence that any of the Baltimore women were molested during the voyage. This may seem at odds with the corsairs' behaviour in Iceland, but there could be a simple explanation: once on board ship, the women were officially State property and the two hundred Janissaries were duty bound to protect them.

Westerners were often surprised to find such discipline. James Cathcart's group of captives included one woman who was given the freedom of the ship and excused the usual shackles. '[She] seemed perfectly reconciled to her situation and endeavoured to reconcile everyone to theirs,' he wrote. '[I] began to thank God that our situation was no worse.'

Joane Broadbrook, in her heavily pregnant state, may have been treated better than the rest. There is some evidence that Morat's men showed respect to expectant mothers.

At the height of the Icelandic raid, for instance, a terrified woman went into labour behind a large rock. Morat's troops soon found her, but to her surprise they spared her life and treated her kindly. This small act of humanity in the midst of atrocity impressed the islanders so much that they preserved the stone as a memorial.

And when the wife of Heimaey parson Ólafur Eigilsson gave birth during the voyage to Algiers, two of Morat's men donated their shirts to serve as baby blankets. In view of these two cases, it's probable that the corsairs showed compassion to Joane. Perhaps the reason was purely commercial: to keep her and her baby alive for sale. Or perhaps, as the captive Fanny Loviot speculated in her own case, the hardened seamen looked at the women and 'thought of their wives, their mothers, their sisters whom they had left at home.'

CHAPTER FOURTEEN

A Remedy For Grief

Back at home, poor William Gunter was inconsolable. The man who had lost more relatives than any other single individual in the Baltimore raid was determined to do everything in his power to bring his loved ones home.

Haggard and grief-stricken, Gunter stood before the powerful Lords of the Privy Council in London and poured his heart out. He told of his great loss and begged that they put pressure on the English consul in Algiers to redeem the captives.

The Lords nodded gravely. But unknown to Gunter, they'd already had their cards marked by their fellow aristocrat, Richard Boyle, the Earl of Cork.

Boyle had written to the Lords asking them to find some way of freeing the 107 captives.

But his tone was strangely lukewarm, and he added with more than a hint of apology: 'Among many others that suffer by that accident there is one William Gunter, who bears the greatest part in that loss, having his wife and seven sons carried away by the Turks. He will not be dissuaded from repairing thither to solicit your Lordships applying some remedy to his grief.'

Will not be dissuaded? Boyle's tone spoke volumes about the attitude of the English aristocracy towards commoners who'd been enslaved in Barbary. The subtext of his message to the Lords was clear: Just humour the old fellow and send him home.

Yet, as Gunter would have discovered, there was talk of little else in London. The raid on Baltimore was far more than a regional nuisance. It was an invasion of the King's territory and an unprecedented humiliation.

The Baltimore incursion was without doubt the greatest Islamist invasion of the British-Irish Isles. True, hundreds of English and Irish sailors had been seized from their ships at sea in the previous decade (up to a thousand in one year alone) but land raids had been rare.

Six years earlier, in 1625, Barbary troops had invaded Mount's Bay in Cornwall and stormed into the local church during service, screaming threats and brandishing their *yatagans* at the terrified worshippers. Corsairs raided the Cornish village of Looe that same year, but the alarm had been raised and they found the town almost empty.

Later, in 1640, corsair ships from Algiers were to swoop

on the Cornish port of Penzance and seize dozens of men, women and children.

It's hard to find reliable statistics on the number of slaves captured in these incidents. While there was a painstaking tally of the 107 captives taken in the Baltimore raid, the figures for Cornwall are vague and suspiciously rounded. They tended to include local fishermen and mariners who'd been seized at sea. We must remember, too, that it was in the interests of local authorities seeking expensive protection from London to beef up their statistics.

One eyewitness reckoned that sixty slaves were taken in the Mount's Bay raid. Eighty were seized at Looe, but this figure included seamen and fishermen who'd presumably been taken at sea. The main source for the Penzance incident in 1640 is a report from London saying that 'those roguish Turkish pirates' had seized from the shore near Penzance 'sixty men, women and children; this was in the night ...'

Even taking these figures at face value we find that no other invasion of these islands matches Baltimore in terms of scale. At the time, officials described it as 'unprecedented'.

Certainly, it caused an economic calamity in Ireland.

As the ever-caring Sir William Hull of Leamcon wrote the day after the raid: 'If these [pirate] ships are not driven off, trade will be ruined and the people will be utterly unable to pay off their debts.'

Tensions were racked up even higher when a Captain William Thomas based in Algiers relayed intelligence of further impending raids on Ireland, sparking off fears of a full-scale Ottoman invasion.

And the Earl of Cork warned: 'I hear on good authority that the Turks intend to surprise the whole southern coast next year, distributing their fleet according to the strengths of the different ports.

'This rumour has stopped trade on the southern coast of Ireland.

'Three evils follow: the depeopling of the harbour towns, and the cessation of the pilchard fishery, which trains men for the Navy and increases the King's customs; and the stoppage of the rapid flow of coin into the Realm.'

The authorities worked hard to find some practical early-warning system that would prevent such a disaster happening again. Beacons appeared on headlands at Baltimore and Cape Clear. '[U]pon the firing of these beacons, [local men] are to assemble under arms at Clonakilty,' the President of Munster ordered.

An ingenious Captain James proposed:

'... a system of flag signals: flags placed on different positions on the poles will indicate whether the ship is a Turk or Dutchman.'

The Earl of Cork begged London for aid. 'We have no means or ships here and look entirely to Your Lordships,' he wrote. 'The sea between England and Ireland must be guarded. Pirates frequently assume command of it in summer time.'

Firmly locking the stable door after the corsairs had bolted, Boyle promised that the few people remaining in Baltimore would 'rebuild, and prepare and hold, at their own expense, a blockhouse' to repel invaders.

The follow-up invasion never came, but that summer Boyle had a different fight on his hands. He was facing the fury of an all-powerful King who saw the Baltimore raid as a personal insult and humiliation ... and who would not rest until he found out who was to blame for the fiasco.

Eight miles northwest of Oxford's dreaming spires lies Blenheim Palace, birthplace of Winston Churchill. On the other side of the lake, a rarely-visited memorial stone stands today as the only remaining relic of the once-grand Royal Manor House of Woodstock.

For six centuries, this sylvan hunting lodge had served as holiday home for English monarchs. It was here that Eleanor of Aquitaine surprised her husband Henry II with his secret lover Rosamund – with fatal consequences for the king's mistress. It was here that the young Princess Elizabeth Tudor – imprisoned by her half-sister Queen Mary – scratched a pathetic poem on a glass window:

Much suspected of me
Little proved can be.
—*quoth Elizabeth, prisoner.*

In the summer of 1631, Woodstock became the setting for another moment of high drama in history.

King Charles was enjoying a midsummer break – perhaps enjoying a glass of claret from the famously well-stocked cellar after a game of tennis in his newly-installed courts – when word reached him of the abduction and naval fiasco at Baltimore.

'This event is absolutely without precedent, even in time of war,' read the despatch from the Earl of Cork and his fellow Lord Justice, Adam Loftus. 'It is a grave loss to the King but, besides, it is an insult to his honour.'

The news did nothing to enhance the quality of the royal holiday. Charles was a small man with a stammer and a notoriously short temper. It was clear from his blistering reply that the monarch was incandescent with rage.

'The invasion [at Baltimore] was no more unusual than the absence of the means of prevention,' his furious letter hissed. 'You shall inform us where responsibility for this negligence lies.

'You blame the two captains appointed to guard the coast and they blame each other, but we are not satisfied with these recriminations. You shall inform us about what was left undone to guard against such a thing.'

The letter put the fear of God into the complacent bureaucrats. For weeks, the courts of Dublin and London were loud with the silken rustle of backsides being covered as almost everyone involved tried to blame somebody else.

As we've seen, Captain Francis Hooke of *The Fifth Whelp* maintained that Admiral Sir Thomas Button had pocketed the money for his supplies, leaving him stuck in port. There was an added complication: Hooke, although a humble captain, was under the special protection of the King's powerful Secretary Of State, Lord Dorchester.

This might explain the strangely mild tone of the Earl of Cork's letter to London eight days after the raid. After asking Dorchester to make a diplomatic complaint to the Ottoman Empire, Boyle broaches the subject hesitantly:

'I think Captain Hooke much to blame; if he had even cruised about, he would have frightened off the Turks. As he is under your special favour, I trust you will admonish him.'

A couple of weeks later, a more comprehensive picture begins to emerge. It is July 14, and the Lords of the Admiralty are writing to the two Lords Justices:

'Captain Hooke complains that he has been badly and dishonestly victualled by Sir Thomas Button and that want of victuals prevents him from dealing with the pirates, of whose depredations we hear daily complaints. It is obviously a bad thing that captains should victual their own ships. A cause of the difficulty is the dispute between Captain Hooke and Sir Thomas. You have done much to make things worse by allowing Sir Thomas to swerve from our instructions. You must take the victualling out of Sir Thomas's hands and give it to Sir Sampson Daydrell ... be strict about this matter.'

Four days later, however, Captain Hooke is once again harbour-bound in Kinsale. He protests to the Admiralty Lords that he has been forced to 'live from hand to mouth' since 4 May.

The same day, he writes another letter to the authorities complaining forthrightly about Button's 'corruption'.

There must have been some substance to Hooke's complaints, because by July 23, he is back at sea, plying between Cork and Waterford. Hooke reveals that he has been given supplies for fourteen days and that Button has promised him six months' pay.

Later that summer, Captain Hooke travelled inland to the town of Mallow for an informal hearing before the Earl of Cork and Boyle's great rival, Munster President William St Leger.

— Captain, you have been accused of negligence over the piratical raid on Baltimore, Boyle said icily. What have you to say?

Hooke tensed. He knew that his entire career hung in the balance. With a dramatic flourish, he produced a battered sea-log.

— This journal has been signed by all the officers on *The Fifth Whelp*, he said. It testifies that since we arrived at Kinsale in April, we have been victualled from hand to mouth and could not leave port.

The book was passed to Boyle and St Leger, who studied it carefully.

— So this was not a case of cowardice, Hooke persisted.

There was a silence as the two officials examined the log.

— In future, the Earl said at last, you shall be victualled for three months.

The Fifth Whelp was soon back at sea, and Captain Hooke was recording in his journal: 'We are today victualled for a month.'

Hooke left the Mallow hearing with his head held high. But if he thought the case was closed, he was wrong. His troubles were far from over.

CHAPTER FIFTEEN

Black Paste and Putrid Water

Life goes on, as it always does. As the corsair ships sailed onwards past La Rochelle, the weather became warmer and Joane, Bessie and the other women were allowed out on deck for prolonged periods. They found themselves growing accustomed to the comforting – if not comfortable – predictability of shipboard routine.

'The morning commences with the watch on deck's 'turning-to' at day-break and washing down, scrubbing, and swabbing the decks,' sailing veteran Richard Dana recalled. 'This, together with [drawing] fresh water, and coiling up the rigging, usually occupies the time until seven bells, (half after seven) when all hands get breakfast. At eight, the day's work begins, and lasts until sundown, with the exception of an hour for dinner.'

Captured European crewmen were confused by the

corsairs' unfamiliar work schedule, which involved two ten-hour watches from 8 pm until 6 am, and 6 am until 4 pm, with a 'dog watch' in between. Some captives could not sleep for fear that they might miss their watch.

On an Islamic ship, there was another routine. Five times a day, after the call to prayer, the faithful would form rows facing in the direction of Mecca and perform the set *rak'ah*, or genuflections: a standing prayer, a kneeling prayer and two prostrations. Like the Flemish captive Emanuel d'Aranda, John Ryder must have been filled with 'fear, wonder and curiosity' at the sight. D'Aranda admitted he felt spellbound by these exotic figures 'talking strange tongues, wearing strange clothes, carrying strange weapons, and praying with odd rituals.'

But within a few days, many captives found their initial terror replaced by a growing curiosity. At least some of the Baltimore hostages must have been moved to ask questions and receive their first instructions about this strange new religion that was to dominate so many of their lives.

At mealtime, Ryder would have queued up with the others to be served from a communal pot. The food was like nothing he had ever seen before. He would probably have agreed with the fastidious Italian captive Filippo Pananti, who recalled his first meal with horror: '[I]t consisted of a black looking paste in an immense pan, which, placed on the deck, was immediately surrounded by a host of hungry Moors and negroes, indiscriminately mixed together and making common cause for the laudable purpose of emptying the platter.'

The captives had to wait 'like timid spaniels' for the leftovers.

'Stretched along the decks in the manner of the Turks, [we were] obliged to eat our wretched meal with the lowest part of the crew.'

And the drink wasn't much better than the food. 'The beverage consisted of putrid water,' he wrote, 'which was handed round to the company in a large earthen pitcher.'

On other ships, dinner consisted of ship's biscuit and a few olives with vinegar and oil. '[They] told us to eat heartily,' the captive John Foss recalled, 'for after our arrival in Algiers we should not be allowed such dainties.'

For the troops, the fare was even more frugal.

'A ration just sufficient to sustain life is daily weighed out to the Janissaries,' writes Ogier Ghiselin de Busbecq, an ambassador to the Ottoman court. '…[T]hey take out a few spoonfuls of flour and put them into water, adding some butter, and seasoning the mess with salt and spices; these ingredients are boiled, and a large bowl of gruel is thus obtained.'

Some European corsairs included less orthodox foods in their diet. In 1623 the Barbary-based pirate John Nutt's stock of food consisted of 'bread … twelve hogsheads of beef, *besides pork* [my italics], and a store of water and some wine … '

Morat's ships continued on their long journey southwards, through the stormy Bay of Biscay and down the western coast of Spain and Portugal. The weather grew hotter and awnings were erected to protect the officers from the blazing sun.

For the fifty Baltimore youngsters, curious despite their situation, there would be a constant unfolding of marvels: perhaps a sighting of a whale or seal, or a school of dolphin flashing by. The corsair crew would very likely have included lads of their own age and we can imagine, for instance, the Gunter boys peering intently as they learned how to fashion a bowline or tie a Turk's head knot.

The deck was a busy and often chaotic place. Ships of the era carried not only humans, but also a wide variety of animals ranging from pet monkeys and parakeets to the hens and goats who were allowed to wander freely on deck.

Anna the maid would probably have relaxed when she saw that her own two young charges were being treated kindly by the crew. The Icelandic captives of 1626 recorded that Morat's pirates began acting like fond uncles to their children, slipping them treats and helping to cheer them up. Pananti confirmed this: he wrote that two child captives in his group were very much the centre of affectionate attention.

From the youngsters' point of view, the corsairs would

have made up a remarkable tableau – faces of nearly every conceivable shape and shade, and voices speaking in at least half a dozen languages. We know for certain that they would have heard people conversing in English, French, Dutch and Portuguese as well as Turkish and Arabic. (D'Aranda heard tongues of seven nations and Pananti noted several Mediterranean and African races.)

In this floating Tower of Babel, communication was made possible only by inventing a common language – *Sabir*, or 'The Knowledge', a mixture of Romance and Arabic tongues. The beauty of *Sabir* was its simplicity. All verbs were infinitive and didn't change tense. '*Mangiar*' always meant 'eat'. 'Drinking' was '*bibir*'. 'To sell' was '*vendir*'. For the future tense, you simply used the word '*bisogno*', 'need', before the verb. Adjectives also remained unchanged.

John, Tom and the other Baltimore captives could quite rapidly have picked up the basics and learned to communicate.

Life on board the slave ship was not all hard work. Morat had far more hands than he was ever likely to need, and in calm weather there would have been plenty of leisure time.

The Janissaries were famous for their ability to do nothing, quite cheerfully, for long periods. European visitors to Algiers were amazed at their ability to sit still for hours on end, calmly smoking a pipe and meditating.

In many cases the captains also adopted this laid-back attitude. If Morat Rais was anything like Pananti's rais, he was quite happy to sit for three or four hours, cross-legged on a mat on deck, occasionally barking out orders but mostly content to smoke or smooth his moustachios.

At night, there might even be entertainment. Pananti reported that the corsair crew treated the captives to a display of songs and dances and then called on the prisoners to sing their own folksongs. Surprisingly enough, many of the slaves obliged.

On a calm evening, this heady mix of western and eastern music would ring out from the open deck and drift up towards the stars.

Perhaps Morat Rais would invite some of the men from Baltimore to join him in his great cabin. This was usually a pleasant and airy chamber placed high on the poop deck and furnished with fine silk cushions and rugs. Barbary captains were often cultured gentlemen and they enjoyed good conversation.

Pananti and a few other favoured captives were regularly invited to the great cabin by their rais. He would serve them coffee and rum (which, the Italian noted cynically, had been stolen from his ship in the first place).

The Irish-born captive James Cathcart recalled how his rais, 'a really good man', served him coffee in his cabin and dispensed some philosophical advice.

'Christians, be consoled,' the captain would say. 'This world is full of vicissitudes. You shall be well used. I have been a slave myself, and will treat you much better than I have been treated; take some bread and honey and a dish of coffee, and God will redeem you from captivity as he has done me twice.'

This is not to imply that the Baltimore captives were having an easy time. The sickness and the squalor remained, along with the rats and the fleas in the miserable cable lockers.

Yet there is plenty of reliable evidence to show that there were tolerable moments amid the horror.

The accounts of Barbary captivity are full of cases in which captives found themselves mellowing towards their captors. Against all the odds, firm friendships could be established.

To his own surprise, even the irascible Filippo Pananti began to adjust to life with the corsairs. 'It is true our diet was not of the finest quality; but hunger, the best of all sauces, made us eat; and though our bed was not of down, yet habit enabled us to sleep,' he wrote. 'Our case was not quite so hopeless as we at first imagined.'

He became friendly with the ship's purser and the Janissary captain, both refined and civilised men. And even the rais eventually earned Pananti's approval: although he was swarthy and fierce looking, he was 'valorous and intelligent'.

'[H]is manners,' the poet admitted grudgingly, 'were by no means repulsive.'

James Cathcart said he too began to forge friendships. '[S]ome Turks who were more charitable than the rest … gave us some onions, oranges, raisins and figs from their own private stores,' he recalled.

'I likewise received relief several times for standing at the helm for the sailors and actually learned to smoke by the kindness of the ship's steward, who gave me a pipe and tobacco.'

And John Foss, who had been left almost naked by his captors, was bowled over by a single unexpected act of compassion. '[A]n old Turk, with an air of kindness, gave me an old shirt without sleeves,' he wrote. 'It was soothing to find a spark of humanity in my barbarous masters.'

Such experiences can trigger off dramatic changes in the human subconscious. Gradually, without realising it, prisoners and hostages can shift towards a position in which they identify more with their captors than with their own countryfolk.

There is a healthy psychological basis for this process of 'survival identification' among captives. It is a syndrome that has always existed – but it has only recently been given a name.

At 10.15 in the morning of 23 August 1973, a burst of automatic gunfire shattered the silence of the business quarter of Stockholm.

At that moment, an escaped convict named Jan-Erik Olsson blasted his way into the Sveriges Kreditbank. Police surrounded the building and for the next 131 hours, he kept four bank employees at gunpoint in a tiny bank vault. As the siege dragged on, the hostages began to side with Olsson. They claimed that the gunman was actually protecting them from the uncaring authorities outside. Surprisingly, their attitude persisted even after the threat had passed. They held no grudge against Olsson, but more than that – they were actually grateful to the convict for 'giving them back their lives'. By this they meant that he had withheld his power to kill them.

As psychologists began to study the phenomenon, they worked out a theoretical explanation. Under the threat of death, the hostages had unconsciously adopted another identity, a pseudo-personality which is sympathetic to the captor and makes it harder for him to harm his victim. For this technique to work, the feelings must not be false or forced, but genuine and heartfelt. This is much deeper than superficial dissembling – it is an age-old coping mechanism with roots deep in the psychology of human evolution.

Other cases were recognised and diagnosed. The most famous was Patty Hearst, the American heiress who joined the terrorists who had abducted her. And during the seizure of a Dutch train in 1975, some of the hostages developed bonds of sympathy with the guerrillas who'd captured them.

Three vital elements are needed for this process to work. First, the hostage must consciously develop positive feelings for the captor, usually after some small act of kindness. In some cases, it is sufficient that the abductors choose not to use their power to kill.

Secondly, the captor must reciprocate these positive feelings.

And thirdly, the prisoners must develop negative feelings towards their own authorities – for example, if they feel that their government has betrayed or forgotten them.

No-one is certain about the deep forces that drive this syndrome. One expert saw it as sexual, part of the same process that attracts some women towards obvious scoundrels. Another has seen it as a return to babyhood, with the helpless captive regressing to an infantile state in which the captor represents the all-powerful parent.

Did the Baltimore hostages experience any of these symptoms? We simply don't know. What we *do* know is that all the elements identified by modern psychologists were in place: an abduction by force; a lengthy confinement with the abductors; captors who turn out to be less brutal than expected; and a feeling that the uncaring authorities at home have let them down.

The subtle shifts that began on board the ship might go a long way to explaining the surprising events that were to unfold more than fifteen years later, when the question might legitimately be asked: was Baltimore an early seventeenth-century example of the Stockholm Syndrome?

As Morat's ships reached Gibraltar and changed course towards the rising sun, the twin coasts of Africa and Europe loomed out of the haze and narrowed to a gap a mere twenty-seven miles wide. On the right, the world of Islam; on the left, the world of Christendom, so close that Ryder and the other captives must have felt they could almost swim to safety. Morat's men tensed and the captives held their breath, both sides knowing that the Straits were regularly patrolled by Spanish gunships and that this represented their last, desperate hope of rescue.

Back home in Baltimore, the relatives of the captives shared this forlorn hope. In such cases, wishful thinking can rapidly translate into rumour. At around this time, Captain Hooke of *The Fifth Whelp* actually reported to London that the Spanish had indeed rescued all 107 captives.

'No pirate has been here since the two Turks,' he wrote, 'and I hear they were captured by Spaniards off the coast of Spain. I hope it is true.'

Hooke would have loved it to be true, but unfortunately it wasn't. We can only imagine how the false report must have lifted the Baltimore relatives to the heights of joy only to plunge them, later, into even deeper gloom.

A contemporary naval officer, one Captain Plumleigh,

summed up their despair. 'I never saw people in whom one disaster had settled so deep an impression,' he wrote, 'as the Turks' last descent has done in these Irish.'

CHAPTER SIXTEEN

The Diamond City

By now, it is late July. Morat's two ships hug the sunbaked Mediterranean coast of Africa, passing bays where the turquoise water reflects cobalt under the wings of wheeling seagulls. The waters are busy with exotic shipping: polacres, tartanes, and *xebec* galleys with banks of slaves straining at the oars.

As they enter the territory of Algiers, the mounting excitement among the crewmen is matched only by the sense of dread and apprehension among their captives.

The approach to the city of Algiers by sea is so dramatic it might almost have been stage managed. A headland withdraws, almost like a curtain, to reveal a beautiful horseshoe-shaped bay; and then, suddenly, a blast of blinding white that assumes the shape of a huge triangle affixed to the green backdrop of the Sahel Hills. Perhaps someone on board makes the usual romantic comparison to a diamond in an emerald frame. As Joane's eyes adjust to the glare, the white triangle defines itself as an ancient city, stretching all the way from the water's edge right up to the hilltop.

Working before the mast, John Ryder, Tom Paine and the Gunter boys watch in sheer awe as the features of the city begin to unfold: the flat-roofed buildings, the squat forts and octagonal minarets, the aqueducts and mosques. The searing white is broken only by terracotta roofs, a red tower, and dusty shade trees.

To the left of the city, they can see a hill with a flattish top, crowned by a fortress with a fluttering flag. To the right lies another hill with a more defined crest. Between the two summits, the city flows like a white hot stream of lava down to the shoreline.

At the top, four hundred feet up, lies the 115-year-old citadel of the Kasbah, forming the apex of the triangle of Algiers. The waterfront forms the base, and all three sides are defined by formidable stone walls. Along the shoreline, the white marble columns of the principal mosque, the Jamaa-el-Kebir, proudly proclaim the city's religious affiliation to the world.

To the right of the waterfront lies the harbour, built in the shelter of the long mole that Barbarossa threw up between the mainland and the the main island. A small forest of masts thrusts skyward, representing just some of the navy of fourscore ships based at Algiers. Protecting this fleet is the latest addition to the Algerines' ring of fortresses – the redoubtable Bordj El Fenar or Fort of the

Lamp, a squat tower topped by a beacon and bristling with fifty-five cannon on four levels. One glance at this fortress would be enough to convince Ryder and the other Baltimore hostages to abandon all hope of a rescue by sea.

For the final stage of the journey, the male captives are manhandled below and clapped in irons. They miss the spectacle, for as Morat's two ships draw nearer, the city explodes in noise. The gunners at the Bordj El Fenar let fly a salvo of fire; the sound of the shots crackles and echoes across the hills. Morat's gunners respond shot for shot. It is the traditional welcome, but it contains a coded message, for the corsair captain's success will be judged by the enthusiasm of his reply.

To Ryder, Paine and the other men confined below, the turmoil is terrifying. Emanuel D'Aranda recalled being awoken by the deafening gunfire as he lay in the hold where 'I slept with thirteen other Christians, each one with a foot in chains ... At this noise, all the curious folk of the town came to the harbour.'

Throughout the city, the atmosphere is electric with anticipation. Shopkeepers are stocking their shelves, tavern owners check their wine cellars, and the whorehouses spruce up their women ready for a brisk trade.

To the cheers of the waiting crowd, the flagship and her consort edge through the packed harbour and toss ashore the lines. Dockhands spring aboard to disable the rudder, a standard precaution to prevent hijacking by runaway slaves. By evening both ships will have been emptied – ballast and all – to be cleaned and waxed ready for the next mission.

The sailors throw their kit ashore and shout greetings to their families and friends. Ryder, Paine and the other men are led up, squinting and blinking, to line up on the deck alongside their women and children. Official auditors come aboard and run a practised eye over the new captives, valuing them as swiftly and accurately as a horse dealer might value a stallion.

The officials leave to take the good news to the Palace. At a nod from Morat, the slaves form a bedraggled line and file miserably down the ship's gangway to the harbour.

It is late morning on Thursday, July 28, 1631, when the first of the slaves sets foot on Algerine soil. Their arduous thirty-eight-day voyage is over; their former lives are fading away like the sea mist on the horizon. It is time to begin their new lives under African skies.

CHAPTER SEVENTEEN

Moving Next Door To Hell

Buried in the vaults of the British National Archives in Kew, near London, lies an extraordinary document. It forms part of the F71/1 collection – the correspondence between London and the Barbary States in the early 1600s. It is the only existing record of the arrival of the Baltimore captives in North Africa.

Folio number 157 is entitled 'A note of such English ships ... brought into Algiers' and is annotated: 'About ships from April 1 1629 to November 26 1637. Admiralty'.

It is a long list, brown with age, and recorded in spidery handwriting. In fact, it looks rather like a page from a child's copybook from a bygone era. There are three columns: date, details and number of people on board. It contains over seventy separate entries for ships from places such as London, Yarmouth and Weymouth, sometimes with dozens of seamen on board, and the speed at which they were flooding in can be judged by the fact that the original final total of '1466' had to be struck out with pen at the last moment and replaced with '1473' as another seven men arrived.

Somewhere in the middle of all this is an entry which reads as follows:

> *1631.*
>
> *July 28. Morrato, [a] Fleming, and his consort brought from Baltimore in Ireland eighty-nine women and children and twenty men, moreover twenty-four men which they took out of a barque of Falmouth, master John [illegible surname], and two fishing boats which they set adrift, in all: 133.*

What I find remarkable is that the Baltimore reference is just another routine item in a list. Although deemed so significant that it takes up three whole lines in a document of mainly single-line records, it is squeezed in between an entry for thirty-eight people who arrived with the *Falcon of London* on April 8, 1631, and another entry for twelve people who arrived on a Weymouth ship later in July. The implication is clear. Baltimore is just one more drop in the ocean. The circumstances may be unique and unprecedented; the arrival of so many women and children may be heartbreaking; but in terms of numbers, in this city of slaves, it is really nothing special.

James Frizell was not a happy man. In the six years he had served in the difficult role of English consul in Algiers, things had never been so bad. The Algerine corsairs were attacking his country's shipping almost at will. New consignments of English slaves were continually arriving in port and the numbers were mounting faster than he could cope. Only five years ago there were fifty or sixty, a manageable number. Now, on this morning of July 28, the figure stood at 207.

The English authorities refused to negotiate ransoms, reasoning that it would merely encourage the corsairs to return and capture more.

Frizell wrote home regularly describing the dreadful conditions of the captives in Algiers and urging that at least some of them be ransomed. It was becoming increasingly clear that he was wasting his time.

Irritated, the corsairs had recently decided to up the ante. They'd warned the English ambassador in Constantinople, Sir Thomas Roe, that if ransom cash didn't arrive soon, they would target English territory with the same sort of devastating land raids they had carried out in the Mediterranean.

Sir Thomas had taken this threat extremely seriously. He had written to his superiors warning that the number of British slaves could soon number a thousand. 'They say that, unless you send [ransom money] speedily, they will go to England and fetch men out of their beds as commonly as they used to in Spain.'

Incredible as it might seem, the figure of a thousand was a mere fraction of the number of captives in Algiers at that time. Every year, hundreds of Europeans were being snatched up and fed into the gaping, insatiable maw of the Algerine slave machine. Between 1621 and 1627, one tally listed 20,000 slaves of all nationalities in Algiers. In the four years since then, the figure had swollen by nearly a quarter. In the early 1630s, a Redemptionist priest, Father Pierre Dan, would estimate the total number of slaves in the city at 25,000 – not counting an extra 8,000 Christians who had changed religion.

As for the English and Irish slaves, Sir Thomas's prediction of a thousand was to prove eerily accurate. That figure would, in fact, be bypassed by the late 1630s, and by 1640 there would be three times that number.

As consul, James Frizell knew there was little he could do to help these people, even though he was their only hope. There was no money in the kitty to buy their freedom, and his own pockets were empty.

Frizell was not paid by his Government, but by the Turkey Company, a commercial shipping firm which was supposed to give him a salary and let him levy fees from English ships. But in Algiers, English merchant ships were rare ... and James Frizell was facing financial ruin. Even his basic salary had dried up and there were times when he was close to starvation.

Frizell could hardly have ended up in a worse place. Algiers was renowned among the diplomatic community as a hell-hole, a place where foreign consuls were regularly jailed, beaten with sticks or publicly humiliated at the whim of some unpredictable governor. Rulers would demand lavish bribes in jewellery, then toss them contemptuously to their servants. The consul's own house might be ransacked and his possessions seized. Diplomats would be abused in the royal court, threatened in the street and, on occasions, executed. When one envoy described Algiers as 'the next step to the infernal regions' he was not joking.

Throughout the centuries, consuls who'd been abandoned for years in this mind-warping city would react in extreme ways. One took to heavy drinking. Another went completely mad and was last seen 'sitting on his bed with a sword and a brace of pistols at his side'.

Frizell himself seems to have reacted by slumping into a chronic depression. His only wish – and he wished it desperately – was to come home. He felt as though he himself were a slave being held 'in thralldom' in Algiers. 'I do verily believe,' he said at one point, 'that never any of His Majesty's ministers hath been so neglected as I am.'

So the last thing James Frizell wanted to hear, on that morning of July 28, 1631, was the news that another slave ship had arrived – carrying so many English and Irish captives that they would boost the total in Algiers by over 60 per cent the moment they stepped ashore.

The arrival of the Baltimore captives also confirmed

Frizell's worst fears. This was something unique. An entire village of civilians – men, women and children – had been 'fetched out of their beds' on land, just as the corsairs had warned they would do.

With a heavy heart, Frizell hurried down to the harbour to perform his duties. He knew his options were limited. He could try to have them released under some technicality of law, but this rarely succeeded. In practical terms, there was nothing he could do but log the slaves' arrival and protest in the strongest terms to the Algerines. Then he would notify the English authorities who would, as usual, ignore his requests for ransom money.

The consul was no doubt sweltering in his English tunic and breeches by the time he reached the Marine Gate and walked the length of the harbour mole to where Morat's ships were berthed. He would have had to elbow his way through the sizeable crowd that gathered on the quayside to gawk at every fresh cargo of infidels. The hubbub would have been deafening. Over the pathetic groans of the new arrivals, and the crying of their children, one could hear the shouts of the slave traders who'd come to inspect the latest prize, and the desperate cries of long-term captives trying to locate anyone with news from home. According to a Spanish monk who spent many years in Barbary, there was even a lowlife contingent among the existing Christian slaves who would 'jeer at the wretches who are brought in captive' and let them know just how dire and hopeless their position was.

There were also conmen – English renegades who would sidle up to the slaves and offer to safeguard their hidden valuables or help them escape. When the seventeenth-century English captive 'T.S.' was taken ashore at Algiers, the first person he met was a Cornishman. Speaking in a broad West Country accent, the man offered to save T.S. and his colleagues by taking them under his own wing. But they suspected his motives when they saw him haggling for prices with other buyers.

'He was a trader in slaves,' wrote T.S., 'and knew well how to make his advantage of his own nation.'

Eventually Frizell would have pushed his way through the throng and introduced himself to the Baltimore captives. Despite his disillusionment, he was a kind-hearted man; it is probable that he was deeply moved by the sight of the emaciated Ryder and Paine, the dishevelled and pregnant Joane Broadbrook, and – worst of all – the dozens of bewildered children clinging pathetically to their mothers' skirts as their eyes gazed up at him in supplication.

Still, he had a job to do. He tallied the numbers and recorded eighty-nine women and children and twenty men from Baltimore, and a further twenty-four English and Irish sailors seized by Morat at sea.

Shouting above the din, he would have promised to

notify London of the captives' plight. In the meantime, however, they must obey instructions and follow Morat Rais to the palace of the Pasha, who would decide their fate.

Once the dockside paperwork had been completed, John Ryder and Tom Paine were ordered to fall into a long line along with the rest of the male captives. Joane, Anna and the womenfolk fell into place behind, with the children in tow. This was a set ritual, for corsair captains loved to show off their prizes and would always conduct their procession of miserable captives on a triumphal tour of the city.

For instance, when the sixteenth-century corsair Murad returned from his spectacular raid on Lanzarote, he led the parade while mounted on the Pasha's own steed and escorted by a phalanx of Janissaries.

'At our first landing, great companies flocked about us to see us,' recalled the captured English merchant T.S. 'Every one of us had great strong chain of about 20lb weight linked to our legs and tied to our girdle, so that if we did meditate on escape, it might not be without difficulty.

'We were conducted next in this strange equipage, with our jingling chains at our sides, to the king's palace.'

Another contemporary account reads: 'We were paraded ... around the town five or six times with chains on our necks ... to show the merchants that we had received no mortal injury.'

The Italian captive Filippo Pananti recalled that *his* corsair captain ordered all the prisoners into a long crocodile, assumed his rightful place at the head of the line, and walked the long way round to the Pasha's mansion, proudly waving to the crowd:

'On the Rais's landing, he immediately ordered us to form a procession in his rear, and then moved on, with as much self importance as [the Egyptian conqueror] Sesostris ... an amazing concourse had collected on the beach, to welcome with acclamations the triumphant return of the pirates: but we were neither plundered nor insulted, a treatment which many Christian slaves are said to have met with on disembarking at this inhospitable place ... In the manner of the Roman ovation, we made a long circuit, to arrive at the palace.'

Unsteady on their land legs, John, Joane and the other newcomers from Baltimore filed down the harbour mole, past the gangs of slaves who sweated as they heaved and cleaved rocks. 'The dreadful clanking of chains,' wrote captive John Foss, 'was the most terrible noise I ever heard.'

On the way they passed an enormous cannon – it was known as 'Blessed Father', but later in the century it would be nicknamed *La Consulaire* when a ruler of Algiers fired the French consul out of it in a fit of pique.

As the captives approached the massive city walls, the Marine Gate opened to swallow them into the belly of

Algiers. Joane found herself in a maze of rat-run alleyways, so narrow that only one person could pass in each direction. Curious eyes stared at her from the darkened interiors of shops and workplaces; above her, balconies met in the centre of the street to block out the sun, turning the streets into shaded tunnels and providing a secret refuge from which the womenfolk of Algiers could critically inspect the fair-skinned European females.

Occasionally she would pass through a square or concourse with shade trees and decorated marble fountains. The streets echoed with the cries of vendors and the grumbling of tetchy camels. Donkeys groaning under impossible burdens trotted past, their owners shouting '*Balak, balak!*' ('Get out of the way!') The smell of dung mingled earthily with the scent of the scrambling jasmine and oleander. Joane's senses were assaulted by sounds, smells and sights that were truly alien to her: a tall minaret with a muezzin calling the faithful to prayer; a masked woman carrying a gift of fruit to a shrine; Japanese sailors, Russian slaves, Central African giants who towered above her, their coal-black skins glistening with sweat.

It's impossible to imagine the effect of such an experience upon simple villagers who'd never ventured beyond their own parish. In fact, it is said that during their first few minutes in Barbary, some new arrivals dropped dead from terror.

In this case, all the Baltimore captives survived to arrive safely at the palace. However, if their experience was anything like that of Pananti, their fears would not have been eased by the sight that confronted them there. The first thing the Italian poet noticed was six bloody heads arranged along the entrance – the grisly remains of half a dozen Janissary captains who had dared to stage a rebellion.

CHAPTER EIGHTEEN

'A Good Prize!
Prisoners! Slaves!'

Visiting diplomats described the Pasha's palace as 'the most beautiful building in all Algiers'. And if John Ryder and Joane Broadbrook had any lingering doubts about their own insignificance in this city of 25,000 slaves, these would have been immediately dispelled when they entered the ruler's domain. The entire palace had been built to inspire awe.

The walls of the three-storey palace were constructed from giant slabs of stone, bleached snow-white with lime. A huge decorated gate opened to admit the ogling captives to a central square paved with white marble and shaded by lemon trees. Elaborate fountains threw handfuls of water at the hot, dry air.

In the women's quarters on the first floor, the Pasha's wives would be inspecting the newcomers from behind copper-latticed windows, eagerly looking out for a new maidservant or companion to provide diversion in the harem. Having earmarked their favourites, they would despatch a eunuch to the Pasha begging the favour.

As workmen piled the meagre booty from the expedition in the courtyard, John, Joane and the rest of the Baltimore villagers filed in to a large room whose walls were covered with hand-painted earthenware tiles and cedar fretwork. Joane stared in wonder at the marble columns that supported its two elegant galleries and soared towards ceilings of gilded olive wood. All around her were the richest furnishings of Africa and Asia: cedar trunks inlaid with pearl, filigree screens, marble fountains, and giant urns containing sago palms.

Officials sat at low tables or reclined on sumptuous sofas. No doubt the Algerine corsair admiral Ali Bichnin was there to greet Morat and congratulate him personally. And at the head of the hall, dominating this exotic scene, was the Governor – His Excellency, Pasha Hussein. There is no record of his appearance on that day, but we have a verbal snapshot of one of his successors:

'[H]is feet [were] shod with buskins bound upon his legs with diamond buttons in loops of pearl; around his waist was brought a sash glittering with jewels, to which was suspended a broad scimitar, its sheath of the finest velvet. Upon [his] head was a turban [with] a large diamond crescent [and] two large ostrich feathers ...'

The English captive T. S. recalled that he and his fellow captives were left to wait for quite some time while the ruler lingered over his morning bath. It wasn't until 2 pm that the courtiers filed in, armed with scimitars.

'Next came a grave fellow with a turban almost as big as our English half bushel,' he wrote. 'At one side of it he had a set of diamonds, that did sparkle as his eyes; his vesture was green, his legs were bare, on his feet he did wear sandals … his pace was slow and grave. I could have numbered twenty between every step. He marched in that manner to the upper end, where there was canopy of State over his head, and two Turk carpets with a large pillow covered with damask under him.'

The ship captain formally presented his bill of lading and invited the turbaned Pasha to inspect the slaves. The ruler left his throne and filed slowly past the captives, pausing to stare into their eyes.

'He cast a jest on every one of us,' the writer recalled, 'which gave the company a great deal of mirth and increased our sadness.'

When the Pasha reached T.S., he joked that that he would not be prepared to trust this man anywhere near his women.

This account matches other versions of the Algerines' vetting procedure. They enjoyed psyching out their captives in this way. The legendary Ali Bichnin wrinkled the truth out of his newly arrived slaves with a simple but effective technique. If he captured someone who appeared to be a middle-class gentleman, he would address him as 'My Lord' or 'Count'. A humble cleric would be flattered with 'Your Eminence'. The horrified captives would rush to correct the mistake, thus giving away their true status.

Some rich aristocrats treated the whole business with contempt. Emmanuel d'Aranda tells of one Portuguese nobleman, captured in 1638, who haughtily reeled off his family pedigree, including the fact that his uncle was General of Brazil.

'Nobility and servility will not do well together,' the shrewd Pasha flattered him, before citing a ludicrously high 4,000 ducats for his freedom.

The wealthy dimwit agreed, thus setting the same impossible rate for his fellow captives.

When the horrified D'Aranda told him he could have got away with only 1,500 ducats, the nobleman shrugged disdainfully. 'To what end should a man have money?' he demanded. 'To work like a dog, or to procure his liberty?'

At these hearings, consuls would desperately try to argue for the release of their citizens. The Algerines loved show-trials and would happily debate the finer points of law for hours before deciding in their own favour.

Filippo Pananti recalled how a nail-biting trial took place before the Divan (the Janissary parliament) to decide whether his consignment of slaves was 'a good prize' – that is, legitimate in international law.

A large crowd waited with bated breath outside the building as the English consul of the day argued that the ship had been seized unlawfully. However, the corsair captain responded with all the skill of a top barrister and 'boldly sustained the remorseless laws of piracy, drawing the finest distinctions imaginable between domiciliation and nationality'.

When the corsair won his case, the news spread out to the waiting crowd.

'"A good prize! Prisoners! Slaves!" was now murmured throughout the councils,' Pananti wrote, 'and soon communicated to the crowd assembled without; which by its cries and vociferation, seemed to demand such a decision.'

Now, in 1631, James Frizell argued with justification that the Baltimore raid had contravened Sir Thomas Roe's peace agreement with the Turkish Emperor. But Algiers was not Constantinople, as the consul had found out many times before.

Another seventeenth-century English diplomat described the tortuous legal situation with an air of weariness. 'The pirates of Algiers and Tunis began to cast off their respect and reverence to the Ottoman Emperor, for being become rich by prizes they had taken on Christian vessels, they resolved to set up for themselves and to esteem the peace which Christian princes had made with the [Emperor], not to concern them,' he wrote.

'[T]he Turks were inwardly pleased with these piracies [but] gave good words to the Christian ambassadors. [They] promised much, and effected nothing.'

Frizell's arguments were soon dismissed. The captives were declared as slaves, and the Pasha could turn his attention to his most important task – selecting the most desirable women.

Joane would have felt a sense of dread as Pasha Hussein surveyed the miserable lineup of women and girls by her side. She probably suspected that this was the last time they would be together as a group: after this, they would be scattered to the four winds.

The Pasha was normally expected to send several female slaves as tribute to the Sultan in Constantinople. He might also need to send two or three women to the harem of a counterpart in Tunis or Tripoli in order to return a favour. And, of course, he must not overlook the needs of his personal harem.

There was a respectful silence as the ruler carefully inspected Anna, Miss Croffine and the rest of the younger women. He was entitled by law to one in eight of the adult females and the older girls, and of course he would choose only the best.

In his eyes, it was not a problem that the chosen

women might have been married, or the mothers of young children. These were not full human beings, after all, but infidel prisoners of war – *tutsaklar.* Their heathen marriages were invalid here, and the Pasha would have felt no more compunction at separating mother from child than a horse-breeder might feel at separating a mare from her foal. Mothers like Mrs John Ryder could be dragged screaming from their children and into an enclosed harem which would be their home for years to come.

There was one way to avoid all this unpleasantness. At any stage of these grim proceedings, a rich woman could announce that her family would pay for her freedom. She would then be escorted to a safe home where she would idle away the weeks until the money arrived.

This was what happened to the optimistic woman on Cathcart's ship. She was sent to a hospital to await the arrival of her ransom. Sadly, the cash never materialised and she was 'purchased by the Regency'.

But without access to 4,000 ducats – or even 1,500 – the Baltimore fisherfolk had no prospect of making such a dignified exit. There were screams and entreaties, tearful supplications and angry struggles as the palace guards enforced the Pasha's whims. None of their pleas made any difference. Afterwards, as Pananti put it, the ruler 'looked at us with a mingled smile of exultation and contempt, and then, making a sign with his hand, we were ordered to depart.'

Once the captives had left the royal palace, all pretence at politeness and civility was abandoned. They were now auction fodder, with no more rights than cattle or sheep. They were bound for the slave market.

CHAPTER NINETEEN

The Slave Market

Father Pierre Dan thought he had seen everything in Algiers, but nothing could have prepared him for the experience of the Baltimore captives being put up for sale in the slave market. These were images that would haunt him for the rest of his days: little girls torn, screaming, from their mothers' arms ... husbands struggling desperately while their wives were sold into the beds of other men. As the French priest took up pen and paper and steeled himself to record their horrific ordeal in a report to his superiors, he found himself almost at a loss for words. First the facts. He must report the basic facts ...

'[I]n the year 1631,' Fr Dan began, 'Morat Rais, a Flemish renegado, went as far as England, and from England to Ireland, where he arrived towards evening, and had put into an open boat some two hundred soldiers who then landed in a small village called Baltimore, where they took by surprise several fishermen of that island.

'That same night they took 237 [sic] people, men, women and children, even those in the cradle.

'This done, they brought them to Algiers ...'

He paused, and his pent-up feelings suddenly flowed out through the pen on to the paper in a torrent of emotion:

'It was a pitiful sight to see them put up for sale. For then, wives were taken from husbands and children from their fathers. Then, I declare, they sold on the one hand the husbands, on the other the wives, ripping their daughters from their arms, leaving them no hope of ever seeing each another again ...'

Fr Dan was no ordinary priest. He was a member of the Trinitarians, an order of courageous volunteers, often from wealthy families, who had chosen to work among the slaves in Algiers, and, in extreme circumstances, to offer themselves as substitutes for enslavement. Dan would later become familiar to the Baltimore captives – a striking figure, pacing through the narrow streets in his distinctive white robe emblazoned with a blue and red cross on the breast. (The Trinitarians were originally a Crusader order.)

His obvious sympathy for the Baltimore villagers, whom his church would have viewed as heretics, was extraordinary and showed just what an impact this episode had had upon the entire European community in Algiers. As Fr Dan put it: '[T]here was not a single Christian who was not weeping and who was not full of sadness at the sight of so many honest maidens and so many good women abandoned to the brutality of these barbarians.'

The villagers' nightmare had lasted for hours. Immediately after leaving the palace, the bedraggled captives from The Cove had been marched along the city's main thoroughfare, Grand Market Street, to a large concourse whose shaded arcades were already filled with excited, shouting dealers. This was the notorious Bedistan slave market. Here, in this sunblasted crucible of human commerce, John Ryder, Tom Paine and the other male captives were stripped almost naked and put through their paces like prancing horses.

'As soon as a vessel arrives from a corsair cruise after having taken a prize,' Chevalier Laurent d'Arvieux, a French diplomat to Barbary in the 1600s, explained, 'the slaves are unloaded and taken to the royal house. From these the Dey [Governor] chooses a fifth, and always the best, to be sold for the profit of the corps of the Militia.

'These were taken to the State bagnios [prisons]; the others were led to the Batistan; it is a long, wide street closed at both ends, where all the captives are sold ...

'There you can find auctioneers or brokers who take the slaves by the hand, walking them from one end to the other and shouting the bids at the top of their voices.

'It is an auction where everyone has the right to bid, and where the goods are delivered to the highest and last bidder, always assuming he has the cash to pay.'

The French diplomat explained that these dealers in human slaves ('and many deal in nothing else') used every trick in the book to find out whether the newcomers came from wealthy backgrounds.

'They examine their teeth, the palms of their hands, to judge by the delicacy of the skin if they are working folk; but they'll pay special attention to those with pierced ears, which implies that they are not common folk but people of quality who've worn earrings since childhood.'

He advised wealthy slaves to pretend they were humble artisans and to say with a weary sigh that it made no odds whether they were free men or slaves – their working conditions would be much the same.

Ottaviano Bon, a Venetian diplomat, had much the same story to tell about the slave market in Constantinople a few years earlier. 'Every Wednesday, in the open street,' he wrote, 'there are bought and sold slaves of all sorts, and every one may freely come to buy for their several uses; some for nurses, some for servants, and some for their lustful appetites …

'[T]hey are examined of what country they are, and what they are good for; either for sewing, spinning, weaving, or the like; buying sometimes the mother with the children, and sometimes the children without the mother, sometimes two or three brothers together, and again sometimes taking the one, and leaving the rest, using no terms of humanity, love, or honesty, but even as the buyer or the seller shall think will best turn them to profit.'

When John Ryder was finally hauled into the auction ring at the Algiers Bedistan, he was put on show like a bull or stallion. His experience would probably have been similar to Emanuel d'Aranda's:

'An old and very decrepit auctioneer with a staff in his hand took me by the arm and led me on various circuits of the market,' d'Aranda wrote, 'and those who felt like buying me asked my homeland, my name and my profession ...

'They felt my hands to see if they were hard and calloused from work. Then they made me open my mouth to establish whether my teeth were strong enough to chew sea-biscuits aboard the galleys.'

After the goods had been well exhibited, the auction began.

'They made us all sit down, and this old auctioneer took the first man in line by the arm, walking him around the market three or four times, shouting, 'Any advance?' As soon as the first man was sold, he was moved to the other side of the market and a new round of bidding began.'

The auctioneer's patter was loud and enthusiastic. 'Behold!' he would shout. 'What a strong man is this!

What limbs he has! He is fit for any work.'

When d'Aranda himself went under the hammer, he became naturally curious. 'I asked an old slave: "How much are they offering?" He told me: "That one is offering 190 patacoons [Spanish dollars], and the one over there is offering 200 patacoons." The closing bid was made for 200.'

Meanwhile Joane, Bessie and the rest of the Baltimore females were being ushered into an enclosed sales room off the main square where buyers queued up to inspect them privately and in intimate detail.

It would have become rapidly apparent to Joane that the buyers were primarily interested in three classes of females: virgin girls, skilled craft workers such as seamstresses, and women whom they regarded as outstandingly beautiful.

In this cultural context, 'beautiful' meant ample and curvaceous. According to one contemporary diplomat, the most desirable concubines had 'big breasts ... [and] they are fat because they eat a lot of rice with beef and butter.'

Porcelain-skinned Cornish women were particularly in demand in Barbary, so the Baltimore women – with their Devon and Cornwall parentage – would have precisely met this demand.

Joane herself may have fallen into this category – or perhaps it was just that the buyers examined her swollen belly and liked the idea of getting two slaves for the price of one. She watched the bidding rise higher and higher, and eventually the hammer fell at 150 Spanish dollars (around £32).

Bessie would probably have been sold as a domestic servant at a much lower price.

We know the sale price of only one other woman from Roaring Water Bay. 'Ellen Hawkins of Baltamore' was sold for $86 – that is, around £18. Since she is not listed among the named Baltimore captives, she may have been one of the nameless domestics.

However, much of the attention at the sale would have focused on the younger women and teenage girls. Joane would have had to watch helplessly as friends such as Miss Croffine and Anna, the Meregeys' maid, were submitted to intimate examinations aimed at confirming their virginity and thus establishing their higher market price.

'[When] there is a virgin that is beautiful and fair, she is held at a high rate, and is sold for far more than any other,' wrote Ottaviano Bon.

A contemporary traveller, Aaron Hill, reported that it was something of an entertainment for men to view these 'miserable Christian captive-virgins':

'[T]hey feel their breasts, hands, cheeks and foreheads; nay, proceed, if curious in the nicety of search, to have the young and wretched creatures taken privately to some convenient place where, undisturbed

... [they can] discover instantly by proofs and demonstration, whether the pretended virgin has as yet been robbed of that so celebrated jewel.'

The English slave Joseph Pitts concurred. He reported that buyers had the right to stick their fingers into the women's mouths, squeeze their breasts and check their virginity 'in a modest way'.

A French traveller, Gerard Nerval, had first-person experience of such a viewing in the 1800s. 'They poked open their mouths so that I could examine their teeth,' he wrote. 'They made them walk up and down and pointed out, above all, the bounciness of their breasts.'

Let's pause at this point and reflect on how much a human being was thought to be worth in financial terms.

First of all, we have to realise that there was a huge difference between the inflated ransom demanded and the purchase price. D'Aranda is careful to draw the distinction between 'the value set according to the body, and not according to the ransom that may be got'. While a good craftsman might fetch, say, £46 in the slave market, his ransom might be set at five or six times that amount. These sums could be hopelessly unrealistic – one impoverished Irish captive wrote to the Earl of Cork to report that his ransom had been set at £200.

As for the value of 'the body', the prices varied widely.

Among those held in high esteem were doctors,

gunsmiths, and barrel makers. Unskilled workers might fetch only a quarter of that price, and the sick and elderly a mere tenth.

Prices could be affected by glut and shortage, or by nationality. D'Aranda claimed that English captives came bottom of the list: 'An Englishman is sold on 60 to 70 patacoons whereas a Spanish or Italian is valued at 150 to 200.'

Bidding took place in the main currency of Algiers, a silver coin known as the Zevu Bucu or 'double bucu'. But as this coin was often adulterated, the hard currencies were the Spanish dollar and the Venetian ducat.

Since the dollar was worth around four shillings and threepence in English money, a captive sold at, say, $215 would be worth just over £45 sterling.

Thanks to a remarkable price-list of English and Irish slaves sold at auction in Algiers in precisely this period, we have an accurate idea of what female slaves such as Bessie Flood, Miss Croffine and Anna were worth.

According to this fascinating document, the price of white female slaves varied from $86 (£18) right up to $357 (£75), a huge amount in those days. That was the sum fetched by a London woman called Elizabeth Alwin, who must have been seen as extraordinarily attractive.

The prices fetched by the other females in this list give some clue to the bidding for the Baltimore women. Alice Heyes from Edinburgh was sold for $258 (£55).

Ursula Corlion of Falmouth fetched $107 (£23), while Sarah Ripley of London was sold for $172 (£36).

Four women from Youghal in Ireland were sold together for $890 (£189) and a family of three women – Anna, Elizabeth and Katherine Wright – fetched $590 (£125).

Sometimes mothers were sold with their children. Mary Weymouth was sold along with her two little boys for $215 and Bridget Randall was sold along with her son for $225.

And what would male slaves like John Ryder and Tom Paine have fetched? None of the twenty Baltimore males features on this list, but, based on the same catalogue, it seems that prices ranged from £7 to £66 and averaged at around £27.

To put these prices in context, a clergyman at that time earned £20 and a labourer around £8 a year. An ox cost £4, a horse £3 and a cow £2.

By that reckoning, Ellen Hawkins was worth six horses and Joane Bradbrook was worth eight oxen. A labouring male would have had to work for more than three years just to repay someone's *sale* price on the slave market.

What do these figures mean today? A price of £32 would equate to nearly £3000, or about €4,500, in our time. So perhaps the clearest parallel is that in seventeenth-century Algiers, a woman like Joane Broadbrook could be sold for the price today of a ten-year-old hatchback car.

🐚 🐚 🐚

'After the slaves are sold at the Badistan, or marketplace,' says an official English report in 1675, 'they are carried to the King's house and entered again, where every farthing that is offered for them more than was at the Badistan, turns to the benefit of the public.'

Emmanuel d'Aranda fell down at this final hurdle. He'd been sold privately, but on the Pasha's whim, he found himself headed for the State galleys.

Then, with all business concluded, the profits were shared out. After expenses, half the proceeds would go to the mission's investors, who usually included the ship's captain. The other half went to the ship's company. Each seaman got three parts and each Janissary got half a seaman's cut since he was already on salary. The captain received forty parts.

The profit from this expedition would certainly have run into thousands of pounds – anywhere between a quarter and half a million in today's money. Morat's shares must have earned him a substantial sum – perhaps £50,000 or more today. This would go a long way in a society where everything ran on slave labour. Corsair captains were rich enough to be able to build lavish suburban mansions. Their lifestyle – on land, at least – was genteel and civilized. In a later era, an English diplomat's daughter would write glowingly of her neighbour, a corsair rais whose home was immaculate and who would occasionally drop in on her father for a glass of port.

The tastes of Morat's crewmen would have been less refined. Renegade sailors on shore leave were the terror of Algiers. They were compared to wild animals and one European observer wrote that all the money they brought to the city was tainted by the 'debauchery' and 'unchecked licence' of their activities on land.

That first night, the noise of their raucous celebrations filtered through the prison bars, adding further misery to the plight of John Ryder and Tom Paine; and rose up from the streets through the carved latticework of the harem screens to taunt Joane and Bessie. Once free human beings, they were now simply items of property, and they could do nothing but await their destinies.

His hectic day over, Consul James Frizell sat down to prepare his official report. The document that reached England later that summer provided surprisingly little information. Instead, it took the form of a heartfelt plea from Frizell on behalf of the Baltimore captives, the 231 other English slaves ... and himself.

> 'Humble petition from James Frizell to the Lords.
> 'Most humbly showeth onto your Lordships that since the receipt of Your Lordships' letter to me [July 22, 1629], here hath been taken to this place of new English captives to this day the number of 340 persons remaining here, of which 89 of them are women and

children taken lately from Baltamore, with 20 men only. The rest
were taken out of several ships and barks which they have sunk at
sea. And this is but a beginning of the mischief that they intend to
do hereafter.'

Frizell finishes his letter by beseeching the Lords to 'commiserate [my] miserable estate and that of our poor distressed captives' and 'to release me out of thraldom.'

In a final, desperately pathetic note, the consul promises that if all of this is done, then he 'with the 340 poor English captives, shall ever pray for Your Lordships' persons' health.'

Amazingly, this brief report represents Frizell's only recorded reference to Baltimore that year. The only other reference is a letter in December from a Captain William Thomas, who refers inaccurately to '170 persons' taken from Baltimore.

And so, against a background of official indifference, the slaves' new lives began. In the next few chapters, we will look at the fates that awaited the various categories of captives – the children, the men and the women. But first, we will examine the most dreaded fate of all: a fate so awful that it has been described over and over again as a living hell.

Yet any man living in the fishing community of The Cove would have been a prime candidate for this particular job. Men like Tom Paine had spent their entire working lives pulling oars at high speed, in furious bursts of energy. They already had all the skills required to become a galley slave.

CHAPTER TWENTY

Condemned To The Oar

He that's condemned to the oar hath first his face,
eyebrows and head close shaven (for no more disgrace
cannot betide a Christian). Then, being stripped to the
girdle (as when rogues are to be whipped), chained they
are to the seats where they sit rowing, five in a row, a
Turk going on a large plank between them, and though
their eyes are ready to start out with pulling, he cries:
'Work, work, you Christian curs!', and though none
needs one blow for loitering, yet his bare back bleeds and
rises up in bunches.
—from The Lamentable Cries Of Prisoners
in Algiers under the Turks, 1624

BEING 'condemned to the oar' was the worst
possible fate in Barbary. Witnesses nearly always
used the same short word to describe life on the galley

bench: it was hell, an unremitting torture of agony and exhaustion. Galley slaves were worked, quite literally, until they dropped dead. Their bodies were dumped into the sea and their place on the bloodied, sweat-stained bench was immediately taken up by another unfortunate slave.

The Baltimore slaves were arriving in Algiers at a time when the glory days of the oar-driven corsair galleys were drawing to an end. As European sailing ships gained popularity, the number of galley slaves dropped from four thousand at the turn of the century to around nine hundred in 1675. Yet at this stage, in the early to mid-1600s, these traditional warships were still favoured for their lightness, speed, manoeuvrability, and the raised beak-like forecastles that could slot over an enemy's deck, allowing the corsairs to jump directly on board. In the 1640s, a tally of English and Irish captives in Algiers recorded that a hundred of the slaves – roughly one in seven – were serving with the Turkish galley fleet.

A skilled Baltimore oarsman like, for instance, Tom Paine would have been highly valued as a galley slave. His first day on board his hell-ship would have been very much like that of Thomas Sanders, an English slave from Devonshire:

'We were forcibly and most violently shaven, head and beard,' Sanders recalled. 'We were chained three and three to an oar, and we rowed naked above the girdle, and the boatswain of the galley walked abaft the mast, and his mate afore the mast, and each of them a whip in their hands, and when their devilish choler rose they would strike the Christians for no cause.'

Living conditions were atrocious. '[O]ur lodging was to lie on the bare boards, with a very simple cape to cover us.'

John Fox of Sussex, whose ship was captured at sea in the same era, was doomed to spend fourteen years as a galley slave. 'They were no sooner in [the galleys], but their garments were pulled over their ears, and torn from their backs, and they set to the oars,' writes his contemporary biographer, '… I think there is no man will judge their fare good, or their bodies unladen of stripes, and not pestered with too much heat, and also with too much cold …'

The French diplomat d'Arvieux said that 'for these wretches, life was a species of hell'.

And the eighteenth-century writer Joseph Morgan wrote movingly that any heart capable of the least drop of compassion would be shocked 'to behold ranks and files of half-naked, half-starved, half-tanned meagre wretches chained to a plank whence they remove not for months together (commonly half a year), urged on, even beyond human strength with cruel and repeated blows on their bare flesh … and this for whole days and nights successively, which often happens in a furious chase …'

During such gruelling sessions, Tom Paine would have had to subsist on lumps of bread, which were soaked in wine and pushed into his gasping mouth to prevent him collapsing with hunger. And throughout it all, two slavedrivers would pace the benches, prodding and lashing him with leather whips.

Jean Marteille de Bergerac, a galley slave in 1701, described the process in a way that leaves even the reader exhausted: 'Think of six men chained to a bench, naked as when they were born, one foot on the stretcher, the other on the bench in front, holding an immensely heavy oar, bending forwards to the stern with arms at full reach to clear the backs of the rowers in front, who bend likewise; and then, having got forward, shoving up the oar's end to let the blade catch the water, then throwing their bodies back on the groaning bench.'

This activity could continue for ten or even twenty hours without a break 'and then the captain shouts the order to redouble the lash … If a slave falls exhausted upon his oar (which often chances) he is flogged until he is taken for dead, and then pitched unceremoniously into the sea.'

For a slave like Tom Paine, the only opportunity to escape would come in the heat of battle. But the slavedrivers took exhaustive precautions against mutiny. '[W]e were not suffered to have neither needle, bodkin, knife, or any other instrument about us … upon pain of one hundred bastinadoes,' wrote Sanders. 'We were then also cruelly manacled, in such sort that we could not put our hands the length of one foot asunder the one from the other.'

Yet for those who had the courage, anything was possible. In 1620, an Englishman named Owen FitzPen was enslaved in Algiers and sentenced to galley oar.

'He projected several plots for his liberty,' says a plaque in his honour, 'and on 27th June, 1627, with ten other Christian captives, Dutch and French (persuaded by his counsel and courage) he began a cruel fight with sixty-five Turks in their own ship which lasted three hours in which five of his company were slain.'

Despite the overwhelming odds, FitzPen took the ship, sold it for £6,000, and returned to England a wealthy man.

For slaves like Tom Paine, there was only one small glimmer of hope. Tradition dictated that the slaves were entitled to a share of any prize taken. This was given to their owners, who for religious reasons would often return a small amount to the oarsmen. In rare cases, a captive on a successful voyage could raise enough cash to escape the hell-ship by paying for another slave to take his place.

Incredibly, some slaves lasted for decades at the oar, so it is probable that these fully-trained, hardy 'lifers' were excused the harshest treatment. This seems the only way to account for John Fox's fourteen-year stint at the oar, or the thirty years chalked up by some slaves on the Maltese galleys. Historian Peter Earle cites one astonishing case in 1682 in which a slave aged over eighty petitioned for release after a full half-century at the oar.

There were break periods during which (according to one 1628 account) the oarsmen were chained together but 'free to walk about the ship.'

And Emmanuel d'Aranda, the young Flemish galley slave, hints that life might even have had its lighter moments.

One of D'Aranda's colleagues on Ali Bichnin's galley was an Italian named Fontimama, a fast-talking but likeable conman. Sent ashore to get fresh water, Fontimama was approached by two local men who offered to buy any smuggled scraps of iron.

Fontimama told them he had just the thing for them … and proceeded to sell them the ship's anchor for five patacoons.

And so the short-tempered slavemaster Ali Bichnin, who'd been enjoying a doze in his cabin, woke up to hear his guards arguing with several locals who were convinced they had the right to remove the galley's anchor.

The locals explained their purchase to Bichnin, who confronted the Italian conman.

'Fontimama replied that he thought the galley would go better being discharged of that weight,' writes d'Aranda. 'All the galley could not forbear laughing at that answer … and Fontimama kept his five patacoons.'

If the sweltering summers at the galley oars did not succeed in killing a man, the winters often did. At the end of the short sailing season, Tom and the other slaves would be put to general work for six or eight months. However, galley life had left many of them so pain-racked they were incapable of other tasks. These unfortunates were often flung into filthy prisons where 'through reason of their ill-usage and worse fare, [they were] miserably starved'.

John Fox, the Sussex slave, was lucky. He was an accomplished barber, a skill that involved surgery as well as haircutting. He was allowed to wander freely during the day with an iron on his leg.

D'Aranda spent one winter in an underground jail in Tetuan in Morocco. The standard slave prison here was a converted grain cellar with a barred hatch in the ceiling. It was intolerably hot, and any rain would flood the pit within hours.

Tensions exploded when the already-overcrowded cell was allocated two extra prisoners – Spanish deserters who'd 'turned Turk'.

'We lay on the floor as close as could be one to another,' says d'Aranda, 'because the room was narrow and nobody would have these two rascals lying near them, and there being no house of office in the prison, every two or three had a pot as they have in Spain, and these two wretches were necessitated to *enfe* themselves. They were extremely put to it, for to do anything on the floor was not permitted, because it was our bed and nobody would lend them a pot.

'One day, their master cast them a little bread at the

grate without anything else … nay, they were forced to beg the water they took off the other slaves.'

The English galley slave Thomas Sanders reported that he spent the off-season on a construction site: '[W]e were put to all manner of slavery … I was put to hew stones, and others to carry stones, and some to draw the cart with earth, and some to make mortar.'

John Fox spent fourteen years sweating at the oars in summer and working as a barber in Alexandria in winter, before deciding that he'd had enough. It was time to break free.

Taking full advantage of his licence to move around the city, Fox managed to obtain a number of metal files and access to a galley. At 8 pm on New Year's Day, all the prisoners filed off their irons and swarmed through the jail searching for weapons and looting the treasury.

The prisoners fought their way through 'a hot skirmish' to the roof, where they had to battle for control of the escape ladders. Many of the looters died because they were too heavily weighted with gold to run quickly.

The noise of the battle raised the alarm all over the city, but by this time the ship was ready:

'Now is this galley afloat, and out of the shelter of the road,' Fox's biographer writes. 'Now have the two castles full power upon the galley … The cannons let fly from both sides, and the galley is even in the midst and between them both … [but] they sail away, being not once touched by the glance of a shot.'

John Fox eventually returned as a hero to his hometown of Woodbridge. He had managed to spirit 266 galley slaves away from a Turkish prison and bring all but eight of them safely across the Mediterranean to freedom.

This, then, was the life that Tom Paine could have expected as a galley slave in Algiers. But it was not the only job in Barbary – far from it.

Let's return to the aftermath of the slave market in July, 1631, and see what sort of fates would have awaited John Ryder and the other men from Baltimore.

CHAPTER TWENTY-ONE

'Dog Of A Christian, To Work!'

AFTER the ordeal of their auction had ended, John Ryder, Corent Croffine and the other male prisoners from Baltimore would have been led on yet another humiliating circuit of the town. Afterwards, they were taken to what Pananti described as 'a large dark looking building'. As they passed through its grim gateway, the guards would sardonically deliver the traditional welcome – words reminiscent of Dante's famous warning 'Abandon hope, all ye who enter here'. They would call out:

'Whoever is brought into this house becomes a slave.'

The slaves were now in the belly of the bagnio – the network of urban prisons that would be their home from this day forth.

As the name suggests, the original bagnios were

bathhouses, but they had developed into a gulag of giant purpose-built prisons. The largest state jail – the Grand Bagnio – held up to two thousand slaves of nearly two dozen nationalities.

Let's see the bagnio from the point of view of a typical slave like John Ryder as he walks through the awesome main gate and into the prison yard for the first time …

Ryder enters a spacious courtyard, which at first resembles a Mediterranean village square. It's surrounded by shops and tavernas run and staffed by slaves. Outside the bars are wooden tables where free men – European mariners, renegadoes, wastrels of all nationalities – sit in the shade drinking flagons of wine and smoking their pipes. Some of the drunker ones are singing and others are huddled together, whispering and plotting. There are public cookhouses, serving out western-style meals to the renegades – even pork sausages are available. The smell of frying food makes Ryder's stomach groan, for he hasn't eaten a decent meal for weeks.

Catholic chaplains in their solemn and elaborate gowns wander past the tables to their quarters at the rear of the shops.

And of course, everywhere there are the slaves themselves, who, in Pananti's words, 'wander like pallid spectres', wrapped up in their melancholy fate.

The jail itself lies beyond the central square, opposite the main gate. It is a three-part structure with two cell blocks to either side and, in the centre, a building that serves as chapel.

The guards herd Ryder towards the barbershop and storeroom where he is shaved of his hair and beard – a humiliation in itself – and issued with blanket and clothes.

A baggy, skirt-like garment, drawn in to form holes for each knee, serves as trousers. A floppy, wide-necked shirt is worn under a waist-length sleeveless jacket. For footwear he gets the ubiquitous pointed Turkish slippers, scuffed and thin-soled, and if he is lucky, a red skullcap to protect his head.

'No sooner is anyone declared a slave,' writes Pananti, 'than he is instantly stripped of his clothes and covered with a species of sackcloth; he is also generally left without shoes or stockings, and often obliged to work bareheaded in the scorching rays of an African sun.'

This gear (already well-worn) is expected to last until the annual reissue of garments in mid-winter. 'I do assure you,' one envoy later wrote of the Baltimore captives, 'their clothes are thin.'

Ryder's right leg is painfully fitted with a metal ring almost as heavy as a modern bag of sugar. During the day the slaves will also be required to drag a length of chain, its weight progressively lightening with good behaviour.

A contemporary illustration shows a captive with a chain as thick as a man's wrist affixed to his leg-ring; this fetter is so long that he has to carry it looped over his left arm.

Ryder is hustled to his quarters. These are described by the French diplomat d'Arvieux as 'terrifying jails where the poor souls are piled on top of each other rather than housed'. His hammock is slung somewhere in a stack between ceiling and floor, with other men sleeping above and below him, and a communal ladder to provide access.

As a new slave, Ryder receives only a minimal serving of bread on his first evening. Someone whispers to him that this is a starvation diet designed to provoke the desire for a speedy ransom. The usual 'menu' in the state bagnio is three loaves of bread a day, served mid-morning, noon and suppertime and occasionally softened by olive oil or vinegar.

Ryder and his fellow newcomers are placed under the tender care of the controlling Guardian Bacha, a sort of boot-camp sergeant major who will make his life miserable until he can afford to bribe his way to a higher standard of living. In some cases, new prisoners are even left to sleep out in the open until they can 'buy' a place in a cell.

In the unlikely event that Ryder has managed to secrete a few scraps of food or valuables, these will be removed under the pretence of safekeeping. (The English slave Thomas Sanders had brought a jar of oil and a basket of bread: 'But before I came to the Banio the Turkish boys had taken away almost all my bread, and the keeper said, 'Deliver me the jar of oil, and when thou comest to the Banio thou shalt have it again'; but I never had it of him any more.')

At least there is one consolation. Men who'd been separated during the auctions are reunited in these bleak cells. The grim walls echo to the sound of weeping and commiseration as men like Richard Lorye and William Arnold try desperately to console each other over the loss of their wives and children.

Sanders tries to convey the gloomy atmosphere: '[W]hen I came to the Banio and saw our merchants and all the rest of our company in chains, and we all ready to receive the same reward, what heart is there so hard but would have pitied our cause, hearing or seeing the lamentable greeting there was betwixt us.'

Sleep is hard to achieve in those dark, airless surroundings, with the weeping of slaves mingling with the raucous din from below. D'Arvieux describes the atmosphere at the bagnios. They are, he says, 'places of horror, what with the smoke of cooking from all around, the noise, the shouting, the blows and the tumult prevailing everywhere'.

But the first dreadful night would be short. The sun has barely begun to tinge the eastern horizon when Ryder is shaken out of his sleep and hustled out into the prison yard. It is 3 am, and time to begin his first day at work.

'A *trabajo cornutos; can d'infidel a trabajo*!'
'Dog of a Christian, to work!'

236

The harsh cries of the Guardian Bacha echo around the walls of the courtyard as Ryder rubs the sleep from his eyes and takes his place among the hundreds of slaves in the courtyard. Above him, stars are only beginning to fade in the pre-dawn light. He is hungry, but there is no time for breakfast – that will come later.

Feeling the weight of his heavy irons, Ryder trudges in line out of the bagnio and into the sleeping city streets.

'Being ordered to proceed to the scene of our labours, a mournful silence marked our progress, which was attended by guards both in front and rear, armed with whips,' recalls Pananti.

Pushing through the narrow streets, the long-term slaves skilfully liberate food from the baskets of deliverymen on their way to market. The alleyways echo to shouts of accusation: 'Which Christian dog [took that]? Infidel, I will have you beaten to death!'

The first stop is the huge bakery where other slaves have been sweating all night to supply the city with bread. Here, two rusks of cheap black bread are thrown at the slaves, 'as if to dogs'. Ryder has scarcely wolfed it down when the pathetic procession moves on down to the Great Hall of the Marine, where the prisoners are formally recorded and allocated their tasks. Some will be sent to sea, others to the farms, still others to the quarries. In many cases this choice will dictate whether they will survive in Algiers, or die gasping from overwork and exhaustion in some hellish quarry pit. This is the moment that decides his future.

A generation after the raid at Baltimore, Samuel Pepys wrote in his diaries of a drunken afternoon in the Fleece Tavern. The unlikely result of this hazy interlude was one of the best summaries we have of slave life in Algiers: 'Captain Mootham and Mr Dawes (who have been both slaves there) did make me fully acquainted with their condition there: as, how they eat nothing but bread and water. At their redemption, they pay so much for the water they drink at the public fountains, during their being slaves. How they are beat upon the soles of their feet and bellies at the liberty of their patron. How they are all, at night, called into their master's *bagnard*; and there they lie. How the poorest men do use their slaves best. How some rogues do live well, if they do invent to bring their masters in so much a week by their industry or theft; and then they are put to no other work at all. And theft there is counted no great crime at all.'

Succinctly put, but true. There was a hierarchy of slave roles.

With the exception of the galley oarsmen, the unluckiest slaves of all were the State labourers, who were treated as beasts of burden. 'I am made daily to grind a mill as a horse,' one English captive wrote pathetically.

Mr T.S., the English captive, began his slave life as a palace cook, but was later put to work in the fields, 'with an ill favoured Turk, leading me by a chain, as a horse or a bullock, through the streets.'

Hundreds were employed on State farms. There are reports of men pulling ploughs like horses, with metal bits in their teeth. Captain John Smith, who was later to colonise Virginia, was at one stage enslaved by the Turks and put to work threshing corn. It was, he said, 'the worst of cruelty' and he was 'treated like a dog'.

Some were put to work at the quarries, where huge rocks weighing 40 tons were blasted out of the cliff. The slaves – working continuously under the lash – had to drag them on sleds for two miles to the harbour where they were loaded on to barges and used to bolster the Mole.

Others laboured on construction works, where they had to carry baskets of earth across high catwalks. As they tried to balance on these planks, sadistic overseers would poke and strike them with sticks.

'Figure to yourself above 1,000 poor wretches,' wrote one slave, 'many of them half naked without hat or shoes, at work in the heat of the sun all day till four and sometimes till five or six o'clock on a summer day, carrying earth in a basket to the top of a high building, exposed to the heat and often blistered with the sun, chafed and scalded with the weight of their load, the perspiration flowing from them … '

These cases represented the blunt and crude end of slavery in Algiers. However, perhaps John Ryder was among the luckier ones. The more enlightened private owners treated their slaves reasonably and encouraged them with a form of incentive deal. The owner or patron (pronounced *patroon*) would advance a loan to the slave to set up as a craft worker or trader. Ryder would have been able to keep a small amount of earnings – up to a third – which he could use to repay his loan and, eventually, start saving towards his own ransom.

Slaves like these were allowed to sleep in open prisons or even in their patron's home. There are reports of owners treating slaves as they would treat their own children. Warm personal relationships were often forged between master and servant.

Richard Joyce, an Irishman captured by Algerine corsairs while on his way to the Caribbean in 1675, was a case in point. His patron was a goldsmith who taught him how to fashion the intricate, symbolic jewellery then fashionable in North Africa. Joyce proved a willing and dextrous pupil and remained with his master for fourteen years.

When at last his ransom was arranged, the goldsmith was heartbroken. He offered Joyce a full partnership and his only daughter in marriage. But the Irishman reluctantly refused and returned to his native Galway to set up his own craft workshop and become a wealthy man.

That much is fact. Legend gives the story another twist, which might well be true. It's said that when Joyce

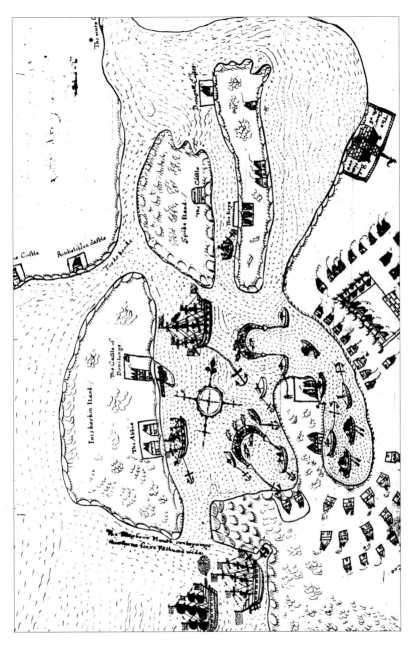

Above: An era frozen in time: this remarkable picture map of Baltimore, clearly showing the modest homes in The Cove and the fishermen seine-netting at sea, was drawn just months before the pirate raid shattered the settlers' lives forever.

Above: A meal in an Algerine household.

Below: 'Whoever enters here becomes a slave': this unique 1631 document records the arrival of the Baltimore slaves in Algiers. The highlighted section reads: *'July 28. Morrato, [a] Fleming, and his consort brought from Baltimore in Ireland 89 women and children and 20 men ...'*

Above Left: Richard Boyle, Great Earl of Cork: the amount he spent on a single present for his daughter could have ransomed all the Baltimore women from slavery. But the main concern for landowners like Boyle was that the raid would affect their tenants' ability to pay their debts.

Above Right: Sir Thomas Button, arctic explorer and war hero: his state-of-the-art navy vessels could have prevented the raid, but he pocketed the money for their supplies, leaving them stranded uselessly in harbour.

Below: A Trinitarian priest, probably Fr Pierre Dan himself, ransoms European slaves in Algiers. Fr Dan was intensely moved by the plight of the Baltimore captives and wrote that it was a pitiful sight to see 'so many honest maidens and so many good women abandoned to the brutality of these barbarians'.

Above: Torments of the slaves: the Trinitarian priest Fr Pierre Dan recorded the sadistically ingenious punishments that were meted out to captives in Algiers.

Below: Sultan Murad, who ruled the Ottoman empire at the time of the Baltimore raid. His boyish face belied a dark and cruel temperament. Fuelled by drink, he would roam the streets at night in search of citizens to impale.

Above: The Stallion of the Seraglio: Sultan Ibrahim, whose notorious orgies were the most debauched since the decadent days of the Roman empire. When he demanded a giantess for his bed, his courtiers obliged … but she was strangled by his jealous mother.

Below: A seventeenth-century waterfront view of the Sultan's seraglio in Constantinople. Once she passed the Gate Of Felicity into the harem, a slave would probably never return to the outside world.

Prospect of the GRAND SIGNIORS SERAGLIO from Galata

To the Right Hon.ble William, Lord Paget.

Barbarÿsche Galejen

Above: A typical corsair galley, low and sleek with a raised prow to lock over the deck of enemy ships and enable its troops to pour on board. Sea chases could continue for days without respite for the exhausted oarsmen.

Below: The 'well-guarded city'. This seventeenth-century plan of Algiers and its fortresses shows how impregnable the corsair base had become. A slave arriving here could abandon all hope of rescue.

Alger

A · Le Château du Mole ·
B · La Porte du Mole ·
C · La Nouuelle batera ·
D · L'entrée du Mole ·
E · La Porte de babason ·
F · La Porte de babaxadit ·
G · La Porte de babaluet ·
H · Le Château Nouueau bati
    lan 1369
I · Tombes des Rois ·
K · Cimétiere ·
L · Deux Forts batis Par les
    Espagnols

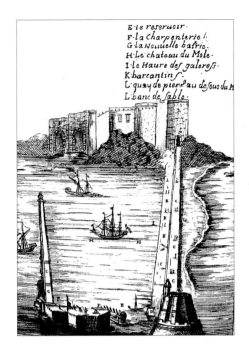

E·le reseruoir·
F·la Charpenterie l·
G·la Nouuelle batrie·
H·Le chateau du Mole·
I·le Haure des galeres·
K·barcantins·
L·quay de pierr au desous du M
L·banc de sable·

Above: Tiny figures guard the harbour and toil to maintain the Mole. It was continually being eroded by the sea, and replenishing it with rocks was one of the worst jobs a slave could expect in Algiers.

Below: Slaves packed like sardines at the oars of an admiral's galley. 'For these wretches', wrote one witness, 'life was a species of hell.'

Above: A seventeenth-century plan showing the layout of the Sultan's Seraglio in Constantinople. Entering at the left, a visitor would progress through a series of guarded portals before reaching the no-go area of the women's harem to the right.

Below: A typical street in Algiers.

left, he took with him a design for jewellery depicting a heart and a protective pair of hands. The result has become familiar to us all as the Claddagh ring.

John Ryder would have rapidly discovered there was good money to be made in bustling, prosperous Algiers by any slave who could spot a business opportunity.

According to d'Aranda, a captive who could borrow enough money to buy a pipe of wine (110 gallons) at $16 in September could retail it later at a profit of $40 or $50. 'The Spaniards who could keep taverns lived like princes among the slaves, and in a short time got as much as paid the ransom,' he wrote.

Or take the case of William Okeley, an English slave who would have been a familiar figure to John and the rest of the Baltimore captives. Enslaved in 1638, Okeley was told to choose any trade that would earn two dollars a month for his master.

He set up shop selling wine and tobacco, then began sewing canvas clothes for seamen. Okeley was sold on to a kind elderly patron who treated him as his own son and whom he was extremely reluctant to leave. By the time he made his spectacular dash for freedom (more of which later) he had secretly amassed a considerable amount of money. The scrupulous Okeley honoured his commitments to his patron and 'paid him his demands duly' but secretly began hiding his own cash in preparation for his moonlight flit. 'I had a trunk [with] a false bottom, into which I put all the silver and gold I had, and into the body of the trunk, what it would hold.'

He entrusted the valuable trunk to his chaplain, Rev Devereux Spratt, who somehow managed to bring it home intact. Okeley was able to return from slavery as a rich man.

Other slaves prospered to the point where they did not wish to return home at all.

The French diplomat d'Arvieux wrote of one French slave who lived in a private apartment complete with library, study and fifteen servants of his own. Although he remained technically enslaved, this man found life so agreeable that he would never have dreamed of squandering his riches on his own ransom.

Similarly, an English envoy named John Braithwaite was astonished when he arrived in Morocco to find an Irish slave who kept his own household of European slaves and threw elaborate parties. Mr Carr (his first name is unknown) treated Braithwaite to 'a very elegant dinner' and fine wine, to the pleasant background music of an ensemble of northern slaves. A convert to Islam, Carr became became drunkenly homesick during the meal and told Braithwaite that he was 'as much a Christian as ever' – a phrase eerily reminiscent of Morat Rais's protestation to Harrison that he was 'ever a Christian at heart'.

Alternatively, John Ryder may have been able to secure

an administrative job and rise up the civil service career ladder. This was what happened to another Irish born slave, James Leander Cathcart.

Cathcart seems to have been one of those unsinkable characters who can adapt to any environment. We've already encountered him on his slave ship just after his capture – he was the one who managed to persuade his captors to give him tobacco and fruit. In Algiers, he was even better at working the system. While remaining a slave, he rose to the pinnacle of power and riches.

Cathcart was born in Mountmurragh in Co. Westmeath, but emigrated to America and served in the Revolutionary War before being captured by corsairs near Portugal in 1785.

The secret of his success was a combination of Irish charm, efficiency ... and bribery. Cathcart understood that everything in Algiers ran on *baksheesh* and skilfully used this to his advantage.

He made friends easily and won over nearly everyone he encountered, up to and including the ruler. While other slaves would react to their new masters with grovelling submission or with seething resentment, Cathcart did neither. He would argue for his rights robustly but politely, and with a touch of dry humour.

At first he was put in charge of a group of American slaves whose job was to maintain the grounds at the royal palace. The garden included a small zoo of pet lions, and Cathcart's enthusiasm to feed them was never regarded as suspicious, even though the lions became increasingly slimmer and the Americans grew healthier on a diet of red meat.

His run of good luck ended when he was transferred to a grim state bagnio and put to hard labour. Undeterred, he used his meagre funds as a bribe to secure a move to a better prison, where his language skills earned him a job as a harbour administrator. From there he rose rapidly up the civil service ladder and ended up back at the palace as Chief Christian Secretary – the highest job that any unconverted slave could get.

Meanwhile, Cathcart had borrowed money to invest in a captured cargo of wine. The move paid off so handsomely that he was able to purchase several taverns. Eventually he became rich enough to buy his own ship.

The ruler of Algiers, who was involved in talks with America at the time, needed a go-between and instructed Cathcart to sail home to discuss treaty terms. Cathcart – who was, remember, still a slave – sailed off to the land of the free, but dutifully returned to Barbary to conclude a peace deal that earned liberty for his countrymen as well as himself. Thomas Jefferson was later to describe him as 'the honestest and ablest consul we have with the Barbary powers'.

Further down the hierarchy of prestige there were good jobs and bad jobs. One of the most coveted positions – and it took a hefty bribe to earn it – was that of servant at the Janissary barracks. But for the ultimate cushy job, it would be hard to beat the task allotted to a young French guitarist who was instructed to provide music in the female baths. The women 'quite naked, took their bath in front of him,' one writer reported enviously.

Since male slaves were regarded almost as domestic animals, they were often given free run of the household – with all the temptations that this entailed.

'*Guarda per ti, et non andar mirar mugeros de los Moros; nous autros pillar multo phantasia de questo conto,*' new slaves were sternly warned in *Sabir*. 'Be careful, and do not go to look at the wives of the Moors. We are very particular on that matter.'

A Christian slave caught with a Muslim wife could expect no mercy from the Algerine authorities. And the risk wasn't all one-sided. Wives caught in adultery would be flung alive into the sea in a weighted sack – often by their own vengeful husbands.

However, relationships were not always discouraged. There were genuine romances between unmarried male slaves – men like Edward Cherry or John Amble – and the eligible daughters or nieces of their masters.

To Europeans, the Algerine women were as exotic and beautiful as the pale-faced northern women appeared to the North Africans. In public, they wore white cloaks, tied tight at the knee over voluminous trousers. A white headdress covered their hair and their face was concealed, except for the eyes, by a white veil.

Europeans compared the floating vision to ships gracefully under sail, or even to Greek goddesses.

Those privileged to see them in private raved about their 'clean and healthy appearance' and their clear skin and flashing eyes. Yet this beauty did not always come directly from nature. They were skilled in cosmetics and took enormous trouble to create the wide-eyed, startled-doe look that was so fashionable in Algiers.

On special occasions they would dress in their finery and wear the *sarma*, a richly worked metal crown, culminating in a peak from which gold and silver coloured ribbons descended almost to the ground. Baltimore bachelors like Edward Cherry, accustomed to the unadorned fish factory workers of their own village, could not have been blamed if they fell head over heels for such exotic visions.

In an era of arranged marriages, owners would often earmark a talented slave as a potential husband for a daughter or niece. A common scenario involved a slave who had learned a trade and was now capable of supporting a family. If he agreed to convert to Islam, he would be given his freedom on his wedding day. Another scenario centred on wealthy young widows – there were plenty in warlike Algiers – who could offer instant wealth and prosperity to an eligible man.

According to D'Arvieux, patrons would give their slaves 'promises, exhortations and everything that was seductive' in a bid to win them over.

And so we see the vast and bewildering variety of lifestyles that could have been open to the male slaves from Baltimore in 1631 – from bathroom balladeer to human mule, from cosseted family babysitter to royal lionkeeper. The fates of the male captives from Roaring Water Bay – ordinary men like John Ryder, Corent Croffine, Edward Cherry and John Amble – could have gone in any of a thousand different directions, but their lives in slavery would at least never have been dull and predictable.

CHAPTER TWENTY-TWO

Beyond The Gate Of Felicity: The Harem Women

[T]o bring forth children to die untimely deaths; and to end their days by prisons, or the bowstring, or to live miserable lives separated from mankind and immured within walls, or entombed whilst they breathed, and not to tremble with horror

— the role of a palace concubine, according to Paul Rycault in 1634.

THERE is no mystery about the fate of Joane Broadbrook, Bessie Flood and the other three dozen Baltimore women who ended up in Algiers – their future had been decided the moment they were herded aboard the corsair boat. They were all destined for the harems: the younger and more attractive women as concubines, the older ones as domestic servants. Some would have ended up in the Pasha's own harem, some at the homes of local merchants, and some would have been sent all the way to the Sultan in Constantinople.

The women who were despatched to the imperial harem in the decade beginning 1631 were both lucky and unlucky in their timing. They were fortunate in that they arrived right in the middle of a period known as 'The Reign Of Women' in which the royal palace, and sometimes even the vast empire itself, was effectively ruled by females. However, they were also unfortunate. For most of its existence, the imperial harem was a comparatively sedate place. It was sheer bad luck that anyone sent from Baltimore would have experienced the reigns of the two craziest and most debauched sultans in the empire's seven hundred-year history. The first was a twisted drunk. The second was a lunatic whose grotesquely inventive sexual orgies shocked even the harem veterans who thought they had seen it all.

In his poem *The Sack Of Baltimore*, Thomas Davis speculated about the fate of the women captives. In his version, a young man from Bandon – a 'gallant' – is due to marry a woman named O'Driscoll. But she is abducted to Algiers, where the governing Dey selects her for his *serai*, or harem:

The maid that Bandon gallant sought is chosen for the Dey,

She's safe – he's dead – she stabbed him in the midst of his
Serai;
And, when to die a death of fire, that noble maid they bore,
She only smiled – O'Driscoll's child – she thought of Baltimore.

His heroine's fate would have been particularly grisly. In this method of execution, victims were tied to a post and surrounded by a ring of bonfires whose heat would roast them slowly to death. O'Driscoll's child would hardly have met her death smiling.

However, this story was pure fiction, since no Algerine governor was ever stabbed by a harem slave. Critics have also pointed out that there were no O'Driscolls in the list of Baltimore captives; but, then again, very few of the women were actually named. It is quite possible that one of the servants was a local O'Driscoll girl and that Davis could have based his work on oral tradition. Whatever the truth, the central theme of his verse is authentic. When Davis suggests that the nubile young women from Baltimore were selected as sexual playthings by rich and powerful men, he is absolutely right.

The rulers of Algiers were notorious for their rapaciousness, and not only towards their slaves and captives. Even diplomats' wives and daughters were targeted.

'Mr McDonell's daughter, pretty and young, for my harem,' a later Dey of Algiers wrote about the English consul's daughter. 'The Spanish consul's daughter, who is ugly, to serve the favourite; I shall have the English consul's head cut off and that of the Spanish consul also … if they dare to complain.'

In the late 1600s, an Irish woman named only as Mrs Shaw was enslaved in Morocco, where the notorious emperor Muley Ismael selected her as a bedmate. Years later, Mrs Shaw confessed to an English envoy that the emperor 'having an inclination to sleep with her, forced her to turn Moor'. The nights they spent together must have left the emperor especially satisfied, because he made her his fourth wife.

However, Muley soon tired of his new bride and sold her to a Spaniard. By the time she met the English envoy, the former empress was wandering the streets half-naked and destitute, with a new baby in her arms.

In 1685, writer Francis Brooks reported that the same emperor chose an English slave for his bedchamber: '[He] had her washed and clothed her in their fashion of apparel and lay with her; having his desire fulfilled, he inhumanly, in great haste, forced her away out of his presence'.

Regional governors like the Pasha of Algiers were always expected to replenish the Sultan's harem with their most beautiful and exotic women. Failure to do so was more than a diplomatic *faux-pas*: it would have been career suicide. Pale-skinned women of English West Country extraction were the cream of the crop, the supermodels of the Barbary world. It would have been unthinkable for

Pasha Hussein to have received a large consignment of such women in 1631 without donating at least some of them – the *best* of them – to his imperial master.

So although this is not specifically recorded, we can speculate with reasonable confidence that perhaps a half-dozen of the female captives from Baltimore would have ended up in the Imperial Harem.

Which of them received the summons? Bessie Peeter's daughter? The Evans's young female servant? Anna, the Meregeys' maid? History doesn't tell us.

Let's follow a typical female slave from Baltimore on that long journey to the imperial palace in Constantinople. (A useful exercise in any event, because the setup in the Sultan's harem was simply a larger-scale version of the Pasha's own harem and much the same rules would have applied to both.)

After the long sea journey across the Mediterranean, the young slave – let's suppose it was Anna – would have found herself in the mighty Ottoman capital on the banks of the Bosphorus. She would have been conveyed in a curtained carriage to the vast city-palace known as the Topkapi Serai. Peering through the veils at her new home, she would have been overwhelmed by the sheer scale of the seaside palace. Three miles in circumference and covering over 170 acres, Topkapi was home to more than 4,000 people ranging from warriors to pen-pushers and from sexless eunuchs to the world's most beautiful and voluptuous concubines.

Anna's carriage would rumble through the white marble portals of the Imperial Gate into the first of four courtyards. The first was a busy public square with all the utilities of imperial power – administrative offices, a mint, a gun store. There was the smell of baking bread from a huge bakery. From here a loftier gate, the Gate Of Peace, led inwards to a second courtyard of gardens and cypress trees. The Square Of The Processions was heavily guarded by Janissaries and restricted to those on legal or government business.

They were moving steadily away from the busy hum of everyday life. The next gate they would enter would mark the boundary between the outside world and the silent, protected world of the inner palace. Once they passed through The Gate Of Felicity, few would ever return. They would spend the rest of their lives in the harem.

The word 'harem' holds a wealth of exotic and decadent associations for westerners. But this would have baffled a typical Muslim husband of the seventeenth-century whose sole wife and daughters resided in a very staid 'harem.'

In any home, the women's quarters was *haram* – an adjective meaning 'forbidden', but in a positive sense, like a protective den or a sanctuary.

Even the smallest living spaces can have their harems or forbidden zones, created simply by drawing a curtain across a room.

The Topkapi harem took this idea to its extreme. Here up to a thousand women were retained for the pleasure of a single male, the Sultan. They ranged from black maidservants from the sub-Sahara all the way up to slave 'queens' with opulent chambers and dozens of staff.

This palace of excess had nothing to do with Islamic teachings. It arose for a quite different reason – national security. Sultans were constantly vulnerable to assassination. If they took wives from prominent families, they created palace power blocs and angered rivals. It was much more convenient – and safer – to father children with slave women.

Think of the implications for a moment. This meant that every new emperor was the result of a union with a slave. It also meant that any slave who bore the firstborn male was rocketed from poverty to the pinnacle of power the moment the infant gave his first cry. If she and her son survived until his accession – a very big *if* – the formerly humble slave girl would become the Queen Mother, the most powerful person in the palace.

The hundreds of women in the harem were divided into clearly-defined classes. At the apex was the current emperor's mother, the Queen Mother or *Sultan Valide*. Counted in her household were the royal sisters and daughters, the Sultanas.

Next in line were the four 'special favourites' (*kadin*), the slave women who were first to bear boy children. They were quasi-wives, hence the number, and they ranked in order of their sons' birth.

After these four came the 'favourites' (*ikbals*), regular consorts of the Sultan. Below them came the chamber women (*odalisks*) who were themselves divided into several ranks. There were hundreds of them, and although they were all available to the Sultan, the vast majority were never expected to sleep with him.

When Anna passed through the Felicity Gate, she would have found herself in a grand courtyard surrounded by a multi-arched arcade. At the far end was what the English traveller Aaron Hill described as a 'wonderful river', an artificial concourse that flowed both ways and marked the dividing line between the Grand Seraglio and the forbidden grounds – the harem.

Passing across a drawbridge guarded by black eunuchs, Anna would have climbed a marble staircase whose walls tumbled with scented jasmine and honeysuckle. Black maidservants, loaded down with towels and clothes, scurried down passages towards the baths and laundries.

The newcomers would have been led past the superintendent's office, and into one of the long, narrow dormitories. Their sleeping arrangements were basic, as Aaron Hill testified:

'Their beds are only quilts or carpets five times doubled, over which is laid a satin coverlet and which, being turned aside, they enter in their shifts and muslin drawers and contentedly repose themselves until the break of day, beyond which hour they seldom are permitted to indulge themselvers in slumber.'

New arrivals to the harem were usually women in their teens, but girls as young as eight could also be inducted for training. Each new batch of entrants always caused a stir among the long-term residents. There were scores of other harem women of all nationalities – Georgians and Carcassians, blond Scandinavians and olive-skinned Latins – and the only thing they had in common was their exceptional beauty. Already the most attractive women in the empire, they now had access to the most skilful beauticians and hairstylists.

As Anna would discover from conversation, not all of them were reluctant captives. Impoverished families would volunteer their daughters for the harem simply to ensure their survival. Even in Christian cities like Venice, powerful families would contrive to have their shrewdest daughters taken in to the harem, arming them with covert connections and a secret bribe-purse to help them rise to key positions of influence.

Anna was in the harem, but she was not yet a member of it. First she had to be medically examined for any illnesses or flaws. After that, she had to meet with the approval of the *Sultan Valide*.

In the 1630s, the Queen Mother was an ambitious and utterly ruthless Greek named Kiosem. For the reign of two Sultans – Murad IV, the current emperor, and later his younger brother Ibrahim – she would rule the palace and much of the empire with an iron hand. Kiosem was a former slave who, at the age of fifteen, had become a favourite of the teenage Sultan Ahmed with whom she had three sons. When Ahmed died, rivals ordered all three sons to be strangled but Kiosem helped to defeat the plot and ensure that Murad became Sultan.

One of the traditional roles of Queen Mother was to act as a procuress for her son, seeking out and training the most beautiful virgin girls for his pleasure. This was a delicate task: the women had to be so devastatingly seductive that they would excite the Sultan's jaded appetite, and yet not so irresistible that they might pose a threat to her own power. To this end, she would inspect each newcomer closely.

The chosen ones were trained as concubines, a process involving personality skills, storytelling, poetry and musicianship as well as the finer arts of seduction. It was by no means inevitable that a concubine would share the Sultan's bed; she might never even meet him.

Once trained, these concubines enjoyed a special prestige. Far from being viewed as second-hand or damaged, they were highly sought after as wives by other men. If a sultan wished to present a special gift to someone, he would donate one of his most prized virgin concubines as a wife.

A newcomer like Anna would probably have started harem life as an ordinary *odalisk* or chamber woman. (An '*oda*' literally means a room.) This did not involve cleaning or routine cooking, but training in specialist skills. Apprenticed to an *oda* or training centre, she would have learned skills ranging from coffee brewing and sherbet making to Koran reading. There were specialist jewel-keepers, bathgivers and wardrobe mistresses. All of these activities were vitally important in the ritual of the harem, and most trainees would aim eventually to become head of her own *oda*.

Twelve of the most talented and personable odalisks would be given the exceptional honour of becoming the Sultan's personal maidservants (*gedikli*).

There were several ways in which an odalisk or concubine could be selected for the royal bedchamber. The first was the traditional ceremony in which the Queen Mother presented her most beautiful virgins to her son after Ramadan. Another came when the Sultan wandered around the harem and made his own choice.

With so much at stake, it is not surprising that there was fierce competition to win the emperor's attention. Prohibited from making eye contact or talking to him, the concubines had to rely on gesture instead: it was said that a simple ripple of a bare arm and wrist could imply such a wealth of erotic meaning that gloves were made compulsory for the sake of decency.

The Sultan enjoyed watching his concubines as they exercised in the garden. Sometimes he'd disrupt their activities with horseplay, chasing them or throwing them into the fountains. On occasions he would ask them to dance:

'[They] practise the most lascivious dances, postures and performances to raise the lustful fire and excite the passion of the amorous Sultan,' wrote Hill. 'He beckons [one woman] from the rest, and leads her to some bower to talk a while in private and prepare her expectation for the honour he allots her to.'

Ottaviano Bon, a top Venetian diplomat, describes another common selection process:

'[W]hen he is prepared for a fresh mate, he gives notice to the *Kahiya Cadun* [harem stewardess] of his purpose; who immediately bestirs herself like a crafty bawd, and chooseth out such as she judgeth to be the most amiable, and fairest of all; and having placed them in good order in a room, in two ranks, like so many pictures, half on the one side, and half on the other; she forthwith brings in the King, who walking four or five times in the midst of them, and having viewed them well, taketh good notice within himself of her that he best liketh, but says nothing; only as he goeth out again, he throweth a handkerchief into that virgin's hand; by which token she knoweth that she is to lie with him that night.'

When he disappeared, there would be a fever of excitement throughout the harem. The woman he had chosen would be immediately elevated in status to a *geuzdé* – literally, one given the eye. She would be given her own room, maidservants and beauticians.

The chosen woman would, according to Bon, be 'exceedingly joyful'. Yet the *geuzdé* must also have experienced shivers of apprehension. Sultan Murad may have been only twenty-one in the year 1633 – he had taken the throne at the tender age of eleven – but his innocent, boyish face belied a sadistic and cruel nature. One witness talked of his rosy face and 'black and lively eye', but added ominously: 'His exterior appearance did not correspond with the internal cruelty of his violent spirit.'

Murad was an active ruler: the last Sultan to lead his troops in battle. He had established his authority by ruthlessly crushing a Janissary mutiny and beheading the fifty ringleaders.

The entire nation lived in terror of his unpredictable rages, but it was his palace staff who bore the brunt. He executed a cook on the spot for preparing a bad dinner. Courtiers who showed the slightest signs of pride had the tips of their ears and nostrils cut off 'to clip the wings of their ambition'. When one slave offered to translate for a French diplomat during a heated dispute, Murad instantly ordered the man to be impaled – a dreadful punishment in which a spike was inserted in the fundament and pushed through the entire body until it emerged at the top. Murad stayed to watch, relishing the grisly spectacle.

Soon cruelty became an end in itself: a vicious royal

entertainment involving innocent passers-by. Murad's favourite pastime was to sit by the seaside randomly shooting his subjects as they rowed past in boats. On one occasion he spotted a boat full of women and sent orders for it to be sunk. 'Among his pastimes,' wrote one contemporary, 'nothing was more pleasing than some divertissement connected with blood.'

Plagued with painful gout, he sought refuge in strong Malvoisia wine, which served only to fuel his violent rages. Even Murad seemed terrified by the changes in his own personality. When sober, he would command his terrified staff to ignore any orders he issued after dinner.

He slapped a nationwide ban on alcohol and tobacco. His soldiers roamed the country, demolishing taverns and spilling wine into the gutters. Anyone ignoring his order had his legs sawn off. A man and woman caught in the act of selling tobacco were 'impaled alive ... with a roll of tobacco about their necks'.

Maddened by constant pain, Murad began stalking the streets in disguise looking for late-night drunks. He met two women wandering in the dark and ordered them to be cut into pieces. A deaf man who couldn't hear his shouted challenge was strangled on the spot and his body left on the road as an example.

As the death-toll mounted, his soldiers would sneak out ahead of the Sultan, driving revellers away with stones in a bid to save their lives. Yet Murad's bloody promenades continued ... until it was said that there was a victim almost every day and a festering corpse strung up at every junction.

And this was the man with whom the *geuzdé* would have to spend the night.

The summons to the royal bedchamber might come that same evening, or the following evening, or not at all. If the call did not come, the chosen one was demoted back to the basic level of *odalisk* – presumably a humiliating and embittering experience.

If the big moment arrived, the *geuzdé* was 'washed from head to floor [and] scented with perfumes' before being escorted to the Sultan's bedroom, where she would knock and enter on her knees. Directed by a row of white candles, she approached deferentially until she reached the end of the royal bed.

'A slave to your commands, great monarch, awaits your beckon,' she would ask ritually. 'May or may not she now be admitted?'

Aaron Hill, the contemporary English traveller, explained what the concubines must do next: 'Dropping off their nightgowns, they must gently raise the bedclothes at the foot, and so creep gradually up to those embraces.'

Ottaviano Bon wrote that two elderly maidservants silently remained in the room all night: '[O]ne of them sits by the light at the bed's feet, and the other by the door.'

Next morning the couple would be awakened by eunuch choristers singing a benediction:

Endless pleasures bless your bed
Angels' wings around you spread
Godlike offspring grace your joys
Heavenly daughters, lovely boys.

The Sultan always rose first, dressing in brand-new silk robes. It was tradition for his bedmate to accept the discarded clothes, including a jewel he'd leave in the pocket.

If she had pleased him, the concubine would be readmitted to the harem as a favourite with her own permanent apartment and staff. More valuable gifts would follow from the Sultan: '... jewels, money and vests of great value,' says Bon, 'agreeable to the satisfaction and content which he received from her that night.'

For the ordinary *odalisk* like Anna, however, life in the harem was as disciplined and humdrum as it might have been in a convent. In fact, Bon makes the direct comparison:

'Now in the women's lodgings, they live just as nuns do in great nunneries, for these virgins have very large rooms to live in, and their bedchambers will hold almost a hundred of them apiece. They sleep upon sofas, which are built longways on both sides of the room, and a large space left in the midst to go to and from about their business.

'Their beds are very coarse and hard ... and by every ten virgins there lies an old woman ... [to] ... keep the young wenches from wantonness.'

According to Hill these matrons were former concubines who took a 'malicious care to hinder [such] wantonness as they are past the task of.'

He said lights burned all night so that the matrons 'may be able to discover all immodest or indecent pastimes'. This caution went to extremes, with orders that any phallic-shaped vegetables must be finely chopped before entering the bedrooms.

Orientalist painters like Ingres and Delacroix imagined voluptuous women lying naked on sofas. In reality, the typical *odalisk* was warmly wrapped up: there are descriptions of them huddled around the charcoal burners, which provided the only heat in the draughty palace.

For exercise, they would play ball or indulge in childlike games of tag. We have a unique description of one of these sessions from an English craftsman named Thomas Dallam who worked near the harem. At one stage he sneaked a look through a grille:

'[T]hrough the grate I did see thirty of the Grand Signor's concubines that were playing with a ball in another court .... They wore upon their heads nothing but a little cap of cloth of gold, which did not cover the crown of her head; no bands about their necks, nor anything but fair chains of pearl and that a jewel hanging on their breast, and jewels in their ears; their coats were like a soldier's mandilion [cloak] ... they wore breeches of scamatie, a fine cloth made of cotton and wool, as white as snow and as fine as lane [muslin]; for I could discern the skin of their thighs through it.'

He confessed he was reluctant to leave the grille, 'for that sight did please me wondrous well.'

Had Dallam been caught, he would have lost his eyes and possibly his life. Sultan Murad once wreaked a terrible revenge on a Venetian merchant who'd built a viewing room with spyglass above his seaside mansion. Murad decided his true motive was to spy into the harem and ordered the merchant to be 'hanged in his shirt'.

Security in the harem was strictly enforced by the black eunuchs. The chief black eunuch was entitled the Master Of The Maids, an immensely powerful figure. Far from being weak and effeminate, eunuchs were tough security specialists who'd been subjected to savage beatings to test their endurance. They often had wives and concubines: and, although neutered, with a little ingenuity they could still enjoy giving and receiving sexual pleasure.

It goes without saying that the harem could be a hotbed of sexual frustration. For most, the sole opportunity for any form of sexual encounter lay in the hammams or baths.

'It's common knowledge,' wrote diplomat Bassano da Zara, 'that as a result of this familiarity in washing and massaging, women fall very much in love with each other. And one often sees a woman in love with another one, just like a man and woman ... on seeing a lovely young girl, [they] seek an excuse to wash with her just to see her naked and handle her.'

Generally, however, the baths were similar to a modern health club, where women could relax and enjoy lively conversation.

Otherwise, Anna would have found the hours and days dragging by. The women would drink endless cups of tea, coffee or chocolate. Some took relief from the boredom in opium. Others would sit smoking tobacco, telling complex stories, or playing elaborate parlour games.

Then in 1640, nine years after the Baltimore raid, Sultan Murad died suddenly at the age of twenty-eight, to be succeeded by his insane brother Ibrahim. And from that point on, life in the harem could never be described as boring.

No-one could have blamed Ibrahim for being as crazy as a barrelful of monkeys. He was by nature a man of gentle and easy temper, but he had already endured enough to send the sanest man screaming up the walls. Along with his elder brother Murad, he had narrowly survived execution as a child. When Murad became Sultan in 1623, the eight-year-old Ibrahim had been locked away in The Golden Cage, a tiny room with only one window for light and air.

In this unreal environment the young Ibrahim had gone completely insane: it was said that his deranged cries echoed around the entire palace. Every time the key turned, he was convinced it was the official strangler.

On February 8, 1640, Murad went on a massive bender of wine and aqua vita. When an eclipse darkened the sky, he was so terrified that he suffered a fatal seizure.

It was only through the intervention of his iron-willed mother that Ibrahim survived the dying emperor's final hours. One of Murad's last acts was to command the execution of his brother and to grant the succession to a foreign ally.

Kiosem moved fast. She summoned a council of state and 'with gentle words, desired them to remember that Ibrahim was the lawful heir and their true Emperor'. In the cold light of her challenging eye, the courtiers backed down and cried: 'Long live Sultan Ibrahim!'

But when Ibraham was informed that Murad had died, he was convinced this was a cruel ruse and refused to come out. In a macabre scene, the icy-veined Kiosem ordered that her eldest son's body be laid outside the Golden Cage. Only then did the whimpering new Sultan leave his cell.

And so began one of the most disastrous reigns in Ottoman history. The twenty-five-year-old sultan was totally unfit to rule an empire. His subjects reacted to his first public appearances with mockery. Kiosem moved rapidly to limit the damage. She decked her son out in the most majestic apparel and, determined that he should be feared as well as respected, she personally strangled two potentially disloyal courtiers.

By making a secret pact with the Grand Vizier, Kiosem was able to consolidate her power as the *de facto* empress. Ibrahim was a mere puppet as the Iron Lady negotiated peace with Persia and Austria. Never had the Reign Of Women been so powerful.

Other problems were not so easily repaired. Ibrahim's ordeal in the Golden Cage had left him impotent, and for almost a year 'the warm embraces of the most inflaming ladies in his Seraglio could not thaw his coldness' until he finally came through and fathered a son.

Ibrahim reacted to freedom by going demob-happy, indulging in every form of excess his inflamed imagination could invent. When someone told him that every strand of his beard should be decorated with jewels, he ordered it done.

He also developed a fetish for sable fur – he wanted it all over the walls and ceiling, even on the floor.

Surrounded by the most beautiful and exotic women in the known world, the Sultan was still not content. His demands became increasingly bizarre. On a whim, he decided he wanted to have sex with a giantess and sent his emissaries in search of the nation's biggest female – not disproportionately wide or tall, but a perfectly shaped Amazon. A nationwide search yielded an enormous Armenian who delighted the Sultan so much that he offered her anything she desired. Revelling in her new status, the newcomer demanded and received the governorship of Damascus. Ibraham cheerfully ordered all his wives and princesses to serve her in court.

Needless to say, the Queen Mother did not take kindly to this. She sweetly invited the new arrival to a private dinner where, between courses, an expert strangler sneaked up to slip a garrotte around the guest's neck. Kiosem sadly informed her son that his giantess had succumbed to a mysterious illness.

Fuelled by aphrodisiacs, Ibrahim demanded full-scale orgies on a Roman scale. His debauches became so grotesque that they shocked his courtiers and alienated the Janissaries, who were eventually to depose him. Worst affected of all were, of course, the concubines themselves. In one notorious orgy, they were required to crawl around neighing like mares while the naked Ibrahim mounted them like a stallion at stud.

Nothing excited him more than a challenge: a woman he could not obtain. For some reason, he wanted to have sex with Murad's widow, who was so horrified by the prospect that she tried to stab him. Noise of the fracas alerted Kiosem, who rushed to the scene and begged her son to back off. This show of disloyalty enraged the Sultan, who had meanwhile learned the truth about his giantess's death. He threw Kiosem in prison and agreed to release her only when she 'submitted herself with all humility to her son, begging his favour and pardon'.

Ibrahim recruited a sweet but poisonous female spy named Shecher Para (Sugar Candy) to trawl the municipal baths looking for the city's most beautiful women. Sugar would find a suitable candidate and return with descriptions so enticing that Ibrahim would soon be head over heels in love. If the woman did not agree to become his bedmate, he would have her arrested. There was outrage when he kidnapped the daughter of a religious leader and had her dragged to his bed.

Then one day, the mad sultan decided on a whim to clear out his entire harem. Hundreds of live women were stuffed into weighted sacks and thrown into the Bosphorus. Only one woman managed to burst free from her grisly shroud and was picked up by a ship. The rest – including, presumably, any of the Baltimore women who had arrived from Algiers in the early 1630s – were drowned.

Years later, according to an unverified folk tale, a salvage diver swam down to the river bed in search of a wrecked ship and was astonished to find the surface covered in vertical body-bags, each held to the ground by a heavy weight and swaying eerily in the current.

CHAPTER TWENTY-THREE

Through The Silk Tunnel: Love And Marriage in Barbary

E ven in the stony soil of enslavement, genuine love could take root and grow. It would be a mistake to think that all the slave women from Baltimore ended up as reluctant concubines or grudging servants. Many would have been chosen as wives, and in some cases they were willing partners.

Remember that these women were prize catches. There are several documented cases of enslaved Englishwomen or Irishwomen marrying the actual rulers of their new countries.

The historian Sir Lambert Playfair refers to an Englishwoman who willingly married the ruler of Algiers in the late 1600s – although he suspected her motives were mercenary.

And from a biographical list of famous Scotswomen there is an intriguing reference to one Helen Glogg, born a blacksmith's daughter in Perthshire in the mid-1700s. Helen was only eighteen when she was captured by corsairs and sold as a slave in Algiers. According to this source, a Moroccan emperor became so besotted by her beauty that he took her as his principal wife and empress.

Another historian, Godfrey Fisher, points out that at one stage in the late 1600s, the rulers of Algiers and Morocco each married an English slave.

According to one history of the Moroccan royal line, the eighteenth-century emperor Muhammad III chose as his second wife an 'English or Irish woman' who took the name of Lalla Sargetta. Their son Mulay al-Yazid became an emperor.

In the late 1600s – as we have seen – an Irish woman named Mrs Shaw agreed to turn Muslim in order to become the fourth wife of the Moroccan emperor Muley Ismael. When the relationship turned sour she claimed to have been forced into it, but Muley was a charismatic figure and it is quite that possible that she married him voluntarily.

Some of these references undoubtedly overlap and point to the same cases. Still, these brief glimpses of extraordinary marriages give some indication of the high regard in which slave women from the British-Irish Isles were held in Barbary.

However, for the best example of a genuine romance between ruler and slave we have to go back three hundred years to an Englishwoman who took the name of Chams ed Douha – 'Dawn Light'. We don't know her original name or how she was captured, but every year thousands of visitors still file respectfully past her royal grave near Sallee.

Abou El Hassan, Sultan of Morocco from 1331 to 1349, was a cultured ruler who created a renowned centre of learning at Chellah. Today his college lies in ruins, but we can still visit the necropolis where he lies at rest beside his adored wife and former slave Dawn Light – her prestigious burial site testifying to the genuine love he held for her.

Marriage in Barbary was a democratic business. While they may not all have married into royalty, it's probable that many of the Baltimore women and girls made good marriages with local men and (dare I say it) lived happily ever after.

There were also romances between the slaves themselves. Slaves were permitted to marry each other, but any children would themselves be slaves. In rare cases, enslaved couples made it out of Algiers and returned home to marry, one waiting faithfully for the other to be ransomed.

Of course, love can strike when you least expect it … as the Icelandic captive Gudrid Simonardottir could testify.

The Baltimore women in Algiers would have been familiar with Gudrid's story, because she was their contemporary. Married with a three-year-old child, she had been torn away from her husband in Morat's Icelandic raid.

This Nordic beauty caught the eye of the Pasha's son, who decided he wanted Gudrid as his wife. She was placed in the royal harem, but for some reason the marriage never took place.

When her ransom arrived nine years later, Gudrid was forced to leave her child (then twelve) behind her on the quayside.

Stopping off at Copenhagen on the way home, she fell in love with a young pastor who offered her spiritual counselling. There was public scandal when she became pregnant. However, it emerged that Gudrid's husband in Iceland had already died and the couple were free to marry.

The pastor became an eminent poet, but Gudrid remains a shadowy figure. One source says that she remained steadfast in her Christian faith in Algiers: she wrote letters in which she said she 'suffered daily' and believed that the captives' ordeal was a direct punishment for their sins. She is said to have left the Algiers quayside instructing her child to remember verses of Scripture.

Another source claims that 'Turk Gudda' – as she became known in Iceland – had converted to Islam in

Algiers, and later caused great embarrassment to her clergyman husband by continuing to practise her Islamic prayer rituals for the rest of her life.

Most of the female Baltimore captives – women like Joane Broadbrook, Bessie Flood, Mrs Corent Croffine and her daughter – would probably have begun their slave lives as servant-companions to wealthy women. They weren't asked to do heavy work, and according to Haedo, they were highly prized for their embroidery, spinning and weaving skills.

D'Aranda tells of one young woman who was on her way to the Algiers palace to be sold as a slave when the Pasha's wife spotted her from a window and requested her as a personal handmaid. As she began service 'the Pasha's wife noticed [she] was an excellent needlewoman and could do embroidery ... so that she was much in her mistress's favour.'

In most cases, however, the women slaves quietly adapted to their new lives. According to d'Arvieux, there was little difference between the routine of a typical domestic servant here and at home. 'They live very commodiously for their state in life,' he reported.

After a few months or years of sewing, Miss Croffine (for example) might be picked out as a potential bride.

To accept, she needed to change religion and become 'purified'.

The weddings themselves were elaborate affairs. The

groom would arrive at the bride's home and host an elaborate feast with musical entertainment.

'He is then conducted into the presence of his wife by four women who are veiled,' wrote the slave John Foss. 'He then retires and goes to his own house, and the bride is set on horseback and led to his house.'

An elaborate tunnel of silk would guide the bride into her new home.

Her female friends would then 'walk through the streets … shouting out together, as loud as they can, with such strong shrill voices that they may be heard two miles.'

Most middle-class brides found themselves in a two-storey house with the women's quarters on the first floor. Furnishings were basic sofas, rugs and roll-up mattresses. Light filtered through stained glass and through latticed windows. These lent their own exotic charm, for the women would wake to find the morning sun scattering handfuls of colour around their white walls like a child flinging brushfuls of paint. As the morning progressed, the coloured light would move around their bedroom like carnival floats.

In wealthier homes, there could be up to four wives, with each spouse entitled to conjugal rights. The French traveller Gerard Nerval once met a sheikh who explained the practicalities of everyday life in a small-scale harem:

'Where do they sleep,' I asked the Sheikh, 'these women and their slaves?'

'On the sofas.'

'But don't they have covers?'

'They sleep fully dressed. However, there are silk or woollen blankets for the winter.'

'But I don't see a place for the husband?'

'Ah! The husband sleeps in his room, the women in theirs, and the slaves on the sofas of the communal rooms. If the sofas and cushions are not comfortable to sleep on, they can set up mattresses in the middle of the room, and sleep there.'

'Fully dressed?'

'Invariably, but they keep on only the most basic clothes: trousers, a jacket, a dress. Both men and women are prohibited by law from revealing their bodies to each other from the neck downwards; if they yield to curiosity, their eyes are accursed: that's a formal text.'

'I understand,' I said, 'that the husband does not particularly want to spend the night in a roomful of fully dressed women, and that he's quite happy to sleep in his own room, taking with him two or three of these ladies …'

'Two or three!' the Sheikh exclaimed indignantly. 'What sort of dogs do you think we are, that we should act like this? By the living God! Is there any woman, even an infidel, who would agree to share with another the honour of sleeping with her husband? Is this how they behave in Europe?'

'In Europe!' I answered. 'Certainly not! But Christian

men have only one wife, and they suppose that the Turks, having several, live with them as they would with one.'

'If it were the case,' said the Sheikh, 'that Muslims were so depraved as to act as Christians suppose they do, their lawful wives would immediately demand a divorce.'

The Sheikh continues:

'In reality, almost all of them live with only one woman. Young women from good homes nearly always make this a condition of their marriage. A man who is rich enough to feed and maintain several women ... can, admittedly, take up to four wives; but he is obliged by law to devote one day a week to each one, which is not always a pleasant task. You also have to consider that the constant intrigues of four women, roughly equal in rights, would generate a very unhappy life for him, unless he were very rich and highly placed. For these people, the number of women in the home is a luxury, like horses.'

Once married, the former Miss Croffine would have found her life reasonably pleasant. The women's quarters were not as isolated as they seemed. They had protruding balconies that almost touched over the street: in fact, they could actually be linked by enclosed ladders, allowing the wives to visit each other. It was said that a determined woman could cross the entire city this way.

But the rooftop gardens, with their cooling sea

breezes and ocean views, were among the favourite spots to socialise. Surrounded by screens of plants, the women could work, relax and chat freely.

As long as they were properly attired, they could take numerous trips out – to the shrines for religious duties, to the baths for steam sessions, or to the suburban vineyards for picnics. In the evenings, there might be dinner gatherings, make-up parties or exhibitions of dancing.

All in all, a typical female captive who'd spent her previous life squelching through boggy fields or labouring at the stinking fish palace, might have considered her new situation in sunny Algiers and concluded that life was at the very least ... not intolerable.

CHAPTER TWENTY-FOUR

The Children

LET'S not forget that fifty of the captives taken from Baltimore were children. The Gunter boys, Joane Broadbrook's children, John Ryder's youngsters – they would have been destined for many fates, not all of them unpleasant.

The boys' ordeal would also have begun in the Badistan, where their heads were shaved except for a long lock of hair that was allowed to fall from under their caps to signify that they were unconverted Christians. If their experience was like that of the teenage Joseph Pitts, the Gunter lads would have been forced to stand for six solid hours under the blazing sun with 'not the least bit of bread allowed us'.

As the sale began, the auctioneer began a well-rehearsed routine. 'See what a pretty boy this is!' he would cry out. 'No doubt his parents are very rich and able to redeem him with a great ransom.'

After returning to the Pasha's palace for a second viewing, they were separated and taken to their new homes.

Poet Thomas Davis speculated that some would have become page boys and spear carriers: 'This boy will bear a Scheik's chibouk, and that a Bey's jereed.' This was quite likely, because Christian boys were highly prized as servants in wealthy households once they converted to Islam and endured the ritual of circumcision. After that they would be accepted as family. They would often grow up in opulent surroundings. Years later, the English envoy who arrived to rescue the Baltimore captives would look at such children and admit: 'They keep [them] very gallant.'

Such boy converts brought great honour to their new masters, and the Pasha would often include them among his personal selection. The Icelandic pastor Ólafur Eigilsson was heartbroken when the Pasha picked out his own eleven-year-old son. He was never to see the boy again:

'My son said sadly: "Father, they can do as they wish with my body, but my soul belongs to the Lord."'

Some, like young Joseph Pitts, would have been passed on from one master to another. The English boy was sold three times: firstly to a sadistic patron who systematically beat him 'until the blood hath run down on the ground' in a bid to force him to turn to Islam.

Pitts finally yielded and agreed to convert. He was

dressed in finery, put on a horse and paraded around the city to scenes of great joy.

Eventually the youngster was sold on as a servant to a household where the owner's wife attempted to seduce him. 'Many temptations did she lay in my way, though not by word of mouth, but by signals,' he recalled, 'but I made myself ignorant of her meaning.'

His third patron was an elderly bachelor who treated him kindly. 'My work with him was to look after his house, dress his meat and wash his clothes,' Pitts recalled.

Pitts said he wanted for nothing and became so close to his patron that he felt as though he were his natural son. After a year, the patron invited him on a pilgrimage to Mecca and afterwards granted him his liberty.

As a free man, Pitts faced a choice 'to go from him or to live with him. I chose the latter … [for] he loved me as I had been his own child.'

Pitts joined the Janissaries at a salary of £20 a year and served throughout the Mediterranean before seizing a chance to escape. After fifteen years in Algiers he was by no means sure that he wanted to return home. His patron had told him he would leave him a substantial legacy and Pitts believed the promise was sincere. 'He was like a father to me.'

A Cornish boy, Thomas Pellow, had a similar experience when he was captured by corsairs at the age of ten. After enduring savage beatings he converted to

Islam and grew up to become a celebrated general in Morocco.

There is a verbal snapshot of him, aged twenty-two, in the journal of an English diplomat: 'Today were visited in Mequinez by one Pilleau [Pellow], a young fellow of good family in Cornwall but now turned Moor ... [He] spoke the Arabic language as well as the Moors.'

Thomas survived in Barbary for nearly a quarter-century before escaping and returning to Cornwall in 1738.

In Algiers, there were other, less savoury, reasons why young European boys were in demand. Paedophilia was widespread. The leaders of the ruling Divan were reputed to be pederasts, and when the English captive T.S. arrived in Algiers he noted that the Pasha singled out a German boy for his personal choice because '... they burn with the unnatural fire which consumed Sodom and Gomorrah.'

Pitts reported that the city contained a notorious ring of paedophiles who used self-mutilation as a form of identification. 'I assure you,' he wrote, 'that I have seen several who have had their arms full of great cuts, as so many tokens of their love or, rather worse, their bestial lust.'

Happily, there is no evidence that any of the Baltimore boys fell into such hands.

And what about the female children? For a start, we have to remember that childhood did not last very long, either in North Africa or in Europe. In both societies, girls were often considered marriageable at twelve or thirteen. (At around this time, the Earl of Cork offered his thirteen-year-old daughter as a bride to his bitter rival Wentworth in a bid to heal the rift between them.) In Algiers, girls of that age were also thought ready for training as concubines.

There is at least one documented case of a girl of twelve who was saved from the harem only when a Christian captive promised to marry her.

The youngest girls faced a variety of fates. They could be put to work as maidservants or purchased and raised by investors.

A winsome child could sell for over £100, twice the price of a beautiful woman, and the cream of the crop were selected as page girls at court.

An English aristocrat, Lady Mary Wortley Montague, met a group of them at a Sultana's court in 1718:

'Her slaves were to the number of thirty, besides ten little ones, the eldest not above seven years old,' she wrote. 'These were the most beautiful girls I ever saw, all richly dressed; and I observed that the Sultana took a great deal of pleasure in these lovely children.'

Let's look at two case histories that illustrate the extreme ends of the spectrum of child slave experience in Algiers.

The first deals with the two little daughters of an Englishwoman named only as Mrs Jones. Captured at sea in 1747, the family was conveyed to the Algiers slave market, where Mrs Jones and her two youngest girls – one aged eight, the other an infant – were sold into domestic service. A clergyman described the older child shivering in a ragged coat as she carried heavy buckets of water.

One day a local man grabbed the infant girl and threatened to kill her if Mrs Jones did not have sex with him. When she refused, he cut off the girl's hand and threw it at her mother, who retaliated by knocking him out with a heavy stone and then despatching him with his own sword.

Our second case history could not have been more different: a captive girl who made a fairytale transition from the rags of slavery to the splendour of the imperial palace.

Naksh-i-idil (her Islamic name) was born in France, although her family may have been American. They were captured at sea by Barbary corsairs and sold on the Algiers market.

Naksh-i-idil's parents died when she was only two. She was a child of exceptional beauty, and she caught the eye of a canny slave trader who bought her as a long-term financial investment.

By the time she was fourteen she was a beautiful and cultured young lady. She caught the eye of the city governor who wanted exceptional females to send as his regular tribute to the Ottoman Sultan Abdulhamid I.

Abdulhamid, who was known as 'pious and benevolent', took her as his wife and she gave birth to a potential heir.

As their son Mahmud II began a reign that would last twenty-one years, Naksh-i-idil automatically assumed the pre-eminent role of Empress Queen Mother.

When she eventually died of a fever, Naksh-i-idil was given a magnificent funeral and laid to rest in an opulent mausoleum. The Sultan draped his own scarf across the coffin.

For two decades, Naksh-i-idil had been the most powerful woman in the Empire – a remarkable accomplishment for the former slave girl who had once stood shivering in the Algiers slave market.

The Baltimore children may not have fared nearly so well, but the experiences of youngsters like Naksh-i-idil, Pellow and Pitts show it was possible for a child captive in Barbary not only to survive and to live well, but even to rise to the highest positions in this strange and hostile land.

CHAPTER TWENTY-FIVE

Cursed With Iscariot

Baltimore, six months after the raid

BACK home, the investigations were continuing into the Baltimore fiasco. It was the end of the year before the inquiry was complete, and on New Year's Day, Hooke received a withering rebuke from the Lords Justices.

The Earl of Cork began by referring to the 'disaster' at Baltimore and then addressed Hooke's role in the fiasco.

'We think that if you had done your duty in plying to and fro, it might have been avoided,' he said.

The captain reeled under this onslaught. He had already explained about his lack of supplies.

'It is folly to say that you were not victualled,' Boyle continued relentlessly. 'When you came over from

England, you had a good supply, and you have since got £100 from us.'

Hooke seethed silently.

'You will at once set out and patrol the sea,' Boyle commanded him. 'And if you do not behave properly, we shall inform the Lords in England.'

The ruling must have left Hooke incensed. It was a classic bureaucratic fudge and it left no-one satisfied: least of all the King.

King Charles was still waiting for an explanation and he did not intend to wait for much longer. The letter he sent to Boyle and Loftus was chillingly polite.

> *January 19, 1632, Whitehall.*
> *Lord Dorchester to Lords Justices. The King is surprised at having had no report from [you] with regard to the Turkish piratical raid at Baltimore. I hope that you will make such report soon.*

Just over three weeks later, a report from Boyle and Loftus was on the desk of the Privy Council in London.

> *February 11 1632, Dublin Castle.*
> *We have inquired into the question of negligence of the captain at the time of the recent piratical raid on Baltimore. Captain Hooke complains that he could not act for want of provisions, but on 28 May 1631 we gave a warrant of £200 to Sir Thomas Button towards victualling both ships.*
> *On the 4th of June he told us that he had taken orders for victualling both ships, so that, on the 20th, when the raid took place, The*

Fifth Whelp, which was lying at Kinsale, should have been able to act.

It must be remembered that the attack was delivered suddenly, that the invaders stayed only a few hours [and] that the harbours in that part are many and yet so far apart that it is impossible to tell either where an attack may be delivered or how it may be fore- stalled.

We have urged vigilance on the captains, and sent you over in- structions to Captain Hooke. On victualling ships we have spent £3,649.3s.6d. We still think Captain Hooke dilatory and at fault ... Sir Thomas Button should be ordered to come here at once.

The dispute over who was to blame for Baltimore did a slow fade-out from history. Hooke, who had friends in high places, seems to have escaped with an admonition.

His ship, *The Fifth Whelp*, wasn't so lucky. Six years later, the curse of the ill-starred fleet struck once more when she sprang a leak near The Brill and sank to the bottom of the ocean.

The case against Sir Thomas Button was pursued until his death. There seems no doubt that the Welshman had been deeply corrupt throughout his entire career. His skimming of supplies to *The Fifth Whelp* came as no surprise to his superiors: Button had been doing the same thing since the early 1600s, when he was keeping his ships undermanned and undersupplied and pocketing the extra money. This was a common scam among naval commanders, but, as one biographer points out, Button had 'acquired a reputation for being especially greedy'. He'd also been taking backhanders from the pirates he was supposed to be suppressing.

Just three months before the Baltimore attack his career was engulfed in scandal when it emerged that he'd stolen part of a cargo intercepted on a corsair ship.

After the raid, his reputation was in tatters. He lost the right to victual his ships, he was deeply in debt and, at the age of fifty-six, his health was failing. By November, his admiralty superiors in London would not even talk to him.

Two years later, Button was formally charged with negligence in failing to forestall the Baltimore attack. He was still preparing his defence when he died in April 1634.

As for Richard Boyle, it was not in his interests to dig too deeply into the Baltimore debacle. He was living on borrowed time and he had many enemies – including Munster president William St Leger – who were keen to expose his own financial irregularities. Perhaps he did not want to open any unpleasant cans of worms with an investigation that was too thorough and detailed for comfort.

Yet the authorities desperately needed a scapegoat for Baltimore. And they found one – in the person of John Hackett.

The trial of John Hackett took place at the next sitting of the Cork County Assizes, where he was condemned as an enemy of the state and put to death, all within eight months.

Hackett never did stand much of a chance. After being returned to shore by Morat Rais, he and the Falmouth captain Edward Fawlett had walked straight into the arms of English interrogators who wasted no time discovering the full story of what happened aboard the corsair ship.

Richard Boyle was later to sum up the case against him:

'Hackett, the fisherman from Dungarvan, was seized by the Turks and piloted them into Baltimore instead of taking them into some other port where they might have been taken. He has been condemned and executed as an enemy to his country.'

It's interesting to note the emphasis. Hackett's main crime, it seems, was not to pilot the corsairs to Baltimore, but to stop them attacking Kinsale, where the Navy supposedly stood some chance of capturing them.

Hackett was taken back from Cork city to Baltimore to die. In those days a condemned criminal would often be dragged across country behind a running horse. At every hamlet and every corner, there would be locals waiting with stones and rotten fruit. John Hackett's last day on earth would not have been a pleasant one.

The sentence was carried out on a hill overlooking the bay. The nineteenth-century historian Daniel Donovan, drawing on local folk memories, describes the scene:

'[Hackett] was taken prisoner, carried to Baltimore, and hung on a high cliff, facing the sea, and looking down to the very channel through which the miscreant had but a short time before so treacherously and cruelly conducted the galleys of the bloodthirsty and marauding tyrants.'

Thomas Davis, writing just two centuries after the event, uses the same oral history as the basis for the climax of his poem:

'Tis two long years [sic] since sunk the town beneath that bloody band,
   And all around its trampled hearths a larger concourse stand,
   Where, high upon a gallows tree, a yelling wretch is seen –
   'Tis Hackett of Dungarvan – he who steered the Algerine!
   He fell amid a sullen shout, with scarce a passing prayer,
   For he hath slain the kith and kin of many a hundred there,
   Some muttered of MacMurchadh, who brought the Norman o'er,
   Some cursed him with Iscariot, that day in Baltimore.

Meanwhile, in Algiers, more slaves kept pouring in from England to join the Baltimore captives. On 1 December 1631, James Frizell wrote home to a Captain Hawkridge referring to the 'miserable thraldom that the 384 now English captives, with myself, lyeth in'.

(Note that the number of slaves had risen by nearly 13 per cent since the summer.)

Frizell complained again that 'not one penny' of his salary had been paid to him.

By the following year, another hundred English slaves had arrived.

The plight of the Baltimore captives is vividly reflected in a heartbreaking petition sent by English slaves in Algiers a year after the raid:

'[We are] lying in most miserable slavery that, by [our] barbarous usage, [we] are ready to famish for want of bread.'

Their bulk ransom had been set at £100 apiece ... an impossible sum. They humbly beseeched that they be released from 'this miserable slavery'.

But like Frizell himself, they were pleading in vain.

The Sweetest Voice

*Of 109 persons taken from Baltamore
(being 89 women and children and no. 20 men)
here remaining now are 70 persons only to be ransomed,*

*40 being dead and turned Turks, perforce. And not one
of them as yet redeemed, but only one woman, by Mr Job
Frogmartino from Loagorno through his Jewish Factor
– James Frizell, English consul at Algiers,
February 18, 1634.*

FRIZELL'S letter to his Secretary of State
thirty-three months after the Baltimore raid
showed just how dire their situation had become. Over
the course of less than three years, almost one in three of
the original captives had either died or converted to
Islam – it's a sign of the times that Frizell doesn't even

bother to distinguish between the two categories. Of the twenty men and eighty-seven women and children in the original batch (eighty-nine if you accept the consul's figure) there were only seventy left available to be ransomed.

The most intriguing part of this document was practically a throwaway line. One woman from the Baltimore contingent had managed to arrange her own ransom via a middleman in the freeport of Leghorn – modern-day Livorno in Italy. This go-between rejoiced in the exotic name of Job Frogmartino, but at least he had a name. The ransomed captive herself was given no name at all.

This brief reference to the lucrative and elaborate ransoming network between Algiers and Leghorn needs a bit of explanation.

In Barbary, there were six main ways out of slavery:

You could be ransomed by your family or friends;

You could save up to buy your own way out;

You could be ransomed through charity;

You could be released by your government under treaty;

You could be released by your patron, usually because you'd agreed to convert;

Or

You could escape.

All of those options were open to Baltimore captives like John Ryder and Joane Broadbrook, although some were more realistic than others.

Let's take them one by one. Ransom by family or friends was an option reserved for the rich. In 1631, a professional man earning £20 a year would have had to save for ten years or more just to free a relative whose ransom was set at a typical £200 to £250. For a labourer on sixpence a day, the prospect was as unrealistic as flying to the moon.

However, there were borderline cases of families who put themselves into debt for life to rescue a loved one from Barbary.

Later in the 1660s, a Cork woman, Mrs Eleanor Walsh, applied for an official pass that would permit her to go to Amsterdam with ransom money for her husband John.

'Last November, when her husband was going to England from Ireland, he was surprised by a Turk man-of-war and carried into Turkey,' reads the petition. 'She has sold all she has to pay his ransom.'

Most people were reduced to pleading for donations from local dignitaries. In the case of the Baltimore captives, the obvious person to approach was the Earl of Cork. Richard Boyle was spectacularly rich and could have afforded to buy back all 107 of these hostages at £38 a head without giving it a second thought. For instance, the £10,000 he lavished on a dowry for his daughter Lettice could have bought these captives their freedom twice over. And the £20 he carelessly expended on one day on a quilt and a useless 'medicinal stone' was more than enough to redeem Ellen Hawkins from the owner who had paid £18 for her in the Bedistan marketplace.

We know that the Earl received petitions from the Baltimore slaves and their relatives. Sadly, all of them seem to have gone missing over the centuries. But we can get a glimpse into their desperate state of mind through similar letters sent to him from Barbary.

Just nine years before Baltimore, Boyle had received a letter of entreaty from Gerald FitzGerald, a Cork man who had been held as a slave in Morocco for five years.

Gerald himself put his case before the Earl in a heartbreaking plea for mercy:

'All my trust is in you, only under God, to have pity upon my poor estate of distress and misery … as for my ransom, it will come near hand £200, little more or less.'

He said he and his fellow slaves were enduring so many hardships 'that to reckon them all were infinite, and to taste one of them, intolerable.'

The process of paying a ransom was sophisticated and complex. It had to be – a relative sailing directly into Algiers with a trunk full of money would simply be relieved of his cash and enslaved himself.

Instead, an intricate network of trusts and sureties was developed via freeports such as Leghorn. This was the route followed by the anonymous Baltimore woman – let's call her Mary – who Frizell says managed to free herself from Algiers within the first thirty-three months.

Mary's husband or family would have gathered her ransom from private funds, or – more likely – taken out a loan. Their banker at home would send a promissory note to a banker in Leghorn. The Leghorn financier would contact his opposite number in Algiers, who would accept a draft for the money and pay the slave's owner. Naturally, everyone took a substantial cut along the way.

Everything could go wrong in this process, and frequently did. Banks could crash, bankers could die, crooked financiers could do a runner. Sometimes bankers in Barbary simply stalled for time hoping that the slave would vanish or die in the interim.

In Mary's case, however, the timing suggests that negotiations through Job Frogmartino's bank had begun quite soon after her arrival in Algiers. If that were the case, her time in Barbary would have been spent in a comfortable safe house.

The most intriguing question is: who was 'Mary'? She obviously came from a family of means, unlike most of the fishing folk from The Cove.

It is tempting to speculate that she may have been the wife of the wealthy William Gunter, but Frizell does not divulge.

Whatever her true identity, her troubles would not be over when the money finally came through to Algiers. There were levies to be paid and palms to be greased. There would have been a 3.5 per cent port duty, after which gifts to the same amount had to be bestowed upon the Pasha and the corsair leader Ali Bichnin.

After that, Mary would have been taken to the *belediye* or city hall, where the Cadi would give her the most coveted document in Barbary – the 'free card', a document that carefully noted her name, country, height, hair colour and distinguishing marks.

Curiously, although this document recognised the bearer's right to avoid slave work, it did not permit her actually to leave the city. To do so, the former slave had to pay a further 10 per cent levy for the 'freedom of the gates'.

After the voyage to Italy, Mary had to be kept in quarantine in Leghorn before she was finally allowed home.

But at the end of it all, she probably shared the feelings of the Italian captive Filipo Pananti. When the poet was at last called aside from the other slaves and told '*Ti star franco*' – you are free – he described it as 'the sweetest voice that can possibly vibrate through the heart of man'.

The second option was to earn your own ransom. We've already seen how men like Cathcart and Joyce were able to raise the cash through their own hard work. However, the international brokerage network offered other possibilities, some of them quite ingenious.

For instance, a slave could arrange to sell his house back at home, or borrow against a future inheritance. Most astonishingly of all, there were cases in which slaves were actually released from Barbary and sent home to England – on assisted passages! – so they could raise their own ransom cash. Of course, a dreadful revenge would be taken on whoever had stood security for them in Algiers if they did not return with the money.

Another possibility was a direct transfer – a swap of a Christian slave in Barbary for an Islamic prisoner in Christendom. However, this practice was discouraged with a high exchange rate in which three or four Muslim slaves were necessary to free a single Christian captive.

This is how Emanuel d'Aranda and his three Flemish comrades eventually regained their liberty. Their families, unable to find the money to pay their ransom, instead offered to repatriate seven Islamic prisoners in Europe. Ali Bichnin reluctantly agreed, but insisted on a sweetener of nearly 3,000 Spanish dollars.

The third main option – often the only option – for slaves seeking their freedom was to be ransomed through an act of charity. The most active agent was the Catholic Church, which had established two orders of friars to work for the redemption of slaves in Barbary. The first was the Trinitarians – the Order Of The Holy Trinity And Redemption Of Slaves – followed by the Mercedarians, or Order Of Our Lady Of Mercy. As the number of slaves grew, the Dominicans and Franciscans joined in. The scale of their operations was enormous. The Trinitarians (Father Dan's order) are estimated to have ransomed as many as 140,000 slaves throughout their history. The Irish Trinitarians alone, with a base at the Black Abbey in Adare, ransomed 6,300 captives and lost forty of their number as martyrs.

The Mercedarians were originally a military order, a tradition that prompted them to wear a white Crusader-style habit with a wide leather belt and chain to symbolise the sword they once carried. They are credited with rescuing up to 70,000 slaves.

The Redemptionists – to give these Orders their umbrella title – would raise money through donations, religious levies and legacies. On arrival in Algiers, they would declare their ransom fund to the authorities and pay enormous levies and bribes before selecting the longest serving slaves for ransom. Clad in symbolic white cloaks, the freed men were marched with religious solemnity to the harbour.

The Redemptionists have been criticised by modern historians for wildly exaggerating conditions in Barbary in order to raise funds. But amid all the revisionism, we should not lose sight of the basic brutality of slavery, and the heroism of these men, at least nine hundred of whom died in the course of their work.

For the Protestant slaves from Ireland and England, charity was far less organised: usually a matter of church gate collections and parish fundraisers. Seven years before the Baltimore raid, in 1624, there had been a nationwide charity collection, but it had rapidly degenerated into a farce. The Navy had snatched most of the money to repay its debts.

In 1628 the philanthropist, Sir Kenelm Digby, spent £1,650 of his own money to ransom slaves from Algiers, and in 1631 King Charles I authorised a nationwide charity collection in aid of slaves in Morocco.

Documents from the era reveal something of the scale of the problem. There seems nothing remarkable about the charity donations that were routinely dispensed to slaves; they simply crop up in the records, hidden among the more mundane cases of orphans and needy widows. And yet what tales of heartbreak must lie behind these dry ledger entries?

These are just some examples:

Fifteen shillings given for a minister, prisoner at Sallee.

Sixpence alms given to a poor Algiers slave.

One shilling alms given to John Williams that had been taken by Algerines.

One shilling alms given to Robert Stout and John Boules with a pass from Algiers.

Two shillings alms given to Henry Sheridan and John Price, two poor Algerine slaves.

One shilling alms given to four poor Algerine slaves with a pass from Leghorn.

One shilling alms given to Peter Steward and John Steward that had been slaves three years in Barbary.

One shilling alms given to a poor Turkey slave that had

his tongue cut out.

One shilling alms given to Markis Thow Jenaki Nicula, who had been fourteen years a slave in Algiers and lately made his escape from thence.

Option number four was to be redeemed by government treaty. Peace treaties would often include an amnesty for slaves of a particular nationality, but these pacts rarely lasted for long. The interesting question was why they were considered necessary at all. If all the Christian nations had combined forces, they could easily have defeated the Barbary menace forever. It seems that each nation cynically sought to gain a commercial edge by achieving immunity for its own shipping while the corsairs continued to attack its rivals.

The problem of ransoming slaves through treaty was exactly the same dilemma that faces modern states dealing with terrorism. Paying money to ransom the Baltimore hostages would simply encourage further raids. Besides, Barbary piracy – like modern terrorism – was international. A nation could forge a treaty with one Barbary state, only to be plagued by the same corsairs who'd moved along the coast to another base.

The families of English and Irish slaves tried every form of protest they could devise a bid to persuade their government to change its 'no negotiation' stance. In the 1620s, it was said that the road to the House of Commons was so packed with the weeping wives of Barbary slaves that the MPs could hardly make their way through.

At one stage, three hundred Algiers captives sent a pitiable petition to the King, making 'supplication to rigid death' for their redemption. They were 'groaning under a woeful and intolerable captivity' and begged to be ransomed since most of them were still 'in the May of their lives'.

Supplications just as sad as this were being received regularly in the 1630s, but they fell for the most part on deaf ears.

Two years after the Baltimore raid, a monumental decision was taken about the future of English slaves in Algiers – although it's not clear whether the slaves themselves were aware of it.

A document dated 1633 reveals that King Charles, responding to complaints from merchants in the West Country, commissioned an expert panel to report on the crisis. The experts began by restating the scale of the problem and by recognising 'the great dishonour and loss already suffered' by England. Their verdict:

'[It is] both impossible and improvident to think of redeeming the captives by collection, retribution [i.e., compensation] or at all by ransom, for that would encourage the pirates …'

Even if such action were taken, they estimated that '50m li [£50,000] would not redeem those already taken at the price mentioned by James Frizell'.

The experts 'declare[d] their judgment that there was no way but one (and it most necessary): to suppress them by force.'

It wasn't going to happen. No nation would manage to suppress the corsairs, by force or otherwise, for another two centuries.

And so the miserable captives from Roaring Water Bay would continue to send petitions pleading for the State to ransom them, but they were simply shouting into the wind. The decision had already been taken at the highest level.

The Baltimore slaves were on their own.

CHAPTER TWENTY-SEVEN

Apostasy Now

Divers of the English slaves have turned Turks, through beating and hard usage — Edmund Cason, the English envoy sent to Algiers to free the Baltimore captives.

THE phrase 'to turn Turk' has entered the English language as an all-purpose phrase to describe an act of defection or treachery. But in the 1600s it had a quite literal meaning: to embrace Islam and become a citizen of the Turkish Ottoman empire.

When consul James Frizell reported in 1634 that forty of the original Baltimore captives had either died or 'turned Turk per force' he meant that the converts had been forced to change their religion through violence.

This may have been the case: we have no evidence one way or the other. But it was always more convenient to believe that all 'renegadoes' had been forced into conversion through torture than to admit the truth that the reasons for apostasy were many and often complex.

During fund-raising drives in Europe, congregations were shown pictures of scenes ostensibly set in Barbary but more inspired by Dante's Inferno. Captives are strung up by the heels while tormentors with demonic faces beat or burn them into submission.

Yet the Spanish monk Diego de Haëdo listed several possible reasons for conversion, including fear of slave life; experiencing temporary freedom; and a taste for the 'vices of the flesh'.

This is from the perspective of a Catholic friar, but at least it admits that apostasy could be voluntary.

Other eyewitnesses confirm this. In 1622, a man named John Rawlins wrote that many Christians 'very voluntarily' became Muslims. And George Sandys, an Englishman, said that the Barbary authorities 'compel no man' to convert.

Sadly, however, there are verified cases of conversion through force. The child slave Thomas Pellow was savagely beaten. And the English captive Joseph Pitts had a sadistic patron who attempted to convert him by slow, measured beatings, interrupted only by smoking breaks.

'He declared that, in short, if I would not turn, he would beat me to death,' Pitts wrote. 'I roared out to feel the pain of his cruel strokes, but the more I cried, the more furiously he laid on, and to stop the noise of my crying, would stamp with his foot on my mouth.'

Women were not excused such treatment. D'Aranda's expert seamstress – the one who was chosen as handmaiden to the Pasha's wife – was given '300 blows of the cudgel' for refusing to convert.

However, even Pitts was fair enough to concede that this treatment was not the norm. 'In Algiers, I confess, it is not common,' he wrote, 'though I myself suffered enough from them, God knows.'

Sometimes trickery was used instead. During a friendly debate on religion, James Cathcart was asked if he knew the Muslim affirmation of faith. When he quoted it, the Algerines instantly declared him a convert. It took a hefty bribe to extract himself from this tight spot.

Yet the missionaries who loved to emphasise the violence and subterfuge couldn't hide the fact that thousands of Christian freemen were becoming Muslims of their own volition.

Throughout the early 1600s, as the opportunities for piracy dried up in Europe, there was a steady southward flow of migrants – mostly seamen and shipworkers – who became Muslims purely to advance their careers in the equal-opportunities atmosphere of Barbary, where they found an early version of the American Dream.

These conversions were not all cynical and self-serving. There were many genuine believers, including the Italian renegado Ali Bichnin, who in 1622 built a mosque so beautiful that it still stands as a source of wonder today.

The first recorded English-speaking convert was named as John Nelson in 1583. Among the hundreds who followed were some high-profile names, including an English consul, Benjamin Bishop.

For a typical slave, conversion was rarely a sudden impulse, and more of a gradual process. At first the 'pull' of home was far more forceful than the 'pull' of life in Algiers, but the former would grow steadily weaker and the latter would grow steadily stronger as new relationships were forged.

In Europe, there were two common myths. The first was that slaves who converted acquired automatic freedom. This was not the case: they enjoyed some extra privileges, but they remained slaves.

The second myth was that most owners of adult slaves *wanted* their slaves to change religion. In fact, the opposite was true, since any prospect of ransom cash would instantly evaporate.

'I have known some Turks who, when they have perceived their slaves inclinable to turn, have forthwith sold them,' Pitts wrote. 'They are more in love with money than with the welfare of their slaves.'

D'Aranda tells the story of a Pasha who was considerably annoyed when a thirteen-year-old boy he'd bought for three hundred ducats decided to convert to Islam.

He says the boy had been 'debauched by a Portuguese renegado for the sum of 40 ducats' and adds:

'The Portuguese renegado who had debauched the lad brought the boy before the Pasha, saying: 'This Christian desires to renounce his religion.' The Pasha was not well pleased because he had proferred his 300 ducats ...'

But the ruler had little choice but to accept the situation.

Owners faced strong social pressure to grant freedom to a converted slave. As Pitts put it: 'It is looked upon as an infamous thing ... to deny them their liberty and to refuse to send them out handsomely into the world.'

There was little patience with Christians who converted simply to avoid the consequences of a crime. Thomas Sanders, the English captive, tells of a Frenchman who was sentenced to death and turned Turk in a bid to save his own life.

'Then said they unto him: "Now thou shalt die in the faith of a Turk" and so he did ...'

In most cases, however, conversion led to an open door of opportunities that people back home could only dream about. Far from being despised as turncoats, renegadoes were welcomed into the highest echelons of

Algerine society. For them, the sky was the limit. Humble fishermen like William Symons or Christopher Norwey from Roaring Water Bay could become great corsair captains and make fortunes virtually overnight – in fact, Fr Dan reported that the greatest corsairs were renegadoes. A man like Edward Cherry could become a soldier and rise through the ranks to the very top. They could work their way up the civil service ladder. None of these things were likely to happen to a lowly-born individual in Europe, where such social mobility would not become commonplace for centuries to come.

Today, those who voluntarily convert from Christianity to Islam talk of a gradual shift, a slow dawning, rather than a sudden dramatic epiphany. The process is eased by the fact that the two faiths have much in common. For women like Bessie Flood or Miss Croffine, there would have been some practical incentives as well.

'What I love about Islam,' one modern female convert told a journalist recently, 'is the sense of respect they have for women. I have felt more respect and dignity as a Muslim woman than I ever had as a non-Muslim woman.'

This could have been one of the driving forces behind the mass conversion of the Baltimore women – whether or not they were actually aware of it.

Back home, a married woman had no property rights: everything she owned was vested in her husband. She would also sacrifice her identity and take her husband's name. In contrast, Islam, in its purest form, emphasised a wife's individuality, encouraging her to retain her own name and property.

While there was no concept of equality between the sexes (and nor was there in Europe at the time) there was the exotic notion of an honourable collaboration in marriage. The woman's role as wife or mother was respected and revered. Not everyone kept to this code, but, all in all, Bessie Flood's position in Algiers was, at the very least, comparable to that of her counterparts at home, and in many cases, infinitely better.

Neither side took kindly to losing someone to the opposition. In England, renegadoes were treated with contempt. Among the European authorities in Barbary, it was felt that any action was justifiable in an effort to prevent a man sacrificing his soul.

The Barbary rulers were equally strict about Muslim converts. Today, revisionist writers stress the religious tolerance in the Barbary states. It is true that they showed a remarkable open-mindedness: they allowed Catholics, Protestants and Jews to practise their religions, and even permitted chapels in the heart of the slave prisons.

'Religion bothers nobody there,' d'Arvieux wrote, no doubt with a Gallic shrug. 'You pray to God if you want, you fast when you can't avoid it, you drink wine if you have the money and you get drunk when you've drunk too much.'

But true tolerance would have allowed Muslim citizens to embrace Christianity, and that's where the Barbary authorities drew the line. In fact, they reserved their worst punishments for those who forsook the crescent for the cross.

The most grisly sentences were carried out in the grim and desolate area outside the Gate Of The Stream. Here the ancient stone walls sprouted gruesome metal hooks or ganches, reserved for those unfortunate converts for whom, in d'Arvieux's words, 'a slow death was intended'.

Those who preached against Islam could be impaled on a stake. One English visitor reported that three people met this horrendous fate during his spell in Barbary.

Haëdo tells of one young Arab man who converted to Christianity in Algiers. He was dragged to a nearby building site, hurled alive into a construction mould, and immersed in molten concrete. Some three hundred years later, workmen demolishing the building found the shape left by the body of the martyr St Geronimo, complete with binding cords.

Ransom, treaty and apostasy: those were the main ways out of slavery and they were all utilised by the captives from Baltimore. But there was another means of exit, one that carried such high risks and such a low chance of success that few captives were crazy enough to try it. This was the option of escape.

CHAPTER TWENTY-EIGHT

Fleeing The Pirates' Nest

Algiers, early 1640s

THE walls of the old workshop building shook and the rafters echoed as the fourscore English and Irish slaves made a joyful noise unto the Lord.

Slaves like John Ryder and Corent Croffine roared out their favourite psalms under the enthusiastic leadership of their young minister, the Reverend Devereux Spratt.

Outside in the sunbaked streets of Algiers, Janissary soldiers and religious police officers walked past, shaking their heads in amused disbelief at the heathen racket.

But unknown to them, the lusty hymn-singing was a cover for one of the most audacious escape plans ever concocted in Barbary.

For in a cellar a few feet beneath the singers, other

slaves were secretly hammering nails, forcing groaning lengths of timber into contorted shapes, and stretching tarred canvas across the framework of a small seagoing vessel that would carry them out of the city of slaves and back to freedom.

It is one of history's most astonishing escape sagas but we can't recount it without first telling the story of Devereux Spratt – the remarkable clergyman-slave who made it all possible.

In the cool marble interior of the Anglican Church of The Holy Trinity in Algiers there are memorials to some of the most remarkable English-speaking citizens who featured in the bloodstained history of the corsair capital.

There's a memorial to John Tipton, the first English consul to be appointed to Algiers. There's a marble slab dedicated to the enslaved villagers of an obscure village called Baltimore. And, fittingly close to them, there's a memorial to an extraordinary cleric named Devereux Spratt.

Spratt was an unusual clergyman in all sorts of ways. He was a strong spiritual leader, and yet he was racked by an all-too-human self-doubt that he admitted with an endearing candour.

As pastor to the English and Irish slaves in Algiers, he used his skills to forge this disparate crowd into a coherent, positive community.

By the time Spratt came to work with the slaves in Algiers in the early 1640s, John Ryder and the other

Baltimore captives were entering their second decade of captivity. Since they were all Anglicans from the same southwestern corner of Ireland as Spratt's own church, they would certainly have been his parishioners in Algiers and probably his friends as well.

Devereux Spratt was only twenty-one when he was seized by Algerine corsairs while sailing from Cork to England around ten years after Baltimore. The newly-ordained cleric had already experienced more than his share of bad luck. He had been forced out of his first parish in Ireland by the bloody 1641 rebellion, and his subsequent abduction by corsairs plunged him into a deep depression accompanied by a major crisis of faith. But his perspective changed when he arrived in Algiers. As soon as he set eyes on the hundreds of English slaves who desperately needed his help, he could no longer sustain his self-pitying opinion that God had 'dealt more hard with me than with other of his servants'.

At first, his own conditions as a slave were reasonably good. 'God was pleased to guide for me and those relations of mine taken with me, in a good ordering of civil patrons for us, who gave me more liberty than ordinary,' Spratt wrote.

But Spratt was not destined to remain in clover for long. As soon as serious negotiations began for his release, he was sold on to a new owner. And during the switchover, thieves ransacked his clothes and stole a £1,000 bond he'd hidden at the time of his capture.

It was back to square one with the release negotiations, and Spratt fell into another slough of depression.

'My patron asked me the reason,' he recalled, 'and withal uttered these comfortable words, *Deus Grande* which took such impressions as strengthened my faith much in God.'

Deus Grande: God is great. The same words were used to comfort many a homesick slave, according to the Spanish missionary Diego de Haedo. Spoken in *Sabir*, (another version is *Dio Grande*) they were used as part of a calming, fatalistic mantra intoned by master to slave:

Non pillar fantasia.
Dio grande.
Mundo cosi, cosi,
Si venir ventura, andar a casa tuya.
Si estar escripto en testa forar, forar.
Dio grande, sentar no piglliar fantasia.
Anchora no estar tempo de parlar questa cosa.
Dio grande.
No pigllar fantesia.
Mundo cosi cosi.
Si estar scripto in testa andar, andar.
Si no, aca morir.

Which translates roughly as:

Don't be stubborn.

God is great.

Such is the world.

If you are fortunate, you will go home.

If it is written on your forehead for you to leave, you will leave.

God is great, don't be stubborn.

Now is not the time to speak of such a thing.

God is great.

Don't be stubborn.

Such is the world.

If it is written on your forehead for you to go, you will go.

If not, you will die here.

After that watershed, Spratt's luck changed. An English captain began raising funds for him among the Leghorn merchants. 'After his return to Algiers, he paid my ransom, which amounted to 200 cobes [around £40],' Spratt recorded.

But then there was an unexpected development. The minister had proved such a comfort to the English slaves that they begged him to stay on as a free man and continue ministering to them. Spratt, who detested Algiers, tried to shift the burden of this awful decision on to the captain, his benefactor.

'I told him that he was the instrument, under God, of my liberty, and I would be at his disposing,' Spratt wrote. 'He answered no; I was a free man, and should be at my own disposing. Then I replied: "I will stay; considering that I might be more serviceable to my country in enduring afflictions with the people of God, than to enjoy liberty at home.""

With this courageous decision, the clergyman's prolonged crisis of faith was finally over. He remained in Algiers for another two years, during which he was said to have pulled back many slaves from the brink of desperation. Perhaps Spratt's own human weakness – his personal familiarity with what Brian Keenan called 'the silent, screaming slide into the bowels of ultimate despair' – enabled him to empathise with them and help them more effectively than any other minister could have done.

During his term there he even conducted slave marriages and baptised their children. In the parish church of Castmell, Lancashire, a number of people were recorded as having been baptised in Algiers by Rev. Devereux Spratt.

But after two years of this voluntary mission, he was effectively expelled from the country for his role in assisting the daring escape of his friend William Okeley and four other English slaves.

We've already touched on Okeley's story. He was the slave who started a tobacco shop and later expanded it into a workshop making waterproof canvas clothes. Over the past few months, he had been making preparations for his escape by converting his assets into cash and stowing it in the false bottom of a trunk which he'd entrusted to Spratt's care.

Now it was time to put all those canvas-sewing skills to better use.

It was a simple but audacious escape plan. If Okeley and his glovemaker friend could make waterproof canvas clothes, they could make a waterproof canvas boat. But it would have to be big enough to carry seven escapers, and such a large craft could never be concealed at the workshop. They needed a place where a group of English slaves could meet without arousing suspicion, and work noisily without anyone hearing.

Okeley gained permission to hold thrice-weekly prayer meetings at his shop's storeroom. Spratt agreed to preside at these meetings and, according to Okeley, 'we found our burthens much lighter and our conditions not pressed so hard upon our spirits'.

The services attracted up to eighty English slaves who no doubt kicked up an almighty noise. 'Though we met next the street,' says Okeley, 'yet we never had the least disturbance from the Turks or Moors.'

Okeley was adamant that the main purpose of the meetings was 'to strengthen our faith'. Yet it's impossible for any modern generation to read this story without thinking of the concert rehearsals that covered the noise of tunnel digs at Colditz.

Eventually, a prototype of the canvas boat was created.

'Having formed the design, or at least the rough draft and general model of it, my first care was whether it was likely to prove leaky or take wind,' says Okeley.

The multi-talented Devereux Spratt was enlisted as marine consultant. He checked over the boat and 'judged it possible'.

Spratt takes up the story, writing years later: 'I remember there was a canvas boat made in our meeting-house in Algiers, which was carried forth and hid in a brake of canes by the seaside.'

The boat had been smuggled down one piece at a time by a laundryman who hid the sections among his heaps of dirty clothes.

The seven conspirators met down at the 'brake of canes' on a dark night in July. Okeley's design had been sound: the boat floated like a dream. But she could handle only five people, so two of the slaves had to trudge back to their lodgings with heavy hearts.

The canvas had been waterproofed with pitch, but water still seeped steadily through the joints. One of the men had to work flat-out to bale out the craft while the others hauled on oars fashioned from sections of wine barrels. However, no matter how hard they rowed, the wind forced the light craft back towards land. The dawn light revealed a scene that plunged the exhausted men into near despair: they were still just outside Algiers harbour.

Fearing capture and torture, they rowed frantically for

their lives and made it over the horizon. But it was blisteringly hot and within a couple of days their drinking water had all gone.

It was at this point, as Spratt wrote later, that there began a series of three 'signal providences' or blessings.

Just as the men were lapsing into 'a despairing and starving condition' a turtle broke through the surface right beside their boat. The desperate men captured it and saved their lives by drinking its blood.

The second break came on the fifth day when the men, adrift on the open sea, sank into an exhausted sleep but managed to wake just as their leaky boat was about to sink beneath them. They spotted land ahead – it was Majorca, and they were safe.

The third item of good fortune related to Spratt himself. The Algerines were no fools, and they knew exactly what had been happening at the clergyman's prayer meetings. Spratt's main fear was that he would be held liable for the men's ransoms, 'seeing I was much suspected to have a hand in contriving the boat'.

His paranoia increased when he was followed down to the harbour by a Moor who lived next door to the storeroom. 'Seeing me one day upon the Mole viewing their ships, [he] frowned and grinded his teeth at me …'

Shortly after that, the Algerines expelled all ransomed slaves from the city. 'I then got my free card which cost 50 cobes [£10], and departed with some of my countrymen to Provence and Marseilles, thence to Toulouse …'

Eventually Spratt made it back to England, to be reunited with Okeley and return his trunk of money to him. He preached at a parish in Devon before being sent back to minister in Mitchelstown in Co. Cork – the same county he had left in such haste, years beforehand. A memorial in the local church pays tribute to him to this day.

Understandably, Spratt had no affection for the corsair capital. He ends his story with a heartfelt prayer: 'The Lord stir up the hearts of Christian princes to root out that nest of pirates.'

'It will perhaps be asked, what facilities of escape a slave has in Algiers,' Filipo Pananti wrote. 'It occasionally happens that a captive saves himself by swimming on board some ship in the bay or Mole; but nearly all the powers of Europe are obliged to give up any slaves that may be found on board their vessels …

'Whenever any armed vessels of [England or France] anchor near the capital, care is taken to keep very strict lookout on the captives, lest they be induced to take advantage of the circumstance; when brought back after having attempted to escape, a slave is well bastinadoed and loaded with a double quantity of irons.'

After a short spell in Algiers, Ryder, Croffine and the rest of the Baltimore slaves would probably have agreed with the Tuscan poet's pessimistic assessment. Escape from the 'well-guarded city' was rare. A combination of factors combined to make it all but impossible – the city itself was clamped shut at night, security on the waterfront was tight, and the inland routes held even more hazards than Algiers itself.

In the remainder of this chapter we'll take a look at the rare ones who did break free, and the determined ones who never gave up trying.

The history of successful escapes from Ottoman slavery shows that a spontaneous dash for freedom often had just as much chance of succeeding as a meticulously planned mission.

The English adventurer Captain John Smith was a case in point. Condemned to thresh corn in a field, he rushed his guard and beat his brains out with the flailing bat. Swapping clothes with his rich master, he galloped off on his horse and wandered lost for sixteen days before encountering some friendly soldiers who helped him escape.

There were other spur-of-the-moment successes. In 1669, a fifty-year-old Portuguese slave working in a garden in Algiers spotted an English ship lying just offshore. Wielding a pruning knife, he hacked his way through the guards, plunged into the sea, and swam out to the vessel.

Perhaps the most colourful of such escapes was that of Ida McDonell, the sixteen-year-old daughter of the British consul in Algiers, during an English blockade of the city. Ida disguised herself as a midshipman and slipped out to the English fleet one step ahead of the lustful Dey, who (you may recall) had earmarked her for his personal harem.

Dey Ali Khoja had thrown the consul into jail and was keeping his family as hostages. However, naval officers manage to disguise the mother and daughter and sneak them out to the ships one by one. During the final run the consul's baby was sedated by a surgeon and hidden in a basket of fruit. But just as the harbour sentry inspected the bundle, the baby began crying and the escapers were hauled before the Dey. In an uncharacteristic display of compassion, the ruler let the child go.

Another option for escape was to try to hijack a local vessel. The Algerines were well aware of this risk and made sure their craft had their rudders removed while in port.

However, mass breakouts of this type did happen. Seventy captives obtained their freedom by hijacking a galley that was being prepared for action. They nearly didn't make it:

'[A]t dead of night they got down through the sewer into the port: but the dogs, which are there very numerous, ran barking at them; some they killed with clubs and stones. At this noise, those who were on guard, as well ashore as in the ships, bawled out with all their might: 'Christians! Christians!''

The escapers stormed the boat and overthrew the

guard, only to find the vessel tangled by the ropes of other craft nearby. With the guards in hot pursuit, they jumped into the shallow water, lifted the boat on their shoulders, and carried it clear of the cables into the open sea. All seventy managed to reach safety in Majorca.

While escape by sea was regarded as dangerous, escape by the landward route was almost suicidal. Walls of up to 40 ft high protected the triangular city, and blind desert warriors, renowned for their sharp hearing, helped to guard its five massive gates at night. Even if they avoided the Algerine patrols and the ferocious Berber tribesmen, they would often succumb to hunger, thirst or disease.

Occasionally someone would make it, trekking across the desert by night and subsisting on roots and snails. But most failed dismally, and were dragged back to Algiers filthy and stinking (they'd often escaped by hiding in the toilet drains) to face the dire consequences.

Joseph Pitts witnessed one recaptured fugitive suffer a horrendous punishment. The man's feet were tied by rope to a mule and he was dragged for hours along the stony streets before being burned at the Bab-el-Oued.

Others would be sentenced to extended beatings to the feet, buttocks and stomach. The sight of these bruised and battered survivors hauling their punitively heavy shackles to work would be enough to make even the most courageous captive think twice before trying to escape.

Despite all the odds, despite the horrendous penalties, there were those who never gave up. Among those heroes, one man stands out as an example of irrepressible courage. A Spaniard named Miguel, he made four daring escape attempts during his five years of captivity in Algiers and never once implicated his co-conspirators.

Although he was only in his late twenties, he was already a celebrated war hero by the time corsairs swooped on his galley ship El Sol near the coast of Catalonia in 1575.

The following year he made his first bid for freedom. He was heading towards Oran with a band of fugitive slaves when their local guide left them in the lurch. The bedraggled group was forced to limp back to Algiers.

Next year, Miguel worked out a better plan. He would find a secure hiding place and lie low for several months until the hue and cry died down, then make a rendezvous on the coast with a boat captained by his brother. The plan worked well; Miguel and his co-conspirators hid in a grotto cave for five months until they were betrayed by a renegado.

A year later, Miguel was caught in a third escape plan and sentenced to a fatal two thousand strokes of the bastinado. The beating was never administered.

In his final escape attempt, Miguel plotted to take command of a galley and flee with sixty other slaves to Spain. Again, he was thwarted by a traitor and was about to be shipped off in irons to Constantinople when two friars appeared with his ransom money, half of which had been donated by his compatriots in Algiers.

Miguel returned to Spain where he tried to resume his previous career as a writer. But his style was regarded as passé, and it wasn't until after his death that Miguel de Cervantes became famous for a novel that he had 'hatched in a prison' in Algiers – the book we now know as *Don Quixote*.

CHAPTER TWENTY-NINE

Bagnio Days, Bagnio Nights

For most of the Baltimore slaves, Algiers was a giant prison and all life centred on the bagnios. Much has been written about these unique Barbary gulags. Depending on your point of view, they were either hellholes or 'universities for life'; either noisy, smelly dives, or the only place in town you could order a decent pork sausage.

Because these massive jails played a dual role in Algiers. By night they kept the captives stacked up in their honeycombed beds like so many worker bees. At dawn the slaves buzzed off on their allotted tasks and the bagnio changed character to become a social centre – a recreational village of taverns, barbershops and kebab houses. Here, according to Emanuel d'Aranda, the best conversation was to be enjoyed as renegade sailors gathered around the bar to drink and swap seagoing yarns. D'Aranda had experienced the bagnio as a slave;

once freed, he chose to return there as a customer.

However pleasant the place seemed to a free man, it was a different story for the slaves when darkness fell and the jail reverted to its true role.

James Cathcart recorded the dramatic moment of transition:

'The Guardian called out in a most tremendous tone ... "We are closing the gate!" when immediately emerged from the taverns a motley crew of Turks, Moors, Arabs and even some Jews, all intoxicated, some half naked, having sold or pawned their clothes to the Christian tavern keepers for liquor, others singing or shouting, some with drawn swords swearing they would kill the first person that offended them ... [T]he gates of the prison were then shut for the night.'

In this chapter will try to recreate the life and colour of the bagnio through the eyes of two witnesses – the French ambassador D'Arvieux, and the wide-eyed, open-eared Flemish slave D'Aranda, who let nothing escape his notice.

Let's begin by allowing D'Arvieux to guide us into a typical bagnio:

'The main bagnios are built uniformly, with little difference between them,' he says. 'As you enter, you find yourself in a large square or rectangular courtyard with stalls all around – these are used by the slaves to keep their taverns. The rear of these stores is separated into several small rooms, mostly occupied by the priests of different nations for the care of the slaves.

'They are rented by the Guardian Bachi, or the concierge of the bagnio. You're perfectly safe inside this place, and you have complete freedom to come and go as you please. The main gate opens at dawn and closes very late at night.

'The courtyard has plenty of tables, and they're always filled with soldiers, seamen and other idle and shiftless types who go there to drink wine, sing, smoke or make deals ...'

The taverns are run by slaves who pay protection money to the Guardian Bachi: 'He earns a considerable revenue from allowing the slaves to keep shops where they sell alcohol, food, tobacco and suchlike.'

The only comfort for slaves lay in their religion, which the authorities permitted to be practised openly in the bagnio. 'There's a chapel and a room which is home to the priest, who says Mass before they are led to work at daybreak,' explains D'Arvieux.

It is almost certain that many of John Ryder's fellow slaves from Baltimore would have ended up in the possession of Ali Bichnin, the sardonic and cynical corsair admiral. Immensely rich, the Italian renegado had hundreds of slaves which he kept in his own private bagnio – a vast complex with stout walls smothered in climbing vines. When d'Aranda was there in the early 1640s, it contained more than 550 Christian captives who spoke twenty-two different languages.

Bichnin once demonstrated the extent of his slave empire by holding a banquet at his country home a considerable distance from Algiers. The food was plated up in the city centre and passed out, hand to hand, by an unbroken human chain comprised solely of his slaves.

Bichnin's attitude to his charges was Darwinian. He refused to feed them, reckoning that the fittest would survive, and the others weren't worth keeping anyway. The captives had to moonlight or scavenge in their time off, either on Fridays or in the few hours between quitting time and sunset lockup.

D'Aranda marvelled at how the slaves rose to this challenge. Cottage industries grew up and flourished.

'There were some employed themselves in footing stockings and others got their livelihood by some kind of games,' d'Aranda recalled, 'but the profession most of us most used was stealing. Every night there was publicly sold what had been stolen the day before …'

The Algerines imposed a curious double standard. In theory, stealing was a serious offence for which a man could have his hands amputated. In practice, as D'Arvieux reported, 'they have only a few blows of a stick to fear, for everyone knows that all Christian slaves are professional thieves'.

There was even a grudging admiration for the best scams and a contempt for moral scruples. We've already seen how Bichnin laughed off an attempt by an Italian slave to sell his galley anchor; and on another occasion he sneered at a slave who passed up on a chance for freedom by returning a diamond he had found.

And so, as dusk fell on Algiers, hundreds of slaves would scurry through the narrow alleyways like plague rats, shoplifting, swiping, eating stolen food on the run and filching anything that wasn't nailed down. After nightfall those slaves who weren't confined to the bagnios went burgling.

Other slaves dreamed up elaborate con tricks. The cleverest conman of all was Fontimama, the irrepressible Italian sparrow who'd tried to sell the anchor. He worked so many rackets that he was able to feed not only himself, but also his friends (including d'Aranda) with delicacies that would 'set their jawbones a-grinding'.

One morning in the bagnio, Fontimama dreamed up a brilliant scam that could be used only once. He was so confident that he invited his accomplice to dine with him that night on the proceeds.

The pair set off towards the street where the moneychangers operated. Fontimama carried with him two Spanish half-dollars – one a genuine coin and the other an obvious counterfeit. He showed the good coin to the first moneychanger and asked him to change it for low-value Algerine aspers. The businessman emptied the aspers in a heap and began counting them out, with Fontimama obligingly helping him.

After the aspers were pushed across the table,

Fontimama offered him the *fake* half dollar in payment. The banker spotted the switch instantly. But this had simply been a decoy ruse. What the moneychanger hadn't noticed was that a good proportion of the aspers had stuck to Fontimama's fingers.

The racket continued until noon when, as d'Aranda recalls, 'Fontimama returned to the bagnio with a couple of pullets and money enough to procure three skins full of wine'.

D'Aranda knew another long-term slave, a French cavalier, who was always immaculately dressed and ate handsomely. In fact, he indulged in a round of endless credit, borrowing money from one French renegado and repaying it with a loan from another. In any ordinary society this scam would soon have collapsed, but Algiers was no ordinary society. '[T]he renegadoes being soldiers and being always abroad at wars by sea and land, it happened that some of his creditors died every year and they, having no relations, wives or children, the debt was paid at their deaths,' d'Aranda explains.

It was difficult enough for able-bodied slaves to get enough food to survive. But the same harsh rule applied to those who were handicapped by age or disability.

D'Aranda tells of an eighty-year-old Russian slave who survived on the tips he earned from cleaning the bagnio toilets. Another slave from Hamburg had lost an arm and was left to starve. When someone lent him a half-dollar, he invested the money in the equipment for a game of ninepin bowls, which he hired out to the local children and so 'lived pretty well'.

One slave who'd been penalised with a 100 foot chain wrote letters home for his illiterate countrymen without any charge except the occasional drink. This magnanimous offer attracted so many grateful customers that he built up a large amount of tavern credit, which he converted into cash for food.

Other slaves 'frequented certain houses where they daily carried water and fetched away the dirt,' writes d'Aranda.

Those slaves who were unable to moonlight or scavenge found that the ruthless Ali Bichnin was not bluffing. In d'Aranda's time, no less than twenty English slaves died 'of pure want'.

D'Aranda was not sympathetic. He claimed that all nations made 'some sort of shift to live' except the English, who wasted their time quarrelling with each other.

At the top of Bichnin's scale of instant evolution were the slaves who'd prospered so well that they could live relatively normal lives. Not for them the dawn assembly and the wretched march to work. Instead, they could bribe the Guardian Basha and devote themselves to the serious business of making money.

The most profitable businesses were tavern keeping,

tobacco selling and the black economy. Fencing stolen or smuggled goods was hugely profitable. Each evening the hot material would be displayed in the prison yard and snapped up at keen prices.

Tobacco selling was also a big moneyspinner: we've seen how William Okeley's trade earned him a trunkful of cash. Other slaves bought shiploads of tobacco at cheap rates in Spain and resold them in Algiers.

Tavern keeping was the best business of all, but it involved special problems. The owners were obliged to keep orderly houses, but could not physically restrain drunken locals, since it was a capital offence for any Christian to raise his hand against a 'Turk'. One slave, Rodrigo, solved this dilemma with an ingenious method.

'[W]hen the drunken Turks drew their knives,' writes d'Aranda, 'Rodrigo came armed with a ladder and, getting the Turks' heads between the rounds, led them all along.'

A little lower down the hierarchy of success in the bagnios were the skilled workers. A special bagnio, more like an open prison, was used for specialists like gunsmiths and shipworkers.

Among D'Aranda's comrades at Bichnin's bagnio were six enslaved surgeons 'who got much money, for they were sent for by the citizens'. Unfortunately they were big spenders who rapidly blew their earnings.

The walls of the Algiers bagnios embraced much human misery ... but they also contained a vibrant, exciting international community, with cookhouses where the food was tasty and varied, alehouses where the wine was of the highest quality, and conversation that never grew dull.

Some locals would come here to enjoy the illicit thrill of eating pork sausages. The American slave John Foss once asked an Algerine customer if he realised what he was eating. 'Hold your tongue,' the man replied. 'If you do not tell me, then I shall not know.'

For his part, Emmanuel d'Aranda enjoyed the banter in the tavernas even after he regained his freedom. He would join his former comrades in discourse, or simply let the conversation wash over him like waves from the ocean:

'[T]here would always be some relating their adventures at sea: the Dutch, on what passed in the East Indies, Japan or China; the Danes and Hamburgers at the whale fishing in Greenland, what time of the year the sun appears in Iceland, and when their six-months night is at an end; or if such conversation pleased not, I went among the Spaniards who covered the dominions of their Kings as they pleased, or talked of the delicacies of Mexico or the wealth of Peru, or if I went among the French we had news from New France, Canada, Virginy; for most of the slaves were people some way related to the sea.'

D'Aranda felt he had learned valuable life lessons in the bagnios. '[It] may be seen what mistress necessity is,' he mused, 'and that there can be no better university to teach men to shift for their livelihood than one of the bagnios of Algiers.'

CHAPTER THIRTY

Habituated To Bondage

Meanwhile, consul James Frizell had been sinking ever deeper into depression. At his wits' end, he had penned a direct plea to King Charles.

> To the King's most excellent Majesty.
> The humble petition of
> James Frizell on behalf of himself and 800 of Your Majesty's subjects now slaves in Algier.
> Most humbly showing:
> That the unfortunate and miserable prisoners and slaves having been taken and being still detained in a most lamentable condition by reason of breaking of the peace formerly made and confirmed by Sir Thomas Roe, then ambassador at Constantinople, betwixt Your Majesty's subjects and the Corsari [corsairs] of Algier, have at divers times requested and long hoped for their redemption of their miserable bondage. But same as not redeemed, no fruits of Your Majesty's intended clemency towards them.

Frizell's tetchy letter showed how hopeless the

situation had become by 1634, when the Baltimore captives marked their third year in captivity, and the number of English slaves in Algiers had more than doubled. It was plain that the prospect of release was receding, and bleak despair was setting in.

Frizell had concluded by pleading with the King to appoint commissioners to 'find out some ways and means for the preservation and deliverance of Your Majesty's miserably suffering subjects.'

His words were wasted. Another three years had passed by without hope. By October 18, 1637, as the autumn winds blew in to herald yet another Algerine winter, Frizell's spirits had reached rock bottom. Writing to the Lords Of The Privy Council in London, he complained strongly about 'the miserable and depressed life' of English subjects in Algiers. He reminded the Lords that he had been in Barbary since October 1625, 'in most miserable and extraordinary troubles, to the danger of my life'.

The consul continued: 'Yea, and I am now brought so low for want of means to maintain my charge withal that I am in condition to starve ... I do verily believe that never any of his Majesty's ministers hath been so neglected as I am.'

However, Frizell had a glimmer of good news to report. After listing the latest batch of captured ships, he added:

'And of all of these captives, there is now of them

ransomed 100 ... by Mr Henry Draxer [?] of Leagorno and his Jewish Factor at costs from 150 to 1600 Rs of eight a head...'

So a hundred of the English slaves, with the aid of their families, had been able to buy their freedom in 1637, using the same Leghorn route used by 'Mary', the unknown Baltimore woman. Their ransom prices had varied from 150 Spanish dollars up to $1600: sums that showed just how much profit their investors had made over typical Badistan sale prices.

The despairing consul had continued to write to London begging for the 'fruits of clemency'. But he was begging in vain. In England, the storm clouds of civil war had started to form on the horizon and the King had far too many problems of his own to worry about some dysfunctional diplomat in North Africa ... or his irksome slaves.

As the months and years passed, Joane Broadbrook and the other Baltimore captives became so accustomed to slavery that they could imagine no other state of existence. The formidable walls of Algiers defined their horizons; their only ambition was to get through another working day. '[We were] so habituated to bondage,' recalled the English slave William Okeley, 'that we almost forgot liberty, and grew stupid and senseless of our slavery.'

Still, there could have been worse places to live.

Algiers, the most civilised of Barbary cities, was often described as a miniature Constantinople.

'The city of Algiers is built upon the declivity of a mountain, in the form of an amphitheatre,' wrote one observer.

'The roofs of houses are flat, and the citizens walk upon them in the evening to take the air. Several of the roofs are thinly covered with mould in which a multitude of flowers and shrubs are planted, which at once delight the eye and perfume the cool sea breezes. From these gardens, there is a most enchanting prospect of the environments of the city, where innumerable villas, gardens, paths, fountains and rivulets exhibit the combined magnificence of nature and art.'

Europeans arriving here for the first time were amazed how a city that had unleashed such terror could be so tiny. 'This place which, for several ages hath braved the greatest powers of Christendom is not above a mile and a half in circuit,' one Englishman marvelled.

Between the two main entrances – Bab-az-Zoun, the Gate Of Grief, and Bab-el-Oued, the Gate Of The Stream – snaked the city's main thoroughfare, Great Market Street. Only 36 feet wide, this steep street was one lengthy souk where tradesmen of all descriptions jostled to sell their wares. There were stalls piled high with herbs and hemp; butchers and cobblers; candlemakers and book binders; earnest tailors and scribes. Colour wash splattered the walls near the dyeing workshops; and in the tanneries the rich smell of hide mingled with the stench of the dog faeces used to soften the leather.

The streets were so notoriously narrow that a horseman found it difficult to go through, and two men could not pass without one giving way.

Yet compared to European capitals, Algiers was a healthy city. Its cobbled streets were kept clean by an army of workers. In an era when Londoners emptied their bedpans in the street, Algiers had piped sewage and fresh running water – James Cathcart described this as 'clear as crystal'.

Europeans ridiculed the citizens' personal hygiene, with one Frenchman deriding the 'foolish conceit' of washing before meals.

Islamic medical science was far ahead of Europe, and had been for centuries. In Baghdad, a thousand years earlier, medical students had been taught the basics of modern anatomy, pharmacology and toxicology. From Cairo to Cordoba, doctors had diagnosed diseases as complex as meningitis.

Sophisticated anaesthetics had turned surgery into an art. Abulcasis, who died in 1013, described more than two hundred fine surgical instruments that could remove kidney stones, strip varicose veins, and excise cancer tumours. Islamic surgeons could even extract eye cataracts by suction through a hollow metallic needle.

While Europeans were tackling the Black Death

through self-flagellation, physicians like Ibn Khatima had discovered that minuscule organisms could invade the body and cause disease.

And long before Jenner 'discovered' vaccination, Turkish women were routinely using small doses of cowpox to protect their faces against smallpox.

A diet rich in vegetables also helped to promote health. The climate was kind and the fields produced prolific yields. According to the Spanish monk Haedo, Algiers had an 'infinite number of gardens and vineyards filled with lemon orange and lime trees [and] flowers of every kind.'

Even the weather was pleasant by North African standards. 'The climate in this country is remarkably delightful,' John Foss wrote. 'The air is pure and serene.'

All these factors had a measurable effect on quality of life and longevity. Even then, Algerines were described as healthier and longer-lived than Europeans.

Westerners sneered at the Algerines' minimalist tastes. 'The furniture consists of carpets and mattresses on which they sit and lie,' sniffed the same observer. 'As for food, they have little taste in the preparation of their dishes, and eat in a manner at once slovenly and disgusting to a European.'

But today, Europeans will visit expensive restaurants to get a similar menu: tajines of lamb, couscous, stuffed tomatoes, stuffed vines, meatballs and vegetable kebabs.

During their set breaks – they were off on Fridays and

public holidays – John Ryder and the other male slaves had the free run of the city. Amazingly, any slave with the money could visit the city's bathhouses, restaurants or cafés without restriction. Anyone with enough change for a cup of coffee could sit at a pavement café, where musicians would play the distinctive Algerine music – a mixture of Spanish and Turkish influences – until late into the night.

Language was no barrier to the slaves. Everyone in Algiers spoke *Sabir* – French diplomats used it in their dealings with locals, thinking they were speaking pure Arabic, and the Algerines used it back, assuming they were speaking French.

Alcohol was commonplace despite the formal ban. There were also drugs, and not only the local *kif*.

One slave from Ireland – and in all likelihood from Baltimore – had an owner who took opium. Returning home after a drug session, the patron held out his own arm and told the slave to place a burning coal on the bare flesh. The slave did so. The master, unflinching, told him to blow on the ember to make it even hotter, and still he showed no evidence of pain.

Algiers had licensed brothels, supposedly reserved for the Janissaries, but also frequented by citizens and (illicitly) by slaves. Thomas Baker, English consul in neighbouring Tripoli, once reported: 'Two whores, being last night taken in a Christian's company, were with him this afternoon, being very wet weather, dragged bare-arsed at a mule's tail through all the streets of town ...'

Algerine justice was notoriously swift and harsh, with punishments ranging from the bizarre to the barbaric. A fraudster might be forced to ride backwards on a donkey. Traitors risked hanging or slow decapitation. Beating with sticks was the most common deterrent: a trivial misdemeanour could earn thirty strokes, and serious offences could warrant a thousand or more.

Life in Algiers was never dull. There were minor earthquakes, famines, plagues, uprisings and coups. In the two decades since 1631, there were no fewer than eight governors. On the plus side, the drudgery of the captives' lives was lightened by the major feast days. These holidays gave the slaves an opportunity to earn extra cash with food or drink stalls. Everybody – captives included – was allowed to join in the fun. There would be wrestlers, stilt walkers, puppet shows and acrobats. 'The oddest thing,' marvelled the French diplomat d'Arvieux, 'was to see old, white-bearded men enjoying themselves on swings like children.'

For Joane and the other women slaves, the dreary plod of domestic chores was also broken by family occasions such as weddings or circumcision ceremonies. Female domestics would accompany their mistresses on ceremonial visits to shrines or graves.

As the weeks turned into months and the months

turned into years, the Baltimore slaves ceased to be surprised at the scenes around them. The exotic sights, the unearthly clamour, the rich smells of Algiers became a mere background to what was increasingly becoming a normal existence. As they walked through those narrow streets, pushing through the shouting street vendors and the braying donkeys, ducking out of the way to avoid a swaggering Janissary, they must have felt at times that they had never known any other life.

Then, after fifteen years in captivity, something happened that had the potential to change their lives forever.

It was a September day in 1646, and Joane was no doubt going about her usual round of duties in Algiers when she heard the news that made her heart pound with excitement and anticipation.

A new ship had appeared in the bay. It was an English ship, the *Charles* – and it was coming to take her home.

CHAPTER THIRTY-ONE

The Redemption Of Captives

Freeing hostages is like putting up a stage set, which you do with the captors, agreeing on each piece as you slowly put it together; then you leave an exit through which both the captor and the captive can walk with sincerity and dignity
—*Terry Waite, hostage negotiator and captive in Beirut.*

I N THE summer of 1645, after Oliver Cromwell's New Model Army had decisively defeated the Royalist forces at Naseby, a ship called the *Honour* set sail from England to Algiers. On board was Edward Cason, an envoy entrusted by Parliament with the difficult task of securing the release of hundreds of

English and Irish slaves.

The intention had been there for years. At the start of the Long Parliament of 1640, while an uneasy peace still existed in England, the House of Commons had passed an Act resolving to redeem captives 'taken by Turkish, Moorish and other pirates from the cruel thraldom which they lay under'.

It had been a dramatic break from the previous policy of laissez-faire and represented a determined effort to bring the hostages home.

The outbreak of full-scale civil war in 1642 had stopped the plan in its tracks, but as Cason put it, they had 'kept up resolve amid the storm'.

The *Honour* would have made a rich prize in itself. The well-armed craft was laden with what Cason described as 'a gargasoon of money and goods to great value'.

Tragically, the mission was plagued by the same bad luck that had dogged the Baltimore captives right from the beginning. Passing Gibraltar, the *Honour* encountered contrary winds that forced her to shelter in the bay.

Someone noticed smoke drifting out from below, and as the crew fought desperately to quench the flames of an onboard fire, they suddenly came under attack from shore. The aggressors overwhelmed the Englishmen and seized the *Honour*'s redemption money.

There was one consolation. The raiders had

overlooked a small amount of cash. Cason transferred it to a nearby English ship, the *Diamond*. We can sense the despondency in his tone as he tells what happened next:

'[T]he *Diamond*, a while after, before her return to England, was cast away near Cadiz and so the monies there were lost. Thus one affliction is added to another, and misery, like waves, tread one on the other's heel.'

Cason returned home, his mercy mission a total disaster. However, his superiors obviously did not blame him for the fiasco, for the following year he was despatched on a similar mission in a 'ship of strength' named the *Charles*.

With the country enjoying comparative calm after four years of bloody Civil War, Cason could concentrate on his mission. His brief was twofold: to organise the captives' release and to negotiate a permanent peace.

'We arrived at this port in safety, thanks to God, on 21 September,' Cason wrote home. 'The Basha and the Duana [i.e., the Divan, the ruling council] sent me safe conduct next day.'

Amid the splendour of the Pasha's court, he presented his letters of credential and launched into an opening gambit of conciliation and wounded rectitude. He said he wished to restore peaceful relations and 'desired the subjects of England to be delivered unto me free, for we had not broke the peace'.

It was worth a try, but the Pasha had a ready answer. He could not hand over the English slaves because they didn't belong to him. They had been sold on to individual buyers who could not give them up without compensation for their original outlay. Records of these sums, the Pasha added helpfully, could easily be obtained from the ledger books.

Cason was not impressed and the meeting ended inconclusively. 'Being not content with this answer, I desired my letters to be read in the Duana, to have an answer from the Basha and Duana when they were in council.'

The English envoy cooled his heels for four days until the next session of the Divan, which was scheduled for Saturday.

Meanwhile, word of the negotiations spread like wildfire among the slave community. For captives like Joane Broadbrook and Ellen Hawkins from Baltimore, this was the most excrutiating time of all. After fourteen years in captivity, freedom lay almost within their grasp – they could actually see the *Charles* lying out in the bay, and watch the English crew going about their work. And yet they knew that everything could still go spectacularly wrong and the *Charles* might still sail away without them. It was a time of exhilaration, but it was also a time of dread.

The slave John Foss recalled one such disappointment. '[At first] our hearts were joy. We imagined ourselves already freemen ... our chains were falling off and our taskmasters no longer at liberty to torture us. In imagination we were already traversing the ocean – hailing our native shore, embracing our children and our wives. This delirium of joy was of short duration, like a dazzling meteor in a dark night, which blazes for a moment, making the succeeding darkness more dreadful.'

Joane and Ellen have left no record of their feelings, but we can get some idea of their emotions through the words of Mary Rowlandson, the minister's wife who was abducted and enslaved in Massachusetts in 1676.

'My heart was so heavy before [I heard of my ransom] that I could scarce speak or go in the path; and yet now so light, that I could run,' she recalled. 'My strength seemed to come again, and recruit my feeble knees, and aching heart …

'Yet I had not a comfortable night's rest … I did not sleep for three nights together … I could not rest, I was so full of fears and troubles.'

Mary's reaction was classic. At the time of imminent rescue, a captive can lose control of her emotions to an extent that she becomes a danger to herself and others. Modern hostage negotiators are well aware of the cruel syndrome that can prompt a captive on the brink of safety to make rash, impulsive gestures. During the siege at Entebbe, for instance, the rescuers accidentally shot a hostage who jumped up with arms outstretched to greet them.

For Ellen and Joane, there was nothing to do but endure the agonising days and the sleepless nights and wait until the vital council meeting at the weekend.

If Edmund Cason attended the meeting of the Divan that Saturday, he would have witnessed an extraordinary spectacle. The Divan's rules of procedure were unique. Everyone shouted at once, and the cacophony was heightened by the cries of the translators. Tempers frayed and speakers would often resort to force. There were bizarre rules dictating exactly how much violence was acceptable. 'Obliged by order of the Divan to keep their thumbs within their girdles,' explained one diplomat, 'they durst express their anger by punches and thrusts of their elbows.'

Another English visitor marvelled: 'They stand in ranks … jetting each other with their arms or elbows, raising their voices as if in a choler, or as a pot boileth with the addition of fire.'

Unsurprisingly, the Divan adopted exactly the same position as the Pasha. Cason was asked to meet the Pasha a second time. These negotiations proved more fruitful, with the English envoy agreeing to pay cost-price for the slaves and the Pasha agreeing a peace which would leave all English ships unmolested. The pact was celebrated with lavish banquets.

'The Basha entertained me with all courtesy, feasted me in his house and afterwards in the fields,' Cason wrote.

The following month, the peace treaty was formalised with a historic letter jointly written by the Pasha, the Divan, the Mufti and the Cadi and addressed to the Parliament in London:

> The agent which it hath pleased God to bring hither from the Parliament and England, we give God thanks, for that he has come hither to make peace and love betwixt us until the end of the world, and that he hath given us a letter: and that Edmund Cason is come agent by consent and allowance of the Grand Signior and safety to the harbour of Algiers ... and that he came ashore unto us in love and peace, and that a good peace was agreed upon by both parts, and he demanded the English Christians that were slaves to be delivered unto him, which could not be granted because they were bought by Turks and soldiers that were in the pay, and they would not deliver them till they had the money they cost them at first in the market: and if he will take them upon those conditions, as they had been upon the former peace, we will have a good peace with them, as they have in Constantinople with the Grand Signior, upon this good peace concluded, we, both small and great in the Duana, were upon those agreements well content, for the slaves as they have been sold first in the market, so shall they have them upon that price again, as shall appear on their books at the time of their sale.
>
> And upon this business that you sent here one of your gentlemen, named Edmund Cason, who took the names of all the Englishmen, except them that were turned Turks and put their names down in his register book ...
>
> In Alger, the 15 of October 1646 &c.

This registration process was not as easy as it sounded.

Cason requested that 'every owner of an English captive might come with his slave before me, and a scrivener [scribe] of this place, to declare his slave's name, and what he had cost him the first penny, the which was regifted by us both; and further took the place he was of, and his age, and what ship he was taken in, and how many years past.'

Joane Broadbrook's patron was there, querulously demanding his 150 dollars back, and Ellen Hawkins's master turned up to present his bill for just under 90 dollars.

However, the honeymoon glow of the peace treaty was already starting to fade. It wasn't long before Cason discovered that, in Barbary, things were never simple or straightforward.

For a start, he suspected that he was being conned by the slave owners. 'I was informed that divers Turks and Moors caused us to set down much more than their slaves cost, the which I did advise the Basha. He swore by the head of his Master, the Great Turk, I should pay not an asper more than they cost in the market, and the first sale when they were brought on shore.'

Secondly, he had to negotiate his way through a tangle of levies, duties and outright bribes.

It was standard practice in Algiers for negotiators to be asked to pay 10 per cent to the State on top of the official ransom price. In this case, the Pasha generously offered to give Cason a bulk discount. For him, it would be a mere six per cent. Cason no doubt gulped at the prospect of paying another £600 on top of the £10,000 fee, but he had no option but to accept.

This was just the beginning of the rip-off. 'Then also we agreed for his duties for exportation of the slaves, 20 pesos per man to the Basha, and to the officers, half duties; all of which comes to 31 dollars per slave, without agreement they would have cost about 50 dollars a man for charges.'

When his register had been completed, Cason found that there was a total of more than 650 English slaves in Algiers, with another hundred serving on the Turkish fleet at Crete.

Many more had converted to Islam, he reported, 'through beating and hard usage'.

There were also the children who were being raised in local households, although Cason generously conceded that they were well treated and kept 'very gallant.'

The envoy reported that many of the older boys who had changed religion had been spirited away to Alexandria and other ports to the east.

There was a sense of acceptance that none of the slaves in these three latter categories could be recovered.

Cason had the unenviable task of explaining the economics of the slave trade to Parliament:

'The greatest part of the inhabitants had rather keep their slaves than permit them to be freed,' he complained. 'They come to much more per head than I expected ... Here be many women and children which cost £50 per head, first penny, [whose investors] might sell them for an hundred.'

Then there was the hierarchy of trades. '[M]asters of ships and carpenters, caulkers, coopers and sailmakers, surgeons and others ... are here highly esteemed; so that they had come unto £32 per man, first penny, and they have rated them one with another, and the port charges is 61s.6d per head, so they will be about £38 per head put a ship board.'

Cason tried to simplify things by negotiating a standard individual price that would take all these variations into account, but the slave owners were having none of it. '[T]hey would not consent ... alleging that they were bought at several prices, and it would make trouble among them; the king hath promised I shall not be wronged.'

Cason knew that he did not have enough money to redeem all the English slaves – only 250 or so. As winter drew in, he sent a heartfelt plea to London urging action before winter.

'[Though] you suffer some inconvenience at home, it will give a great reputation to the better purpose of the peace ... I beseech your Honours not to think that this redemption may be part one year and part another: and I desire your people may go home in summer, for I do assure you, their clothes are thin.'

Cason's pitiful lineup contained hundreds of captives from all over the British Isles ... from Youghal in Ireland, from Hull in England, and from Edinburgh in Scotland. But from Baltimore, there were only two.

With the *Charles* waiting to take away the first contingent, Cason faced the heartbreaking decision of selecting who should go, and who should remain.

His orders had been to select according to class status, but Cason was either unable or unwilling to obey. 'I thought to have taken away the better sort of people first, and the rest afterwards, the which I understood to be the command given to me,' he wrote, 'but it pleases God to order that I must take away those I could have for cloth, and leave the rest 'til afterwards ... I think two good ships and a pinnace will be fit to fetch away the rest of the slaves.'

London responded generously to the request, and an official document recorded later that '264 persons, men, women and children, are redeemed and sent home.'

The report warmly praised Cason for his role in the mission. The treaty had been 'long and difficult', it added, but the money had been well utilised.

Meanwhile, two more ships were preparing to sail for Algiers to bring home the remainder of the English slaves ... all of them, that is, who actually *wanted* to come home.

CHAPTER THIRTY-TWO

Homeward Bound

WHEN Joane Broadbrook and Ellen Hawkins of Baltimore finally walked on board their homebound vessel, they were the sole representatives of the village that had been devastated by the raid of 1631.

We can only guess their feelings as they stood on the deck watching the white triangular shape of Algiers recede into the distance. Joane was no doubt looking forward to being reunited with her husband Stephen – but what had happened to the two children who'd been abducted with her in 1631? What happened to her baby? Were they among the children who, according to Cason, were being raised 'very gallant' in local households? Had they been moved to the east, along with so many others? Had they died? All we know is that they do not appear on Cason's list.

As the children had probably grown up in Algiers, it is possible that they had chosen to stay there. Some other slave histories tell of heartbreaking farewell scenes by the dockside as a parent would sail home and a child would remain behind.

And what about Ellen Hawkins? Was she overwhelmingly delighted to leave Algiers? Or in some small corner of her heart, did she harbour a sneaking doubt about the wisdom of the choice she'd made?

We'll never know. Just as we'll never know the answer to the biggest question of all.

What happened to the other men, women and children – more than a hundred of them – who were seized from their beds by Morat Rais's corsairs on the night of June 20, 1631?

What happened to Bessie Flood and her son? John Ryder and his wife? Mrs Tim Curlew? Anna the maid? Corent Croffine, Mrs Croffine and their daughter Miss Croffine? What happened to the seven Gunter boys or the six members of Stephen Pierse's family? The entire Payne family, the entire Watts family? Mr and Mrs Evans with their cook, boy and maid? Did they all just fade away?

We know the fate of only one of them: 'Mary', the unnamed woman who was ransomed via Leghorn just a few years after the raid.

As for the rest, they appear to have vanished from history as mysteriously as the lost tribes in the deserts.

It is unlikely that they all died in the course of fifteen years. Algiers was, at that particular time, one of the world's healthiest places to live, and the majority of the Baltimore captives were young people – in fact, fifty of them were children and young boys. Most of the adults were young married couples. The average post-infancy life expectancy in the 1600s was around sixty.

Admittedly, some might have died 'of pure want' as d'Aranda put it, and others may have succumbed to the lash. Still others may have been spirited away from Algiers.

But others stayed in the city and tried to make the best of their new lives. We know from Frizell's records that many of the Baltimore captives embraced Islam, presumably with the intention of settling down permanently in Algiers.

There seems a consensus among historians who have studied the 1631 raid that quite a number of the Baltimore captives remained behind voluntarily. John de Courcy Ireland, one of the authorities on the subject, has commented that 'few of [them] showed much enthusiasm about returning'.

Henry Barnby, in his meticulously researched article *The Sack of Baltimore*, talks of 'half a hundred northern women passively and sensibly adapting to a new life in a new environment' in Algiers.

Why did this happen? I would suggest two likely explanations – one psychological and the other purely practical.

I've already referred to the phenomenon known as

Stockholm Syndrome, an unconscious response to the trauma of captivity. Without realising it, the victim begins to identify with the captor. This requires positive feelings between captive and captor. The captive must also develop negative feelings towards the authorities at home.

Certain factors make the syndrome more likely to develop. These include duration of captivity, the degree of dependence upon the captor, the extent of abuse, the amount of communication, and the physical distance between captive and home. If we check off this list, we can see that it is almost tailor-made for the Baltimore captives.

Duration: They were in captivity for fifteen years. One contemporary envoy, Sir Thomas Shirley, warned that the more time Englishmen spent in an Islamic country, the more they were likely to adopt the local manners and customs.

Dependence: Their Algerine masters had total power over them, from food allocation and discipline right down to their basic right to live or die.

Extent of abuse: While there were accounts of savage beatings, it seems that most private slaves in domestic employ were reasonably well treated.

Communication: Domestic slaves were treated like family members and there are numerous accounts of lengthy dialogues and strong relationships between masters and slaves.

Distance between the captor and any assisting authorities: The Baltimore captives were many miles from their homeland and, as we have seen from Frizell's correspondence, there was little positive feedback from home.

This final factor seems likely to have been one of the most powerful driving forces for the syndrome. We don't know whether the Baltimore slaves felt anger towards the authorities who had abandoned them to their fate for fifteen long years, but it would have been no surprise if they had felt betrayed and abandoned. A greedy and corrupt Navy had failed to do its duty to protect them; it had failed to pursue Morat's ship; and the Government's apparent indifference to their plight had prompted William Gunter to go to extraordinary lengths to plead his case. All the signs of abandonment were there. For a decade and a half, they were offered no hope. If some of the captives had given up in angry despair, it would have been perfectly understandable.

The slave James Cathcart voiced this emotion in an uncharacteristic outburst directed towards his countrymen at home: 'No notice whatever [has been] taken of us for years ... Thou art the people that now leave us neglected, buried in oblivion in the dungeons of Algiers, suffering the most ignominious captivity, when [a] paltry sum ... would have redeemed us years ago.'

One common symptom of Stockholm Syndrome is that

the captive appears to adopt a different personality, a 'pseudo-identity' which becomes harder and harder to discard with time.

Is this what happened to some of the Baltimore slaves? Did captives like Bessie Flood, Corent Croffine and Stephen Pierce adapt to the stress of their new lives by forging new personalities sympathetic to Islam and Algiers – personalities they were incapable of discarding when Cason's ship sailed in to their rescue?

No-one knows, but it is a fact that some long-term hostages will refuse to allow themselves to be rescued and, in extreme cases, will actually join their captors in resisting any attempts to free them.

The English slave Joseph Pitts confessed that he suffered an agonising internal conflict when he had the chance of freedom. He described this battle between his two personalities in Biblical terms: 'The devil was very busy with me, tempting me to lay aside all thoughts of escape and to return to Algiers ... I was very melancholy.'

Bearing this in mind, it does not seem beyond possibility that some of the Baltimore people simply turned away from the prospect of rescue. There was no need to make a conscious decision: all that was needed was to do nothing.

There were also many sound, practical reasons why the Baltimore captives might not have wanted to go home.

The most obvious reason is that they had entered into

new relationships and perhaps had children with local partners. In such circumstances, it would have been extremely difficult to return home.

There are parallels to illustrate this. The historian Peter Earle refers to a 1604 case of two young women who were enslaved in separate incidents. One was held by Islamic corsairs in Barbary, the other by Christian slavers in Malta. Their fathers organised a direct exchange, but one of the women refused to participate. She had married and settled in her new home and did not want to return.

But perhaps the best parallel is the eighteenth-century case of Mary Jemison, the Northern Ireland emigrant girl who was abducted in Pennsylvania at the age of fifteen. Adopted by the peaceful Seneca tribe, Mary was so impressed by their culture and lifestyle that she decided to stay with them even when offered the prospect of freedom.

'I was ever considered and treated by them as a real sister, the same as though I had been born of their mother,' she wrote later. '... I had no particular hardships to endure.'

Mary married twice, had a total of nine children and became a prosperous landowner. But the main reason she refused to return was that 'I had got a large family of Indian children that I must take with me; and that, if I should be so fortunate as to find my relatives, *they would despise them, if not myself, and treat us as enemies, or, at least, with a degree of cold indifference, which I thought I could not endure.'* [My italics].

Wise Mary Jamison had put a perceptive finger right on the centre of the problem. She could never return to the world she had left behind, because it had changed, and she had changed. If she went back, she would be treated with hostility and suspicion or, at the very least, pitied and patronised. Perhaps the worst treatment of all would be 'cold indifference', the silent shunning of anyone who had escaped, however unwillingly, to a different culture. She would always be an outsider.

The same thoughts must have crossed the minds of the Baltimore women who had been torn away from their husbands in 1631. For captives like Mrs Alex Pumery these unbearable anxieties must have mingled with the guilt that is part of a hostage's burden. How could they return and face their husbands, their sweethearts, their parents, after fifteen years of sleeping with the enemy – sometimes figuratively, but often literally?

How could a woman like Bessie Flood explain, in the cold light of a Puritan church, how she had felt sincerely drawn towards the teachings of Islam, or how she had taken to wearing Turkish dress so happily that she would forever feel naked without her veil?

Some of the cultural rifts were beyond healing. How, for instance, could the pious neighbours back home be expected to understand that a woman remained respectable and marriageable after spending years as a harem concubine? For most people, this prospect would have been impossible to face.

Even without such complications, life for a returning captive was never easy. In the 1600s, ransomed Barbary captives were referred to as 'poor slaves', forced to exist on handouts, and even expected to wear shackles to re-enact their experiences at fundraising events. Some complained that the chains they wore in liberty were, literally, heavier than the ones they'd borne in captivity.

So we can imagine captives like John Ryder or Bessie Flood glancing at Cason's ship, and then back towards Algiers, in an agony of indecision. The point hardly needs to be made that life in this ancient Mediterranean town was, in many ways, superior to life in rainy, wind-blasted Baltimore. How many men, now accustomed to solid and comfortable homes in Algiers, recalled their draughty damp-ridden shacks in The Cove and gave an involuntary shiver? How many women, now used to being awakened by the bright African sun chasing the coloured light around their silk-draped bedrooms, felt like returning to a land where the sun was a mere ghost in a leaden grey sky?

For those women who had laboured in the fish factory or led lives of drudgery as domestic servants, slave life would actually have been an improvement. Here, there was fresh running water; it did not have to be humped from springs in slopping buckets. Here, even the chore of laundry was a reasonably pleasant social activity carried out in a roof garden where clothes would dry rapidly in the warm sun.

There may also have been some dramatic reversals of fortune since 1631. Mrs Harris's domestic maid might have married a well-to-do merchant and become much wealthier than her former mistress. The former fisherman Tom Paine might have become a wealthy captain in his own right; Bessie Flood might have built up a lucrative business selling tobacco. Who knows? Anything was possible in this fluid city where the last could rapidly become first. Whatever way the dice had rolled, few of these people would have wanted to return to a bleak life of shovelling salt or scraping fish-scales.

And so they watched Edmund Cason's rescue ship retreat into the blue distance, knowing that they had permanently severed the umbilical cord to their former lives and their former identities. There would be no second chance, no going back on their choice.

Then, no doubt, they returned to their homes in Algiers, embraced their lovers and kissed their children, and accepted the new destiny they had chosen.

We've discussed many possible reasons for this decision, but they can all be summed up in the words of Lady Mary Wortley Montague, an Englishwoman who visited the Turkish Empire about seventy years later. She confessed – heretically for the age – that she felt drawn towards the Islamic culture and enjoyed the unhurried lifestyle of Constantinople in which leisure time was agreeably passed 'in music, gardens, wine and delicate eating'.

'I am almost of the opinion,' she concluded wistfully, 'that they have a right notion of life.'

Perhaps the Baltimore captives simply agreed.

CHAPTER THIRTY-THREE

The Legacy Of Baltimore

OF COURSE, the men, women and children of Baltimore did not disappear. Their legacy remains among the children of Algiers, among whom there must be some of the descendants of the 107 captives who were torn from their beds on the night of June 20, 1631. It is comforting to think that, in some newly-married Algerian bride of today, there are traces of the genes of Mrs Tim Curlew or some other bride from Roaring Water Bay; and that when some proud Islamic father holds his newborn baby up against the same stars that witnessed the Sack of Baltimore, his child's veins are coursing with the blood of northern fathers like John Ryder whose children were ripped away from them in the Badistan slave market.

There's a facetious story to illustrate this. The eminent historian John de Courcy Ireland, an authority on the Baltimore raid, was strolling through Algiers with a group of local academics when they noticed a child with striking red hair.

'That's because your ancestors came to Algiers,' one of them joked.

'No,' countered the Irish historian. 'That's because *your* ancestors came to Baltimore.'

The Baltimore captives weren't the only ones who left a blood legacy. Their captor, the rapacious arch-pirate Morat Rais, may also have left a remarkable genetic inheritance.

First a brief word about the fate of Morat himself. The former Jan Jansen appears to have continued to prosper in his predatory trade, moving back and forth between Sallee and Algiers. In the autumn of 1631, only a hundred days after the raid, he crops up again in the correspondence of the English envoy John Harrison. With almost incredible brass neck, Morat complains to London that two English pirates, Maddick and Wye, had taken a ship of Sallee and sold its crew as slaves. Morat the master slave-trader refers to Sallee's peace treaty with London and fumes that the English behaved 'treacherously'. This was coming from the man who had personally conducted the greatest ever slave raid on English territory, only a few weeks beforehand. Yet the tone of Harrison's letter is conciliatory and it is possible he did not realise that his friend 'Captain John' was one and the same person as the 'Matthew Rice' who the English blamed for the raid on Baltimore.

Four years later, in 1635, Morat crops up again in less self-righteous mood – his time in the memoirs of the priest Father Pierre Dan. Morat appears to have moved temporarily back to Algiers with his North African wife, and, although he must have been in his mid-sixties, he seems to have embarked on yet another corsair mission.

While his wife was awaiting his return, she received devastating news. Father Dan actually witnessed the drama:

'I saw more than a hundred women hurrying helter-skelter through the streets to commiserate with the wife of that renegado and corsair [Morat] ... they tried to outdo each other in demonstrations of sorrow and woe, shedding tears that were either real or forced, since that is their custom.'

The pirate mastermind had been captured by his most dreaded enemies – the Christian corsairs of Malta.

Yet the wily Morat managed to extract himself from this situation – presumably by paying an enormous ransom – and by 1638 the records show Morat back in Morocco and enjoying the high life. He had set up home at a castle in El-Oualidiya, a pleasant seaside resort thirty miles north of Sallee. Typically for Morat, he had managed to persuade someone else to pay for his retirement home:

'This haven, he during his residence there took special notice of,' said one English dispatch, 'and, understanding it a place probably advantageous to the

[Moroccan] King, persuaded him to fortify it.'

We have a snapshot of him in his new home a couple of years later, in 1640. A new Dutch consul arrived, bringing with him Morat's adult daughter Lysbeth, one of the children he'd left behind in Haarlem.

Their reunion at Morat's castle left everyone moved with emotion. When Lysbeth arrived, Morat 'was seated in great pomp on a carpet, with silk cushions, the servants all round him.' Both burst into tears and they spent some time engrossed in conversation. Yet Morat remained formally aloof and 'took his leave in the manner of royalty'.

Morat seemed keen for his daughter to settle down in Morocco, for she stayed with him for eight months at his country residence. However, she did not take to life in North Africa and decided to return home. Perhaps, as in many family reunions, the dream seemed much more attractive than the reality.

And so Morat settled back into his comfortable retirement, at times, no doubt, gazing wistfully over the horizon of the vast ocean he had once roamed at will with his corsairs.

We don't know how Morat died. One source maintained that 'his end was very bad', but left no further details. A bad end was always a possibility in the stormy politics of Morocco. But some modern historians believe it was simply an invention, a conventional moral ending to serve as a warning to others.

What we *do* know is that Morat's two sons were no more content with life in Barbary than their half-sister Lysbeth. Anthony Jansen, born in 1607, and his brother Abraham Jansen both emigrated to America. In the Dutch colony of New Amsterdam (later New York City) their surname was so common that they adopted the suffix Van Salee ('from Sallee') and under this name they founded several important family dynasties. According to a *Frontline* TV documentary aired by the Public Service Broadcasting Network in the USA, Anthony and Abraham became 'the ancestors of the Vanderbilts, the Whitneys, Jacqueline Kennedy Onassis and Humphrey Bogart'.

Little is known of Anthony's and Abraham's mother except that she was a concubine of Morat's. Tradition says she was Moroccan. Against this, it has been pointed out that Anthony Jansen was born more than a decade before Morat settled in Morocco; however, this evidence in itself does not prove or disprove anything. It seems that the two sons were dark skinned, since they were classed in contemporary documents as 'mulatto farbig' (swarthy mixed race) or by the catch-all term 'Turk'.

The documentary named actor Humphrey Bogart and the music icon John Hammond as Van Salee descendants. Hammond, whose mother was a Vanderbilt, is famous as the producer who first recognised the talents of Billie Holiday and Bob Dylan;

perhaps he had inherited Morat's nose for commercial success. As for Bogart, it seems fitting that he was always most at home in the movie role of a sea captain operating on the fringes of the law.

Anthony and Abraham were interesting characters in their own right.

According to the PBS documentary, Abraham had a love child with an unknown black woman and one of their descendants – John Van Salee De Grasse, born in 1825 – became the first black man in the USA to be formally educated as a medical doctor.

Anthony Jansen Van Salee warrants a special place in New York history as the first man to settle in Brooklyn; it is also probable that the original name of Coney Island ('Turk's Island') referred to him.

When the Van Salees arrived in Manhattan Island in 1630 – a mere four years after Peter Minuit famously bought the island for trinkets worth $24 – they found a semi-deserted rural settlement with no hint of its future pivotal role. Anthony was able to obtain large tracts of land in the lower island. He had a fine anchorage where, it was said, questionable ships would come and go in the dead of night. Since Anthony seemed to have no shortage of money, there is an intriguing theory that he was actually acting as a front man for his father Morat, who was gradually shifting the family fortune to the New World.

Whatever the reason, Anthony became financially

secure. Socially, he had more of a problem fitting in to the strait-laced New Amsterdam society with his free-spirited Dutch wife Grietje, a former barmaid whom he'd married during the voyage out. Anthony was only twenty-three, but Grietje, at twenty-eight, was already a widow and a source of some scandal in the Netherlands.

Anthony seems to have been an irascible individual who would quarrel and fire off a lawsuit at the drop of a hat. Grietje erred in the opposite extreme, becoming so intimate with the island's menfolk that she has been described by one historian as 'Manhattan's first and most famous prostitute'. In 1639 they were denounced as slanderous and troublesome and asked to leave.

They established a 200-acre farm called 'Turk's Plantation' on western Long Island and became the first settlers in present-day Brooklyn. Their increasing prosperity mirrored that of the colony, which was renamed New York with English rule in 1674. Anthony and Grietje had four daughters and two sons: they made good marriages and launched several New York family dynasties whose lines continue today. Grietje died at the age of sixty-seven. Anthony remarried in his early sixties and died in 1676. Intriguingly, his legacy included a beautiful copy of the Koran, an indication to some that he had secretly maintained his Islamic faith. The volume survives to this day.

So much for Morat's line in New York. But what about

the main town in our story – Baltimore?

The raid had delivered a crushing blow to the once-prosperous port. It seems that most of the survivors, dreading another invasion, moved further inland to establish a new colony at Skibbereen.

Thus began Baltimore's long process of decline. In 1745, exactly one hundred years after Cason's first expedition, historian Charles Smith wrote: 'Baltimore never recovered itself … it is now a poor, decayed fishing town, with not one tolerable house in it.'

Another report in the 1700s described it as a 'poor shrunken village'. One visitor sniffed that it was a miserable collection of huts which had no basis to claim urban status.

By 1800, not a single resident had means to pay local taxes and Baltimore was declared a rotten borough, unable to justify its own MPs in Parliament.

By 1837 there was a temporary recovery. The town had a thriving port and its 460 inhabitants had invested in a new schoolhouse. One report said it was 'increasing rapidly in size and importance.'

Then came the Great Hunger. As the bodies piled up in mass graves, the famine ships *Melvina* and *Leviathan* regularly left Baltimore for New Brunswick with thousands of refugees.

In the 1860s a German newsman, Paul Julius Reuter, scooped his rivals in Europe by tossing news despatches into the sea in sealed canisters as transatlantic ships passed Fastnet. Retrieved by fishermen, the despatches were rowed to Baltimore and telegraphed to London. Using this means, Reuter was twenty-four hours ahead with the news of Lincoln's assassination – and for one brief, glorious moment, Baltimore became the nerve centre of news for the entire western world.

By 1876, it was back in the doldrums. 'Baltimore never recovered from the shock of the Algerine invasion,' wrote Dr Dan Donovan. 'Its energies became paralysed, its wealth and prosperity vanished.'

Another nineteenth-century historian, J. E. O'Mahony, agreed. 'Agony upon agony, sorrow upon sorrow ensued,' he wrote dolefully.

Fishing and small-scale shipbuilding helped Baltimore to survive until the tourist boom of the modern era, when a new breed of 'invader' began to arrive, sailing luxury yachts instead of warships, and carrying gold credit cards instead of pirate bullion. Sadly, their insatiable demand for property in beautiful Roaring Water Bay has forced the indigenous young people out of Baltimore even more effectively than Morat managed to do in 1631.

The Algerine slave trade left another type of legacy: the opening of Northern Europe to Islamic influences. Returning captives like Ellen Hawkins, Joane Broadbrook and thousands of others must have brought back tales of an equal-opportunity society in which wealth and status was determined by ability rather than by accident of birth. These were dangerous ideas. For instance, Islamist ideals of equality may have indirectly influenced the creators of the American Declaration of Independence.

Eastern learning shook western science to its foundations. European scholars pored through Islamic writings, gaining new insights into chemistry, mathematics, astronomy and medicine. Again, this was dangerous knowledge. The English academic Dr Henry Stubbe (1632-1676), who openly admitted his debt to Islamic teachings, had his work suppressed and was jailed for heresy.

Another academic who studied the experimental work of Islamic scientists went on to create the West's first objective, verifiable 'scientific method' and became a major influence on the great astronomer Sir Isaac Newton. He was Robert Boyle, the famous chemist ... and the son of Richard Boyle, the Great Earl Of Cork.

For me, the most intriguing twist in our tale began back in the 1630s. It has been suggested that the raid was the main factor that provoked King Charles I to revive the ancient Ship Money tax in 1634. This tax, designed to equip warships, was normally imposed on coastal towns, but Charles extended it to inland communities. Levied in Parliament's absence, this 'taxation without representation' provoked a legal challenge by John

Hampden (Oliver Cromwell's cousin) and became a test case to decide the extent of the King's power. Hampden lost by a narrow margin – and left a deeply divided nation headed on an almost inevitable course towards civil war.

Historian W. J. Kingston was convinced that this was one of the 'important results' of the Baltimore raid: 'Charles I, fearing such raids might be repeated … proceeded to levy Ship Money to equip his Navy, which produced such opposition that it eventually led to the Civil War in England, the beheading of Charles himself, and the raising of Cromwell to power as Protector of the English Commonwealth.'

We could take this further. The establishment of a democracy, however briefly, in England showed that it was possible to do the same thing elsewhere, in America and in France. When he signed the first writ for Ship Money, Charles I effectively signed his own death warrant – and from that turbulent era onward, no autocrat in Europe would be able to sleep comfortably in his bed.

It would be wrong to overemphasise the role of the Baltimore incident in the great march towards freedom. No doubt this process would have happened anyway.

And yet …

And yet, I like to think that there is a sense in which the flames that leapt high over the thatched roofs of Baltimore on the night of 20 June 1631 sent out a bright spark that helped to light the flaming torch of democracy.

CHAPTER THIRTY-FOUR

The Three Knights

The fact that they [the corsairs] were given local assistance and that the captives were all English settlers suggests that there was far more involved than a chance slave raid.

— Dr Liam Irwin, Politics, Religion And Economy: Cork In The 17th Century

THERE'S always been a suspicion that what happened on June 20, 1631 was a set-up job: a pirate raid engineered to remove the English settlers from Baltimore. Although the phrase did not exist in the 1600s, we would now describe it as the 'ethnic cleansing' of an entire town.

The conspiracy theory has never been proven, and yet it has been astonishingly persistent. To this day, visitors seeking information about Baltimore are given tantalising hints. For example, this is from the tourist website baltimore-ireland.com:

'The allegation is sometimes made that the raid may have been orchestrated by the O'Driscolls, who did not care to see their lands being taken over by English settlers – you'd never know.'

Or from another tourist website:

'As the pirates had a pilot from Dungarvan to guide them, and those kidnapped were English settlers, theories abound as to how and why the Sack Of Baltimore was organised.'

Even the Automobile Association's guidebook refers to the theory:

'Some believe the raid may have been orchestrated by the fierce O'Driscolls, to frighten off English settlers. If so, it worked: many of them moved upstream where they felt less threatened.'

None of this proves anything – except that the conspiracy theories passed down through the generations are still very much alive.

There is no doubt that in the decades leading up to the raid, there was a bitter, no-holds-barred battle for control of Baltimore – a battle that ended only when the corsairs arrived. It was a major power struggle involving a Gaelic chieftain, an English planter and an unscrupulous financier. None of these players was a model of virtue, and the tensions between them erupted into a dirty war of attrition. It was a major *cause célèbre* at the time: even the King became involved.

Initially, I was sceptical about the set-up theory. To my mind, the historical record was fascinating enough: why add fanciful conspiracies?

Besides, how could anyone in Ireland have possibly *arranged* with pirates from North Africa to sail north and settle a problem?

But as I delved deeper into my researches, I realised that communication with the Barbary corsairs was not a problem. They had been frequenting Baltimore for so long that they had many contacts and relatives there.

Nor was it unusual for people in the early 1600s to 'arrange' corsair raids against their enemies.

For example, in the early 1600s, a man named Andrew Gray was sentenced to death in Edinburgh for riot and arson. Gray escaped to Morocco, where he nursed his burning grudge for twenty years before leading the Sallee corsairs on a revenge raid on the Scots capital. Lying offshore, he threatened to level Leith port unless he received a huge payoff.

The Italian historian Salvatore Bono has described several cases in which corsair attacks were engineered to settle vendettas among Christians in Mediterranean countries. These could also be viewed, from a modern standpoint, as a common man's protest against a feudal society.

Just seven years after the Baltimore raid, sixteen galleys of corsairs swooped on Nicotera in Calabria, Italy. The raid had been organised and led by a local man after a nobleman seduced his daughter.

And in the 1640s, another disgruntled local organised a revenge corsair raid in Catanzaro.

But the closest parallel to Baltimore occurred in the Sardinian island of San Pietro in 1798, when Barbary corsairs carried off nine hundred people – mostly women and children. It turned out that the attack was organised by a local man with a grudge.

So it seems the idea of a deliberately engineered corsair raid on Baltimore is not so far-fetched after all.

If we accept that all this is feasible, it is just a matter of examining all the evidence with an open mind.

However, the political backdrop of Baltimore makes this difficult. The subject of English involvement in Ireland is still emotive, and there is often a temptation to choose your good guys and bad guys in advance.

But history has shown that there were monsters and heroes on both sides, and if we are to understand the fascinating story behind the Baltimore raid we need to look beyond the clichés.

Writers who have tackled this subject agree on very little, but they concur on one point: none of the players in this saga was a candidate for sainthood.

In this chapter, I'm going to look in turn at the three men – all knights – who were involved in the titanic struggle for control of Baltimore. I want to abandon the chronological sequence of events in order to create a portrait of each of them and to describe their ambitions, their failings and their motivations.

THE FIRST KNIGHT: SIR FINEEN O'DRISCOLL, GAELIC CHIEFTAIN

The poet Edmund Spenser once described the investiture of a typical Irish chieftain in Elizabethan times. The new leader would step on a sacred stone and receive the symbol of his office – in the O'Driscolls' case, a white rod. Then, 'descending from the stone, he turns himself round, thrice forward and thrice backward.'

As Fineen did so, he must have felt the dizzying sensation of a world that was shifting beneath his feet. Foreign customs and manners were being imposed on his people. English fortune hunters were casting covetous eyes on his castle and lands. The golden age of the Gael was fading into twilight.

In fact, the O'Driscolls' power had been on the wane for centuries. Rival Irish clans had forced them out of their extensive ancestral territory into a much smaller coastal area. But they had suffered most at the hands of the merchants of Waterford, whose ships they had harassed and attacked for centuries.

This grudge dated all the way back to 1368, when the Cork clan had helped to attack Waterford town. In 1413, a Waterford mayor named Simon Wickens paid a 'friendly' visit to Baltimore on Christmas Day with a consignment of fine wine. Invited to feast in the O'Driscolls' Great Hall, Wickens downed a cup of wine and danced to a Christmas carol … before arresting the O'Driscolls and marching them down to his ship in chains.

One stormy February in 1537, a Portuguese ship was carrying wine towards Waterford when fierce winds forced it towards Baltimore. The O'Driscolls offered assistance and helped the ship into harbour. Then, treacherously, they imprisoned the crew and seized the cargo for themselves.

The O'Driscolls hadn't even finished unloading the wine when the Waterford men hit back with a lightning raid. Two dozen hand-picked men under Captain Pierce Doblyn sneaked into Baltimore in a light, fast sailing craft named *Sunday*. As the O'Driscolls fled in panic, the commando raiders took back their stolen ship.

Determined to wipe out the O'Driscoll menace forever, the Waterford merchants then sent a full-scale punitive expedition to Baltimore. Three warships carrying four hundred men blasted a relentless barrage of artillery at the O'Driscoll castles. They dismantled the castle of Dún na Long stone by stone and, finally, 'they burned and destroyed Baltimore'.

By the time Fineen assumed power over a rebuilt Baltimore three decades later, the stability of the clan was under threat both from without and within.

Fineen's second cousin, Conor Mac Fineen O'Driscoll, had also sought to be chieftain. The leader of a branch of the clan known as the Carragh O'Driscolls, he claimed superiority in lineage. The clan elders had negotiated a compromise in which Fineen would become chieftain, but Conor Mac Fineen would get half the rents and harbour dues. Neither man was happy with the arrangement.

Meanwhile, opportunities for piracy had dried up as the English asserted their power. Most of the clan's legitimate income came from the fishing industry. Every fishing boat had to pay the chieftain almost £1, plus levies of flour, salt, beer and a dish of fish.

Now even that source was under threat. As early as 1569, a group of English entrepreneurs had asked the Queen to grant them the town of Baltimore and its lucrative fishing rights.

Fineen moved swiftly to forestall this. He asked Sir John Perrot, President of Munster, to allow him to surrender O'Driscoll territory to the Queen, who would then formally re-grant it to him personally.

Perrot, who was probably a love child of Henry VIII, regarded this as an important test case that would help eradicate the ancient Gaelic chieftainship system known as *tanistry*. As he wrote in October 1573:

'Touching Fineen O'Driscoll's suit, it is reasonable ... to drown the custom of the *tanistry*.'

Yet the matter lapsed, and Fineen became almost tetchy in his next petition. '[I have] been a suitor for a long time,' he wrote to the Queen, 'which delay of answer and detracting of time is a great hindrance and not without sore losses to [me], considering [my] dutiful and obedient service ... '

This was a pointed reference to his neutral stance during a recent rebellion.

In 1576, Fineen formally pledged allegiance to the Crown. Three years later, when a second rebellion swept Munster, Fineen was positively enthusiastic in his loyalty. He shopped Spanish spies, supplied intelligence on the activities of Irish plotters overseas, and helped defeat the rebels by allowing Perrot to use his harbour as his main western base. The English governors praised his 'loyalty in this dangerous time'.

In 1582, Fineen sailed to London carrying a suit 'to surrender all his possessions' and was knighted by the Queen.

Three years later he was 'invited' with other Gaelic chieftains to attend the Dublin Parliament, where – forced into uncomfortably tight English clothing – he formally 'took his lands in letter patent from Queen Elizabeth ... thereby extinguishing the Irish rite ...'

Under Gaelic law, he had no right to do this, and some of his kinsmen reacted with fury. Worst affected were the Carragh O'Driscolls.

Throughout the 1580s, even as the Spanish Armada threatened to invade England, Fineen remained steadfast. A military surveyor, Geoffrey Fenton, reported that Fineen had pledged to give the English the strategic fort of Dún na Long if they needed it.

By 1592, the former piratical rover had become respectable as Cork High Sheriff and was one of the most prominent men in the English administration. Even when Fineen was persuaded by his son to hand his castles over to the Spanish invaders, still the English treated him remarkably sympathetically when the rebellion was crushed.

General Sir George Carew wrote that Fineen was 'an ancient civil gentleman that, until this hour, hath evermore held firm to the state and is now grown wild ... the poor old man was overruled by his son and hath no disposition to be a traitor'.

It was a tribute to Fineen's charm and ingenuity that he managed to escape from this situation with his head still affixed to his neck. Forced to surrender his castles to the English troops, he cheekily assumed the role of the generous host, feasting the battle-weary men and holding banquets for their officers. It's said that he even filled the town well with wine and coins, causing it to be nicknamed 'the silver well'.

The tactic worked. The English launched savage reprisals in the area, but his clan was given 'all kind and mild usage'. It was pointed out that Fineen had 'never in the course of his whole life been tainted by the least spot of disloyalty' and had been 'very odious to the rebels'.

Queen Elizabeth pardoned his temporary lapse and summoned him to visit her in London. However, she died before he could receive the formal pardon.

The cost of the trip to London and the expense of restoring his reputation had left Fineen almost penniless.

For the first time, he became vulnerable to fortune hunters.

According to one historian, it was during his absence in England that one of his trusted servants began to 'intrude' into his affairs.

This servant was a native Irishman and a staunch Catholic, but he was as cruel and acquisitive as the worst of the English Protestant invaders.

His name was Walter Coppinger.

THE SECOND KNIGHT: SIR WALTER COPPINGER, IRISH MONEYLENDER

Two and a half centuries after his death, the name of Walter Coppinger was still being spoken with a shudder in Baltimore. His notoriety lived on in oral histories recorded as late as the 1800s:

'No Russian nobleman of former times lorded it over his serfs with such despotic sway as Coppinger,' historian Dr Daniel Donovan wrote in 1876.

'It is related how he had a yard-arm extended from one of the gable ends of his mansion ... a gallows wherewith to hang the victims of his unlicensed power.'

The stories claimed Coppinger's enemies were thrown into a dark dungeon to 'pine for years in wretchedness and chains'.

While Donovan admitted that these tales may have been exaggerated, they probably contained some grain of truth. And we can find other, well-documented evidence of the unsavoury character of this prominent lawyer and moneylender.

Take, for instance, the case of Jeanette Grant, Coppinger's niece, who claimed in 1630 that he had cheated her out of her inheritance.

When she was only fourteen, Coppinger had given her in marriage to a wealthy gentleman named Walter Grant – aged almost eighty.

This grotesque marriage between teenager and octogenarian did not last long, but after Grant died, she trusted Coppinger to manage her estate.

Years later, when she found herself penniless, Jeanette discovered she had been robbed by her own uncle. Coppinger had simply altered the legal documents to replace Grant's surname with his own.

Realising she could never get justice in Coppinger's home county – he was notorious for nobbling juries – the resourceful widow took her case to Dublin. The furious Coppinger reacted by smashing his great fist in her mouth and knocking her teeth out.

When he returned to Cork, he trumped up some charge against Jeanette. She was thrown into prison for four years … the price of crossing Walter Coppinger.

On her release, Jeanette pleaded for justice. She accused Coppinger of 'corrupt practices' and fraud.

In a separate case, a young Cork woman named Ellen ní Driscoll came into a substantial inheritance and sought legal advice from Coppinger. Instead, he tampered with the deeds to put her estate in his own name.

Ellen complained: '[I] cannot get justice from him on account of his power with jurors, and [I am] afraid of [my] life if I should sue.'

At one stage Ellen, then heavily pregnant, begged the Coppinger family for some money to tide her over.

The man she approached may have been Walter himself, or his brother Richard (the wording is ambiguous). His response was horrific:

'[He] did batter [Ellen] in a most cruel manner, and threw her over the cliff into the sea.'

By some miracle Ellen survived, but she lost her baby.

These cases sum up Walter Coppinger: his greed, his corruption, his violent rages, and his utter ruthlessness.

When Coppinger wanted something, he would let nothing stand in his way.

And in 1631, what Coppinger wanted more than anything else was Baltimore.

Coppinger was a complex and fascinating character. His family – of Viking stock – was neither planter nor Gael, but had carved out a formidable niche in local politics. There had been no fewer than eight Coppinger mayors of Cork city.

Walter began his career as a valet. Tradition says he was a page-boy to Walter Raleigh. If so, he would have had an early taste of the high life: Raleigh's court was so opulent that even his servants wore chains of gold.

Later he became page to Fineen O'Driscoll, and secured an entrée to the aristocracy when his brother Richard Coppinger married O'Driscoll's daughter. It was the only opening he needed. Before long, the servant would become the master of the lord.

Over the next ten years, Coppinger made a fortune from moneylending. His technique was simple. He would offer loans to Gaelic gentry who'd been left destitute by the great rebellion. Many had no intention of paying him back. These men thought they were taking out loans secured against their property, which was worth far more. But they were mistaken. As they found out when Coppinger brandished one of his notoriously complex and impenetrable legal agreements, they had actually *sold* their entire property to Coppinger in a deal that would be cancelled only if the money was repaid on time.

By the early 1600s, Coppinger had already gained his first stately home in this way: Cloughane Castle, ancestral home of the McCarthys.

Meanwhile, Coppinger – a staunch Catholic – was clashing with the authorities over his refusal to attend Protestant church services. Hauled before the courts, he responded proudly and defiantly.

—My forefathers practised the Catholic religion, he said. And my conscience ties me to do the same.

—What is your conscience? his interrogators asked.

The record showed he did not reply.

Coppinger was ordered to pay a savage fine of £100.

This case in 1605 may have proved a watershed for Coppinger. During the O'Neill rising he had actually assisted the English forces. Like most Catholics, he had expected greater tolerance from King James. Instead, he found himself stalked and persecuted like a criminal for his religious faith. He had every reason to feel bitter and resentful towards the English.

A few years later, Coppinger felt confident enough to tackle one of the most powerful organisations of the era – the mighty East India Company.

In the early 1600s, the company bought Dundaniel Woods in Cork for £7000 and set up a major shipbuilding operation there. Three new townships – named Thomas, Hope and Bantam – were built to house three hundred specialist workers. They created a dam on the Bandon River, built a dockyard and laid down the keels on the first two ships – substantial merchantmen of 400 and 500 tons.

As carpenters hewed the oaks and elms and smoke rose from the ironworks forges, Coppinger appeared on the scene with a legal deed that claimed the woods were his.

He began with his usual tactic: the long, wearisome law dispute. The Company complained that he was 'continually indicting the workmen through corrupt oaths' and 'intending to weary out the [Company] and force the English from the works.'

Although the shipbuilders had leased a nearby castle,

Coppinger persuaded the owner to evict them.

'[This] would render the English plantation incapable of defending themselves,' the Company complained.

One morning, the shipbuilders arrived at the yard to find that Coppinger's men had destroyed the vital river dam. It had been smashed to pieces in the night.

Was Coppinger an eco-warrior, fighting to preserve the woodlands? The answer is a definite no. Later, he himself attempted to devastate the beautiful Rowry river valley and turn it into a similar industrial zone for his own profit. It is more likely that he simply wanted to drive out the English and take over their lucrative operation.

If so, he failed spectacularly. The two great ships were completed by 1613. Coppinger had probably conceded that he'd met his match: these were tough shipbuilders, not so easily intimidated as pregnant women and widows.

By 1610, Coppinger had matured into an accomplished political activist. They were traits that he was to pass on to a dynasty of Coppinger insurgents: his son, grandson and great-grandson were all to be outlawed for high treason.

Coppinger had learned that you didn't need to fight the English openly on the field of battle.

By the time he set his sights on Baltimore, he knew that there were other ways to get rid of their troublesome settlers.

Like the dam at the shipyard, they could simply be made to vanish quietly in the night.

THE THIRD KNIGHT:
SIR THOMAS CROOKE, ENGLISH PLANTER

'Mr Crooke … hath, at his own charges, within two years, gathered out of England a whole town of English people, larger and more religiously organised than any town in this Province.'

This resounding testimony, signed by a bishop, two knights and a military officer, sums up what Thomas Crooke achieved (for good or for ill) in Baltimore within a mere twenty-four months up to 1608.

As we've seen, Crooke was a prominent London lawyer, and a member of a family of intellectuals and religious freethinkers whose Calvinist views had put them on a collision course with the authorities.

When Crooke came to Baltimore with his fellow settler leaders – John Winthropp, Thomas Notte and James Salmon – his motive was not only to establish a fishing colony, but also to achieve freedom of religion.

However, some say there was a third motive: to facilitate pirates and fence their stolen property.

The accusation was made at the time. Crooke hotly denied it and he was ultimately cleared by the highest authorities in the land.

Many influential people testified to his integrity, including Lord Deputy Sir Arthur Chichester, and the Bishop of Cork. In his own defence, Crooke pointed out that he had raised Baltimore's customs duties from zero to £200 a year – hardly the work of a successful contrabander.

On the other hand, there is strong evidence that he enjoyed an unhealthily close relationship with English and Dutch pirates. In his book *A Nation Of Pirates*, historian Clive Senior quotes contemporary Admiralty sources as saying that Crooke and Salmon bought cloth from pirate ships, supplied them with food, and entertained them at home. In order to provide the pirates with fresh beef, the local butcher was said to have slaughtered two hundred cows in Crooke's backyard.

Other sources tell similar stories. The State Papers tell how, in 1608, pirates landed near Baltimore and burned a dwelling house:

'Hereupon Crooke and other Englishmen went soon after aboard the pirate [ship] to demand restitution. For conferring therefore with these pirates (now traitors) Crooke and the rest were accused of treason.'

In a controversy over the release of a notorious pirate named Captain Coward, the Privy Council stated that Thomas Crooke:

'... has been the chief maintainer and abettor of Coward and other notorious pirates.'

Summoned to England to answer a charge of treason, Crooke enlisted some heavy-hitting character witnesses.

'[T]his is the first time [I] heard of any such charge against him,' Lord Deputy Chichester told London.

The Bishop of Cork claimed Crooke's many enemies had instigated the accusations. He testified to Crooke's achievement at Baltimore and added: 'This has made him violently opposed and accused by divers persons who would weaken him in his good work ...'

He said he trusted that the accusations against Crooke had 'no grounds but the malice of his adversaries'.

Far from collaborating with outlaws, Crooke had been 'continually employed against pirates' and was actually hated by the corsairs.

The Bishop pleaded: '[H]asten his return, lest his absence be the ruin of his good work...which is the thing his adversaries aim at.'

With that, the atmosphere in London began to thaw. In September the Lords issued a thunderous warning to anyone who collaborated with 'the notorious pirates that lately visited Baltimore'. But they said Crooke 'appears guiltless' and would be released to continue his work.

It was an agonising seven weeks before Crooke was finally acquitted. 'Report the return of Thomas Crooke of Baltimore,' wrote the Privy Council, 'who is declared free of all imputations. Desire that he may be aided.'

While this may seem like a clear and unambiguous acquittal, some modern writers have seen it as exactly the opposite. They believe Crooke was guilty and that his crimes were overlooked because his work at Baltimore was vital to the national interest.

Yet it's hard to believe that his high-profile supporters

would have been so enthusiastic about testifying in his favour if they had really believed him guilty. Munster President Lord Danvers, for instance – he had been personally humiliated by the pirates, whom he described bitterly as 'caterpillars' and 'weeds'. Would he really have supported a man who worked hand in glove with his greatest enemies?

And the authorities in London, whose letters constantly spit with fury over the activities of the pirates – were they really likely to turn a blind eye to such blatant treachery? After all, the Baltimore plantation was important, but Crooke *personally* was not indispensable.

We may never learn the full story, but from a strictly legal point of view, Crooke's name had been cleared. He was now free to concentrate on his greatest challenge: the battle for control of Baltimore.

CHAPTER THIRTY-FIVE

Endgame: The Battle For Control Of Baltimore

The manor, castle, town, lands, tenements and
heraditaments of Dún na Sead in Carbery ... with all
and singular the houses, buildings, harbours, creeks,
stones, wrecks of the sea, fishings, woods, underwoods,
fiscarries, mountains, orchards, meadows, advowsons,
mills, seats of Millnes, curtelages, toffs, perquisites ...
—an unexpectedly poetic extract from the crucial
deed deciding Baltimore's future

THE Three Knights – Fineen O'Driscoll, Walter
Coppinger and Thomas Crooke – are the players.
Baltimore is the prize.

THOMAS CROOKE LEASES BALTIMORE

The battle began as early as August 1600, when Sir Fineen signed some obscure deed leasing his lands to Thomas Crooke. But the crisis of war intervened. When Fineen gave his castles to the Spanish invaders and later surrendered them to the English, he may have voided this initial agreement.

After the war, Dún na Séad became an English garrison and most of the native Irish moved out of town. The abandonment was so complete that, a few years later, visitors were told that there were 'few Irish' in Baltimore.

When peace returned, the humiliated Fineen was able to remain in his own castle only by paying £500 for 'conditional letting' of the building. These demeaning terms were dictated on behalf of the English Privy Council by a planter named Sir Henry Becher.

In 1605, Crooke moved to clarify his position. He surrendered all his rights in Fineen's lands to the Crown, and had them re-granted to him by King James.

However, he hadn't reckoned on the problem of Sir Fineen's disgruntled relatives, the Carragh O'Driscolls. Their current head, Donagh Carragh, had good reason to complain. Sir Fineen had broken his promise to share the rents with the Carraghs. Donagh's father had taken the dispute to arbitration, and won a complex settlement giving his branch of the family ownership of Baltimore after Sir Fineen's death.

But, unforeseeably, the ageing Sir Fineen had outlived his younger kinsman and the dispute had passed on to a third generation of Carraghs, as represented by Donagh. He took the case before another panel of arbitrators.

The panel decided the estate should be split: Donagh Carragh was to get the main islands and Dún na Long. Sir Fineen was to get all the rest, including Baltimore and Dún na Séad.

This ruling left nobody satisfied, because in the early 1600s we find Sir Fineen and Donagh Carragh each cheerfully entering into agreements as though he owns the lot. Each was being dishonest with the other, and in the end, each destroyed the other.

Significantly, one man sat on both arbitration panels – Sir Walter Coppinger.

THE COPPINGER-CARRAGH PACT

In 1608, Coppinger negotiated a deal with the pretender Donagh Carragh. It was a meeting of two con-men, and it's likely that each believed he was fleecing the other. Donagh Carragh knew his claim under Gaelic law was largely academic, and welcomed a chance to screw some money out of his hopeless situation. Coppinger, on the other hand, wanted Baltimore so badly that he was prepared to play sucker to Donagh Carragh in order to get some sort of legal leverage on the territory.

We can imagine the two men walking along the ramparts of Dún na Long, pointing across the strait to the glittering prize of Baltimore, the 'fort of the jewels'. Donagh Carragh in his traditional saffron mantle, Coppinger in his modern tunic and stovepipe hat – they would have watched the construction of the English-style homes and agreed that this must be stopped. They eventually shook hands on a curious deal:

> Donagh [Carragh] O'Driscoll ... in consideration of £300, grants to Walter Coppinger ... all that manor, castle, town, lands, tenements and heriditaments of Dun na Sead ...

In exchange for £300 (£37,000 today) Donagh Carragh was mortgaging something he claimed but didn't actually own: the castle and town of Baltimore.

Unless that money was repaid – and it never would be – Walter Coppinger could argue that Baltimore belonged to him.

COPPINGER DEMANDS BALTIMORE

Coppinger was on familiar ground now, in the courts. He prepared a formidable case to prove that the true clan chieftain was Donagh Carragh. Any deal Sir Fineen had signed with Crooke was null and void. Now, could the settlers vacate his property?

To back up this rather flimsy case, Coppinger needed every dubious weapon in his legal armoury. According to the settlers, he used '... feigned surmises and corrupt oaths ... forgeries, champerties, maintainers and other like corrupt and unlawful practices ...'

We already know that Coppinger had a habit of forging documents. A surmise is a false charge. A champerty or maintainer occurs when a lawyer stokes up a case in return for a share of the profits. In other words, the settlers knew that Donagh Carragh was a mere puppet. The real force behind this legal action, and the real beneficiary, was Walter Coppinger.

THEY CUT A DEAL

After a complex and fruitless legal inquiry between 1608 and 1609, the three parties decided to reach a compromise. Effectively, it meant that the English settlers would lease Baltimore afresh for twenty-one years, after which the property would revert to Coppinger.

The year 1610 saw a flurry of legal activity. First, Crooke had to relinquish his previous agreements. He 'alienated' [transferred] his local lands back to the O'Driscolls, thereby cancelling out Fineen's original deal of 1600.

Then, on June 20, 1610, the crucial deal was signed. All three interested parties agreed to a twenty-one-year lease to the settlers, as represented by Thomas Bennett:

'Thomas Crooke and Sir Fineen O'Driscoll, Knt. and Walter Coppinger, Esq. by deed indented, dated the 20th June, 1610, demised to Thomas Bennett, his executors and assigns, all that castle, town and harbour of Baltimore ... to hold the same to the said Thomas Bennett, his executors and assigns, from the feast day of St

Philip and Jacob then last past for a term of 21 years ...'

To demise simply means to transfer for a limited period – in this case twenty-one years, after which the property would revert to Coppinger 'for ever', with Sir Fineen's blessing.

The deal, which involved a payment of just over £185 by Coppinger, also gave Crooke possession of Dun na Sead castle.

This was the vital document, and it was merely underlined by two other subsidiary agreements signed in 1611 and 1612 – the first obtaining the consent of Fineen's wife, and the second making provision for the death of Thomas Bennett in the interim.

The deal meant the settlers could go ahead and develop Baltimore, knowing that they could enjoy at least twenty-one years of security. They paid a substantial sum for this privilege. A figure of £2000 (around a quarter-million pounds today) has been mentioned in early histories and seems credible.

Carragh had got his £300. And Coppinger had a solid long term investment – he would eventually get full control of Baltimore.

The only losers seemed to be the O'Driscoll clan, who had just signed away their ancient homeland forever.

Or so it seemed.

Perhaps *they* had other ideas.

THE PLANTERS DIG IN

Secure at last, the settlers set to build their new colony. Stout homes were thrown up, gardens created, hedges planted, fields tilled and sown.

To be an 'improving tenant' was the ideal for the era. The records clearly show that – whatever the dubious ethics of some of their leaders – the ordinary settlers were prepared to work extremely hard at making a better life for themselves.

A contemporary document gives some idea of the task facing a typical family:

'Breaking the rocks and stoning [i.e., removing stones from] the land five times all over to make it arable land, and so divide it into fields of eight, ten, fifteen and twenty acres per field; also in draining the bogs and making gutters underground ... Ditching and hedging the land, besides sanding ...'

These settlers were willing to put in this backbreaking labour because they'd been assured that they would be 'estated', or given their own homes. As historian Charles Smith explained in 1750:

'He [Crooke] divided the town into several tenements, with lots for gardens; and gave to each inhabitant convenient land for building and grazing, estating them in leases for his own time; and to encourage them to build and plant, he procured a patent for the town, to him and his heirs forever, and promised to make over to each of the tenants an estate in fee farm of the proportion he held; but death prevented his undertaking.'

Baltimore went from strength to strength. Sixty new houses were constructed in neat rows. Added together, the amount spent on building work and land enclosures was estimated at between £1,600 and £2,000 (that is, up to a quarter-million today).

In September 1612, Baltimore was made into a self-governing Borough with its own 'Sovereign', Thomas Crooke.

In fact, the outlook seemed bright for the new-look Fort Of The Jewels ... until Walter Coppinger began to cut rough.

COPPINGER'S RIOTS

Despite the twenty-one-year lease he'd signed, Coppinger soon made it clear that he wanted Baltimore right away – and he wanted the new settlers out.

To achieve this aim, he used the same tactics that any modern slum landlord might use against unwanted tenants. He made life difficult for them. He hit them with individual lawsuits and saw to it that there would be sudden outbreaks of violence.

It was a long, violent war of attrition that began in 1608 (coinciding with Coppinger's interest in Baltimore) and lasted for more than two decades. A petition lodged by the settlers in April 1618 shows that the harassment – which at times escalated to full-scale riots – was part of a well-organised protest campaign involving several politically active religious dissidents:

'[D]ivers Irish recusants have combined themselves to oppose the plantation, amongst whom one Walter Coppinger, of Cloghan, gent., was and is the principal,' says the petition. '[T]hey have for these ten years past sought by manifold unlawful means to banish all the English people out of those parts, and by their continual corrupt and violent courses have undone many ...'

Coppinger was brought before the Star Chamber and censured for 'procuring multitudes of indictments of treasons, felonies, riots and other crimes'.

But the harassment had continued and the settlers claimed they would be driven out 'unless their Lordships shall afford them relief in their accustomed justice and wisdom.'

THE KING BROUGHT INTO PLAY

A few years later, Thomas Crooke took his plea directly to King James I: '[I have] worked twenty years in making the town of Baltimore and [have] raised the customs there from nothing to £200,' he wrote to the monarch. '[I have] hired seamen to serve King James against traitors and pirates.

'Sir Walter Coppinger ... and his adherents, being Papists, have for many years endeavoured ... to supplant and expatriate [me]; and to return these places to superstition and barbarism.'

Characteristically, James responded by postponing the issue.

'We desire, seeing our court of Castle Chamber was lately divided on the question, to have it tried before us and our Privy Council in our court of Star Chamber. All cases between petitioner [Crooke] and Sir Walter, and between Sir Walter and his tenants, to be stayed meanwhile.'

In the real world, it seems that the settlers got no joy from either of these petitions. The message from London was unspoken but clear: the settlers were on their own.

THE O'DRISCOLLS IN EXILE

Sir Fineen was now an old man in his seventies and no longer stood 'tall as the mast of his galleys'. His financial situation was so dire that he was forced to borrow nearly £1,700 from Coppinger. Fineen would later vow 'confidently' that this was a mortgage with part of his land as security. Coppinger asserted, equally confidently, that it was a straight sale of this land.

Meanwhile, under the Spanish sun, the exiled O'Driscolls were patiently waiting.

Conor O'Driscoll, Fineen's eldest son and heir, had fought courageously in the last rebellion and held out to the very last. Together with his son Conor Og and his brother Donal, he had founded an O'Driscoll dynasty in exile who were determined to return and seize control of their birthright.

They would have kept in close touch with events at home – perhaps it was even they who were behind the war of attrition against the Baltimore settlers. But this was just a minor holding action. One day they would get their revenge. One day, the hated English settlers would be driven into the sea.

BALTIMORE ACHIEVES PROSPERITY

Against all the odds, the English plantation at Baltimore thrived and prospered. Babies were born. Sons matured to help their fathers at their boats, and daughters grew up to help their mothers at the fish palace. A new generation was preparing to take over.

Meanwhile, vast shoals of pilchards were practically hurling themselves into their nets. 'Ireland yields a great deal [of cod, herring and pilchards], the best in Europe,' enthused one survey in 1620.

It was reckoned that 30,000 tons of dried fish could be produced each year at £20 a ton (over £2,500 today). Ships loaded with salted fish sailed regularly from Baltimore to Bridgewater and Bristol. Everyone was prospering from Baltimore – except Walter Coppinger.

COPPINGER BACKS FINEEN

Coppinger changed tack completely. He took a legal action seeking to re-establish that *Sir Fineen O'Driscoll* was the true owner of Baltimore.

This may seem like an extraordinary about-turn, until you remember that Fineen owed Coppinger £1,693. If Baltimore belonged to Fineen, and Fineen was unable to repay the money, then Baltimore now belonged to Coppinger.

After examining the dusty tomes, the court ruled in Coppinger's favour. It seems the settlers only heard about this afterwards; they weren't even invited to reply.

Armed with his court order, Coppinger reacted with speed and severity. He moved into the castle and ordered the settlers off his land.

At that stage, two things happened in parallel.

The settlers lodged an appeal against the court order, arguing that they'd invested too much in the property to be thrown out at the side of the road.

Meanwhile, Coppinger and Fineen O'Driscoll became locked in a familiar legal argument over the nature of the £1,693 loan. Sir Walter contended that Fineen had actually *sold* his estate to him for £1,693. Fineen maintained it was a mortgage. Four arbitrators were appointed to resolve the dispute. They found that each was sincere in his interpretation.

Fineen was ordered to repay a mere £1,300 out of the £1,693 in full settlement of the debt. The arbitrators made this concession 'knowing the great and decrepit age of Sir Fineen, together with his present disability and want of means'.

And so, on April 14, 1629, both parties signed a legal agreement (a 'deed of defeasance') setting aside Coppinger's claim to Fineen's estate, on condition that this £1,300 was paid. This was by no means a defeat for Coppinger, because both parties knew he would never get the money. Within a year, Sir Fineen had died in poverty and the arguments were set to begin all over again.

Meanwhile, the settlers were continuing their appeal against eviction. They took their plea before the Lords Justices, one of who was Richard Boyle. The eighteenth-century historian Charles Smith summed up the settlers' case in 1750:

'They proved that they had made a civil plantation of English Protestants there; that His Majesty had incorporated them; that Sir Thomas Crooke had showed them a patent, whereby the town was granted to him and his heirs, and that he had promised to estate them and their heirs, in consideration of which they had expended £2,000 in buildings and other improvements; but that Sir Walter Coppinger had got possession of the castle of Baltimore ...'

The argument centred on how much the settlers had invested. The Lords decided to get an independent valuation from a panel of auditors: Sir William Hull of Leamcon; Sir Henry Becher, the planter mentioned earlier in this chapter; and a Mr Barham. In the meantime:

'Sir Walter was dismissed upon his promise to reinstate the English, at such rents ... as the Council Board should think proper.'

The panel estimated the settlers' investment at around £1,640.

What happened next was quite bizarre. One of the 'independent' auditors, Sir Henry Becher, liked the figures he saw. Without consulting anyone, he cut a private deal leasing the town directly from Coppinger.

Incensed by this action, the Lords ordered Coppinger and Becher to appear before them to explain.

Coppinger refused and was flung into a cell in Dublin Castle for contempt.

Boyle told Becher (who happened to be a friend) that he had two choices. He could either return the lease to Coppinger, who would then be obliged to reinstate the tenants; or he could keep the lease and estate the tenants himself.

Becher refused point blank to give up the lucrative fishery operation.

The case went back to court. This time tempers were running even hotter and, says Smith, 'many voices were given for Becher's being committed to the Castle'.

Boyle leaped to the rescue, suggesting that 'since the season for fishing was come, they might all be licensed home, where they might amicably make up matters among themselves.'

Neither of these two courtroom battles seemed to

have a definite outcome, and the bickering would have continued for years if the Algerine corsairs had not arrived.

Daniel Donovan, the nineteenth-century historian, summed up the whole affair in a parody verse. The three Latin words mean mine, yours and theirs:

> '*The colonists kicked up a deuce of a clatter*
> *And quarrelled and fought over meum and tuum,*
> *The Algerines came and decided the matter,*
> *By kindly converting it all into suum.*'

There had been only one solid, undeniable result of all this legal wrangling. It rises above all the petty rivalries and disputes and, from our point of view, it is pivotal:

Walter Coppinger's ownership of Baltimore was no longer in doubt. It had been copperfastened by the Chancery order and upheld by the Lords Justices. *The only thing that stood in his way was the settlers.*

He had tried the legal route. He had tried harassment and intimidation. None of these tactics had worked. So long as those irksome English planters remained in *his* village, waving their receipts for the money they'd invested, Coppinger would be prevented from gaining total control of Baltimore and its lucrative fishing industry.

He had signed a lease in 1610, which he'd believed would end the settlers' involvement in Baltimore after twenty-one years. But now this agreement was worthless. The court had decided that the settlers had invested too much sweat and money to be evicted, even after the lease expired in 1631.

Coppinger could not live alongside these odious *Sassenachs*. What he wanted was a racially pure Baltimore cleansed of English settlers and populated by Irish.

Perhaps, at some stage in 1629 or 1630, Coppinger thought long and hard and suddenly realised that the solution was staring him in the face.

No settlers – no problem.

There is no concrete evidence that Coppinger had any role in organising the Algerine raid of 1631. But it conveniently removed the only obstacle to his total control of Baltimore. Coppinger was the only man in Ireland who materially benefited from the raid. A mere eight months after the Algerines removed the settlers, the Earl of Cork reported: 'It appears that Sir Walter Coppinger claims it [Baltimore].'

However, it did him little good. In the 1630s the vast pilchard shoals, which had visited Baltimore regularly every year, suddenly stopped coming. A few years later, in 1636, he leased out the castle and village.

Yes, Coppinger had the motive. He also had the means – he was a fabulously wealthy man and he could well afford to pay big money for a grudge to be settled. As someone who regular hired musclemen, he also seems to have had plenty of contacts in the criminal underworld –

which in this era included the pirate world.

But was he capable of organising such an atrocity?

Looking at the near-psychopathic personality of the man, the answer is clear: it wouldn't have cost him a moment's sleep. Morally and ethically, the raid on Baltimore was no different to anything he'd done before – the only difference was in scale.

In Spain, the O'Driscoll émigrés happened to share his ambitions. Sir Fineen had died in poverty in 1630, one year before the raid. In normal times, it would have been either Fineen's son Conor, or *his* son Conor Óg, who would then have stepped forward to receive the symbolic rod of power and the village that came with it.

The exiles would have heard about Coppinger's war of attrition against the settlers and approved wholeheartedly. It would have been no surprise if they had discovered a common motive and dreamed up a grand conspiracy – a time bomb set to explode just after the old man's death had freed them to seek revenge.

This is not a new theory. Historian W. J. Kingston, author of *The Story Of West Carbery*, has speculated that the O'Driscoll exiles organised the raid from Spain as revenge against the English: 'Probably the raiders were told glowing tales of the wealth of the place, and, this not materialising, they took persons instead of gold in the hope of obtaining fat ransoms for them, which they do not seem to have got.'

In his chapter on Baltimore in *Pirate Utopias*, author Peter Lamborn Wilson agrees that the motive was loot: 'Perhaps he [Coppinger] painted it a richer prize than it proved in fact ...'

Alternatively, perhaps Morat Rais was just paid to do the job. The corsair admiral would not have been too proud to accept a fat purse as payment for a contract raid – particularly since he was also striking a blow for the *jihad* at the same time.

Remember, too, that Morat had every reason to hate the English at this time. He had offered to renounce his Islamic faith and serve King Charles, but this offer had been thrown back in his face.

None of the Barbary corsairs would have had any love for Baltimore, a village that had first entertained the pirates and then frozen them out. Corsair historian Edward Lucie-Smith has described the pirates' turning upon Baltimore as 'tit for tat' – and that may be how Morat Rais saw it, too.

If we accept the official explanation of the Baltimore raid, none of Morat's actions make any sense.

Here we have a top corsair admiral and 280 elite fighting troops setting forth in two serious warships bristling with guns. This is clearly an important mission. But no – instead, they just spend their time faffing vaguely about the English coast, picking on minor merchantmen and stinking little fishing boats. Wandering around without direction, pathologically indecisive, Morat suddenly decides to attack the best-defended port on the entire coast – Kinsale – and then changes his mind on the advice of some humble fisherman who persuades him to sail fifty miles west, to a little village where there are nothing but pilchards.

Even if we believe that Morat set out with the specific intention of attacking Baltimore, his actions *still* don't make sense. Why did he waste his energy with these diversions? Why didn't he head directly for his main target?

The explanation could be that he was simply filling in time. Perhaps Morat had agreed not only to attack Baltimore ... but to attack it *on a specific date*.

If we work on the basis of this theory, suddenly all becomes clear.

Morat agrees to the contract sometime in 1630 and makes preparations to sail in the spring in 1631.

In February, the Earl Of Cork's agents in Algiers get wind of the plan, but mistakenly assume that the targets must be Kinsale or Cork.

Morat sets sail in the knowledge that he has a date at Baltimore on 20 June 1631 – no earlier, no later. Like all prudent mariners, he leaves enough time to allow for the unexpected. He makes it to Land's End early, around June 17. He picks up an expert on Baltimore, Edward Fawlett, in what might even have been a pre-arranged meeting. He heads towards the prominent landmark of Kinsale Head, where he arrives by June 19.

Reaching Roaring Water Bay in good time, the corsairs have to cool their heels for a couple or hours until the day ends. Allowing for mustering troops, preparing the boats and rowing to shore, their 'invasion' would have begun almost as soon as the trickling sand in the hourglass showed midnight on the crucial date of June 20, 1631.

Is that how it happened? It's sad to think that we may never find definite evidence. If Morat ever kept a journal, it has long since disappeared.

So of course the reader may be excused for dismissing this entire theory as fanciful speculation.

Except for one curious fact.

It is quite an astounding fact.

In all of the books and articles I have read about the Baltimore raid, no-one seems to have remarked upon it. But it struck me so forcibly that, when I stumbled upon it in a list of ancient deeds, it was all I could do to prevent myself shattering the silence of the National Library with a cry of pure astonishment.

In the great religious wars of the 1600s, dates and anniversaries were highly potent. We need look no further than Guy Fawkes's Day ('Remember, remember, the Fifth of November') or the later Battle of the Boyne whose anniversary ('The Glorious Twelfth of July') is commemorated in Northern Ireland to this day.

This was also an era in which pirates deliberately chose anniversary dates to avenge ancient grudges. For instance, when the privateer Sir Edward

Mansfield launched a raid on the Spanish-held Caribbean island of Santa Catalina in 1666, he timed his attack for May 26 – the precise twenty-fifth anniversary of the date (May 26, 1641) when the Spanish had consolidated their victory over the island's English inhabitants.

Similarly, if Walter Coppinger had inflicted the vengeance of the corsairs upon the settlers, he would not have chosen any old date. He would have made it a grand gesture, a permanent reminder to the English of how he had been wronged.

We've seen that the crucial date in this whole business was June 20, 1610: the date that Crooke and O'Driscoll signed an agreement to hand over Baltimore to Coppinger in twenty-one years' time.

The same date of June 20, 1610 crops up again and again in all the legal documents that follow. To Walter Coppinger, that date was a symbol – of a deal that had been broken, of good faith that had been betrayed.

For the O'Driscoll exiles, too, June 20, 1610 would have been a date that lived on in infamy. It was the day the turncoat Sir Fineen had finally and irrevocably sold out the O'Driscoll clan's ancient heritage, together with his own birthright, to the hated *Sassenach*.

A twenty-one year lease. Signed on June 20, 1610.

If it was a coincidence, it was a truly staggering one.

Morat Rais's corsairs arrived to remove the English

settlers from Baltimore on June 20, 1631 – twenty-one years, *to the very day*, from the date that agreement was signed.

Appendix

The Taken

This is the definitive tally of the enslaved, as compiled by the burghers of Baltimore just a few days after the raid and recorded in *The Council Book of Kinsale*. Confusingly, each line begins with the head of the household, whether or not that individual was personally captured.

A list of Baltimore people who were carried away by the Turk, the 20th June 1631.

William Mould	2	himself and a boy
Ould Osburne	2	himself and maid
Alexander Pumery	1	his wife
John Ryder	4	himself, wife and two children

Robert Hunt	1	his wife
Abram Roberts	5	himself, wife and three children
Corent Croffine	6	himself, wife, daughter and three men
John Harris	6	his wife, mother, three children and maid
Dermot Meregey	3	two children and maid
Richard Meade	5	himself, wife, and three children
Richard Lorye	7	himself, wife, sister and four children
Stephen Broddebrooke	3	his wife and two children (she great with child)
Ould Haunkin	3	himself, his wife and daughter
Evans & The Cook	5	Evans and his boy, cook, his wife and maid
Bessie Flodd	2	herself and son
William Arnold	5	himself, wife and three children
Michaell Amble	3	himself, wife and son
Stephen Pierse	6	himself, wife, mother and three children
William Symons	4	himself, wife and two children

Christopher Norwey	3	himself, wife and child
Sampson Rogers	2	himself and son
Besse Peeter	1	her daughter
Thomas Payne	4	himself, wife and two children
Richard Watts	4	himself, wife and two children
William Gunter	9	his wife, maid and seven sons
John Amble	1	himself
Edward Cherrye	1	himself
Robert Chimor	5	his wife and four children
Timothy Corlew	1	his wife
John Slyman	4	himself, wife and two children
Morris Power	1	his wife

The sum of all carried away from Baltimore: 107*

Timothy Curlew, slain
John Davys, slain
Ould Osburne, sent ashore
Alice Heard, sent ashore
Two of Dungarvan, sent ashore
One of Dartmouth, sent ashore

Portingales	9
Pallicians	3
Frenchmen	17
Englishmen of Dartmouth	9
From boats of Dungarvan	9
This total	47

The sum of all captives: 154

[*Note: the main list actually totals 109, not 107. The compiler is obviously discounting Mr Osburne and Ms Heard, who were set free.]

Bibliography And Recommended Reading

As far as I am aware, no full-length factual book has ever been written about the pirate raid on Baltimore. Few books give it more than a passing mention. I would recommend Donovan, Coppinger, *The Council Book of the Corporation of Kinsale* and Smith, all books dating from the Victorian era or earlier; and in the modern age, de Courcy Ireland, Kingston, Wilson and Healy.

The best academic works on the subject are to be found in the *Cork Historical and Architectural Society Journal* (CHASJ). The most extensive are Raymond Caulfield's 1892 newspaper article and Henry Barnby's 1969 treatise. I am particularly indebted to Barnby's work, a rare blend of academic discipline and easy readability, for giving me an overview of the subject and pointing me towards some of the main sources. Articles by Mark Samuel and Rev J. Coombes also threw light on aspects of the raid.

The history of Fineen and the O'Driscolls has been well documented in the 'Genealogy of Corca Laidhe' (O'Donovan) in Coppinger and Donovan, and more recently by Burke, Coleman, Healy, Kingston and Edward O'Mahony (2000 and 2001).

The best sources on Morat Rais are the correspondence in Castries; Fr Dan; and Gosse.

For more on Algiers and the Barbary corsairs, I would highly recommend Earle, Lane-Poole, Gosse, Clissold, Lucie-Smith, Spencer and Fisher; and on English and Irish pirates in general, Senior and Cordingly.

Other recommended works will be obvious from this bibliography and from my source notes.

Annals of the Kingdom of Ireland by The Four Masters. (1848). Dublin: Hodges & Smith.

Anonymous (1804) *The Captives: An Account of the Sufferings of Twenty Christian Slaves Taken By Algerine Corsairs*. London: Cape Macclesfield.

Baepler, Paul (1999) (ed) *White Slaves, African Masters*. Chicago: University Of Chicago Press.

Bamford, Paul W. (1972) *The Barbary Pirates*. Minneapolis: University Of Minnesota.

Barnard, T. C. (1993): 'The Political, Material and Mental Culture of the Cork Settlers', c 1650-1700, in O'Flanagan, P.; Buttimer, C. G.; O'Brien, G. (1993) (eds): *Cork History and Society*. Dublin: Geography Publications.

Barnby, Henry (1969) 'The Sack of Baltimore'. CHASJ: vol lxxiv part 2, no. 220, pp100-129.

Berleth, Richard J (1977) *The Twilight Lords*. London: Allen Lane.

Bon, Ottaviano (1608) *A Description of the Grand Signor's Seraglio* translated by Withers, Robert and Greaves, John (1650). London: John Greaves.

Brady, Ciaran, and Gillespie, Raymond (1975) (eds) *Natives and Newcomers, Essays in The Making of Irish Colonial Society*, 1534-1641 (Dublin: Irish Academic Press).

Brooks, Francis (1693) *Barbarian Cruelty*. London: Salusbury & Newman.

Burke, James M. 'Sir Fineen O'Driscoll' in CHASJ.

Canny, Nicholas (1993) 'The 1641 Depositions' in O'Flanagan, Patrick; Buttimer, Cornelius G.; and O'Brien, Gerard (1993) (eds): *Cork History and Society*. Dublin, Geography Publications. Chapter 8.

Cason, Edmond (1647) *Relation [of] the Redemption of Captives in Algiers and Tunis, With a List of Captives Redeemed and Prices*. London: F.L.L. Blaikelock.

Castries, Henry de, Count (1905) *Les Sources Inédites de l'Histoire du Maroc de 1530 à 1845*. Paris: Pierre de Cenival and Philippe de Cossé Brissac. Book 3.

Cathcart, James Leander (c.1785) and J. B. Newkirk (1899) (ed) *The Captives*. USA: J. B. Newkirk; also contained in Baepler, Paul (1999) (ed) *White Slaves, African Masters*. Chicago: University Of Chicago Press, pp105-146.

Caulfield, Richard (1892) 'Notes on Dr Smith's History of Cork'. CHASJ: vol 1, p263.

Caulfield, Richard (1892) 'The Sack of Baltimore'. Cork: *Munster Journal* [newspaper]. Reprinted (1892) in CHASJ: vol 1.

[CHASJ] *The Cork Historical and Architectural Society Journal* (1891-present). Cork. (Several references in this bibliography.)

Clissold, Stephen (1977) *The Barbary Slaves*. London: Paul Elek.

Coleman, J. (1924) 'Old Castles of South West Cork'. CHASJ: xxix pp45-51.

Connolly, S. J. (1999) (ed): *Oxford Companion To Irish History* Oxford: University Press.

Coombes, J., Rev. (1972) 'The Sack of Baltimore: A Forewarning'. CHASJ: lxxvii. pp 60-61.

Coppinger, Walter Arthur (1884) (ed) *History of the Copingers Or Coppingers of Co. Cork*. Manchester, London: H. Sotheran.

Cordingly, David (1996) *Life Among The Pirates*. London: Warner Books.

Croutier, Alev Lyle (1989) *Harem: The World Behind The Veil*. London: Bloomsbury.

[CSPI] *Calendar of State Papers*, Ireland. Dublin: The National Library of Ireland.

Cullen, L. M (1981) *The Emergence of Modern Ireland 1600-1900*. Dublin: Gill & McMillan.

Dan, Pierre, Fr (1637) *Histoire de Barbarie et Ses Corsaires*. Paris: Pierre Riolet.

D'Aranda, Emanuel (1662) *Relation De La Captivité*. Brussels.

D'Aranda, Emanuel (1666) *History of Algiers and Its Slavery, english'd by John Davies*. London: John Starkey.

D'Arvieux, Laurent (1735) *Mémoires du Chevalier d'Arvieux*. Paris.

Davis, Thomas (1844) 'The Sack of Baltimore (a poem)'. Dublin: *The Nation*.

De Courcy Ireland, John (1986) *Ireland and The Irish in Maritime History*. Dublin: Glendale Press.

Donovan, Daniel (1876) *Sketches in Carbery, Co. Cork* Dublin: McGlashan and Gill.

Earle, Peter (1970) *Corsairs of Malta and Barbary* London: Sidgwick & Jackson.

Eigilsson, Ólafur (1627) and Magnússon, Gisli (1852) (ed) *Litil Saga Umm Herhlaup Tyrkjans á Íslandí*. Reykjavik.

Fisher, Godfrey (1957) *Barbary Legend*. Oxford: Clarendon Press.

FitzGerald, Brian (1952) *The Anglo-Irish, 1602-1745*. London: Staples Press.

Fitzgerald, Seamus (1999) *Mackerel and the Making of Baltimore*. Dublin: Irish Academic Press.

Ford, Alan (1975): 'The Protestant Reformation in Ireland', in Brady, C., and Gillespie, R. (1975) (eds) *Natives and Newcomers*. Dublin: Irish Academic.

Foss, John (1798) *Journal of the Captivity and Sufferings*. Newburyport, Mass. Also contained in Baepler, Paul (1999) (ed) *White Slaves, African Masters*. Chicago: University Of Chicago Press.

Fox, John (1582) 'The Worthy Enterprise of John Fox' in Hakluyt, Richard (1582+) *Voyagers' Tales*. London.

Gallwey, Thomas (1879) *Richard Boyle, First Earl of Cork*. Dublin: The Monitor.

'Genealogy of Corca Laidhe, The', or 'O'Driscoll's Country', in O'Donovan, John (1849) (ed) *Miscellany of the Celtic Society*. Dublin:

Celtic Society.

Gibson, Charles, Rev. (1861) *History of City and County of Cork* London: T. C. Newby.

Gjerset, Knut (1924) *History of Iceland*. London: Unwin.

Gosse, Philip (1932) *A History of Piracy*. London: Longman, Green.

Grosart, Alexander (1886-88) (ed) *The Lismore Papers of Sir Richard Boyle, The First and Great Earl of Cork*. London: Chiswick Press.

Haedo, Diego de, Fray (1612) *Topography and General History of Algiers*. Spain, 1612; Paris 1870.

Healy, James N. (1998) *The Castles of County Cork*. Cork: Mercier.

Hill, Aaron (1709) *A Full and Just Account of the Present State of the Ottoman Empire*. London.

Irwin, Liam (1980) 'Politics, Religion and Economy: Cork in the 17th Century'. CHASJ: lxxxv, pp7-29.

Kingston, W. J (1985) *The Story of West Carbery*. Waterford: Friendly Press.

Kinsale, Corporation Of (1652+) and Caulfield, Richard (1879) (ed) *The Council Book of the Corporation of Kinsale 1652-1800*. Guildford, Surrey.

Lacy, Terry G. (1998) *Ring of Seasons: Iceland, Its Culture and History*. Ann Arbor: University Of Michigan Press.

Lane-Poole, Stanley (1890) *The Barbary Corsairs*. London: T. Fisher Unwin.

Lewis, W. H. (1962) *Levantine Adventurer: The Travels and Missings of the Chevalier D'Arvieux*. London: Andre Deutch.

Lucie-Smith, Edward (1978) *Outcasts of the Sea*. London: Paddington Press.

Lurting, Thomas (1711) *The Fighting Sailor Turned Peaceable Christian*. London: J. Sowle.

McCarthy-Murrogh, Michael (1975) 'The English Presence in 17th Century Munster' in Brady, C., and Gillespie, R. (1975) (eds) *Natives and Newcomers*. (Dublin: Irish Academic).

Map of Baltimore (c. 1630), draughtsman unknown, Str P 24-5/100
from the Earl of Strafford's Papers (Str P), Wentworth Woodhouse
Muniments at Sheffield Archives, copy obtained by author
(15/11/05) by kind permission of the Head of Sheffield Libraries,
Archives and Information.

Milton, Giles (2004) *White Gold*. London: Hodder & Stoughton.

Moore, Canon Courteness, Rev. (1891) *A Sidelight on Irish Clerical Life*
[i.e., Rev. Devereux Spratt]. Dublin: 1891.

Morgan, Joseph (a.k.a. John) (1732) *A Complete History of Algiers*.
London.

O'Dowd, Mary (1975) 'Gaelic Economy and Society' in Brady, C., and
Gillespie, R. (1975) (eds) *Natives and Newcomers* Dublin: Irish
Academic.

'Official Report of the Raid on Baltimore' (1631) in *Kinsale,
Corporation of* (1652+) and Caulfield, R. (1879) (ed) *The Council
Book of the Corporation of Kinsale, 1652-1800*. Guildford, pp xxxiv to
xxxv; also in CSPI 1625-32 pp 621-2.

O'Flanagan, Patrick (1993) 'Town and Village Life' in O'Flanagan,
Patrick; Buttimer, Cornelius G.; O'Brien, Gerard (1993) (eds): *Cork
History and Society*. Dublin: Geography Publications.

O'Flanagan, Patrick; Buttimer, Cornelius G.; O'Brien, Gerard (1993)
(eds): *Cork History and Society*. Dublin: Geography Publications.

Okeley, William (1675) *Eben-Ezer Or A Small Monument of Great Mercy*.
London.

O'Mahony, Edward (2000) 'Baltimore, The O'Driscolls and the End of
Gaelic Civilisation 1538-1615'. *Mizen Journal*: 8, pp 110-127.

O'Mahony, Edward (2001) 'The Battle of Castlehaven'. Transcript of
lecture to Castlehaven Commemoration Committee, 9/12/2001.

O'Mahony, J. E. (1887) 'Baltimore, Its Past, Present and Future'.
Cork: *The Eagle* [newspaper].

Oxford Dictionary of National Biography 7th ed (2004). Oxford: Oxford
University Press.

Pananti, Filippo (1818) and Edward Blaquiere (1818) (trs.) *Narrative of A
Residence in Algiers*. London.

Pellow, Thomas (c. 1740) and Brown, Robert, Dr (1890) (ed) *The Adventures of Thomas Pellow of Penryn*, Mariner. London: T. Fisher Unwin.

Penzer, Norman (1965) *The Harem: An Account of the Institution*. London: Spring Books.

Pétis de La Croix, Francois (1688) *Relation Universelle de l'Afrique*. Lyon.

Phelan, Andrew (1999) *Ireland From The Sea*. Dublin: Wolfhound Press.

Pitts, Joseph (1738) 'An Account of the Religion and Manners of the Mohametans' in Maundrell, Henry (1810) *A Journey From Aleppo To Jerusalem*. London.

Playfair, Robert Lambert, Sir (1884) *The Scourge of Christendom* [Algiers]. London: Smith, Elder.

'Present State of Algiers, The' (1676) London: English Government report signed 'G.P.', appendix to The Present State of Tangier etc. London.

Priestly, E. J. (1984) *An Early 17th Century Map of Baltimore*, CHASJ: lxxxix pp55-58.

PRO 71/1 (series) The State Papers Relating to the Barbary Nations. Kew: National Archives [UK].

Russell, Michael (1844) *History and Present Condition of the Barbary States*. Edinburgh.

Rycault, Paul (1680) *The History of the Turkish Empire 1623-77*. London.

Samuel, Mark (1984) 'Coppinger's Court: a Document in Stone'. CHASJ: lxxxix, pp59-76.

Sanders, Thomas (1583) 'The Unfortunate Voyage Made With The Jesus' in Hakluyt, Richard (1589) (ed) *Principal Navigations, Africa*.

Senior, Clive (1976) *A Nation of Pirates*. London: Newton Abbot.

Seymour, St. John D. (1909) *Adventures and Experiences of a 17th Century Clergyman* [i.e., Rev. Devereux Spratt]. Dublin: Church Of Ireland.

Sheehan, Anthony: 'Irish Towns in A Period of Change', in Brady, C., and Gillespie, R. (1975) (eds) *Natives and Newcomers*. Dublin: Irish

Academic.

Shaw, Thomas (1738) *Travels Relating To Several Parts of Barbary*. Oxford.

Smith, Charles (1750) *The Ancient and Present State of the County and City of Cork*. Cork.

Spencer, William (1976) *Algiers in the Age of the Corsairs*. Oklahoma: University of Oklahoma Press.

Spenser, Edmund (1596) *A View of the Present State of Ireland*. London.

Spratt, Devereux, Rev. (c.1670) *Diary* [aka *Autobiography*], first published privately 1886, Tunbridge Wells.

Stafford, Thomas, Sir (1633) *Pacata Hibernia, A History of the Wars in Ireland*. Dublin: Hibernia Press.

Templeman, Eleanor Lee (1959) *Arlington Heritage: Vignettes of A Virginia County*. New York: Avenel Books.

T. S., Mr (1670) and Roberts, A. (1670) (ed) *An English Merchant Taken Prisoner By The Turks of Algiers*. London: M. Pitt.

'Tyrkjaránid á Íslandi' (1627) *Sogurit*. vol. 4. Reykjavik.

Went, A. E. J (1946) 'Pilchards in The South of Ireland'. CHASJ: vol 51, pp137-44.

Wilson, Peter Lamborn (1995) *Pirate Utopias, Moorish Corsairs and European Renegadoes*. New York: Autonomedia.

Youghal, Corporation of (1610-1659) and Caulfield, Richard (1878) (ed) *The Council Book of Youghal*. Guildford.

Zara, Bassano Luigi da (1545) *I Costumi & I Modi Particolari De La Vita De Turchi*. Rome.

TELEVISION

Atlantic Jihad (Tyrkjáranid) (2003) director and script, Thorsteinn Helgason, Seylan/Hjálmtyr Heiddal, broadcast on RTÉ TG4 Spring 2003.

The Battle of Kinsale (2001) RTÉ1 documentary.

Harem (2003) Paladin Invision documentary for Channel 4, UK.

White Slaves, Pirate Gold (10/1/2003) BBC Timewatch documentary.

WEBSITES
Rootsweb genealogical website, www.rootsweb.com
Old Algeria website, www.algerie.info
Vieil Alger, www.vieilalger.free.fr
Wikipedia open-source encyclopaedia, www.wikipedia.org.

Source Notes

The main sources for this book are the original documents, reports and letters from the period; the personal reminiscences of slaves in Algiers; and some histories written during the Barbary era. However, in these notes I also use the abbreviation 'rec', which refers to modern works and should be taken to mean 'recommended reading for anyone who wishes to read more about this particular topic'.

PREFACE

Greatest invasion: King Charles used word 'invasion' (CSPI 1625-32, 23/8/1631); Lords Justice said 'absolutely without precedent', (ibid, 10/7/31). See ch 14 .

200-strong force, no. of captives: Official Report (for details see chapter 1).

King's rage: CSPI 1625-31, 23/8/1631).

King's reaction … seeds democracy: See ch 33.

English settlers: CSPI 1606-08 p100

Dutch renegade: Jan Jansen. See ch 4.

Ethnic cleansing plot: Discussed in ch 34.

Radio programme: On RTÉ 1. I believe the interviewee was Dr Patricia Casey.

Books with old Irish, Latin: i.e., Genealogy, Coppinger.

List of names: Based on the official list of captives compiled only days after the raid. I have found four different versions of this list. The one I use is from the *Council Book Of Kinsale*, which is similar to CSPI 1625-32 pp621-22. The list in J. E. O'Mahony's Victorian document is inaccurate in that it lists William Gunter as captured. Finally there is Richard Caulfield's 1892 list.

CHAPTER 1
The Sack of Baltimore

Overview: Most of this chapter drawn directly from the Official Report of the Baltimore raid (hereafter 'Report'). There are several versions of this report, differing in minor detail. I have used the version in *The Council Book Of Kinsale*, pp. xxxiv to xxxv, which is signed by the burghers of Baltimore as the latest and most reliable. Another is to be found in CSPI 1625-32 pp 621-2.

Spanish invasion: ie, Sept 1601. See ch 4 and ch 34.

Troops' appearance: Dan; Lane-Poole p224; rec, Turkish Cultural Foundation website, www.turkishculture.org, Earle p62, Spencer p42, Pananti p32+.

Music struck fear: Dan, 1634; Lane-Poole p253; rec, Wilson pp32-33, Spencer p51.

'The famous Janissaries ...' De Busbecq, Augier Ghislain de (1522-92) *Life And Letters*. London: Keegan Paul, 1881.

Threats and obscenities: see chs 10-11; also Pitts p302.

Harris mentioned: ie, Report.

Worst fate: eg, Pitts p302; also see illustrations in Dan.

Nothing like this before: See note above, 'unprecedented'.

Naval bungling, delay: Report; and see chs 8, 12, 14.

CHAPTER 2
The Last Day

Overview: In this chapter and in ch 9 I have tried to recreate a typical Sunday among the settlers of Munster in the early 1600s, drawing evidence from disparate sources, notably CSPI, the Earl of Cork's letters and the *Council Books* of Kinsale and Youghal. The topography of The Cove, the main town and Tullagh church and the main descriptions are all clearly shown in the Map of Baltimore (hereafter

'Map'). Depictions of the landscape and coast in the pre-development era have been gleaned from a wide spectrum of sources both contemporary and later. Donovan was especially helpful in evoking the atmosphere, mood and climate of old West Cork. O'Flanagan was of great assistance, especially the description of 1600s Baltimore by O'Flanagan on pp404-5 and his general notes on layout of towns; Canny's depiction of village life in general on pp262-278; Barnard's chapter 9 on Cork settler culture; and the notes on town layout and house style on p180+. Cullen and Brady also provided background. Modern re-creations of seventeenth-century villages were also helpful. The people, their names and their family circumstances are accurate and are taken from the list in Report. The Meregeys' maid, who is nameless in this list, has been given the only pseudonym – 'Anna'. See special note on Joane in chs 31-32.

Farm animals: It is clear from the Map, from Smith and from the 1641 depositions that the settlers had to augment their fishing by keeping livestock. Also rec, CHASJ LII pp55-56, also Canny in O'Flanagan pp265-270.

Fair: Genealogy p99; rec, Kingston p46.

Fairs in general: rec, O'Flanagan p336.

Midsummer customs: Donovan p235.

Long-term lease/no blow-ins: See chs 34-35.

Dissenters/Crooke family: For more, see entries for Thomas Snr, Samuel and Helkiah Crooke in *Oxford Dictionary of National Biography*.

Secret printers: ie, the so-called Martin Marprelate letters in 1589. Rec, www.anglicanlibrary.org.

Executed: i.e., William Hackett in the Cheapside uprising 1591. One seditious clergyman was also hanged and another died in prison.

Seditious sermon: i.e, J. Field, 1570s.

Primary motive religious: Petitions in CSPI 1615-25 pp190-1; Copinger; also rec, E. O'Mahony, who says one of the motives was religious freedom.

Crooke deal with Fineen: See chs 34-35.

From West Country: See discussions in 'The Politics Of The Protestants In Munster', p1-20 in CHASJ LXXVI July-Dec 1971;

also Canny in O'Flanagan p258-262.

Borough status/pirates: See chs 34-35.

Church Hierarchy shared outlook: See Ford.

Harassed/Coppinger: See chs 34-35.

Crooke died: *Oxford Dictionary Of National Biography*. As above. (Samuel Crooke died in 1635: Kinsale.)

Fishing process and fish palace: Smith vol 2 pp310-11. Rec, Arthur Went in CHASJ vol 51 1946. Rec, Patrick O'Flanagan, 'Town And Village Life' p398 in O'Flanagan. Rec, Canny's 1641 Depositions p262 in O'Flanagan. Layout of Cove, Map.

Smell intolerable: Rev S. S. Shaw, 1788, quoted in St Ives And Hayle tourist literature.

Description of castle, surrounds: Map; Donovan p93; also rec, O'Flanagan p405.

Jobs in fishing town: Richard Whitbourne, *Discourse And Discovery Of Newfoundland* London, 1620. For more, read Canny in O'Flanagan pp262-270 and Liam Irwin.

Chasten delinquents: Kinsale entry for 26/9/1612.

Tullagh description: Map.

Gunter 'credit': Smith pp268+.

CHAPTER 3
Hunting For Humans

Departure ritual for corsairs: Pitts p313, Lane-Poole p221-3; rec, Clissold p35.

City gates: Pétis p45-48; Shaw pp68-9; rec, Spencer p29

City guns: Pétis p53; Russell p322; rec, Spencer p30; 'red mouthed', rec Vieil Alger.

Morat's ships/guns: Report

Two volleys etc: See departure ritual above.

'Legendary' Morat: 'He grew to great esteem among them', from 1638 despatch in Castries, p485-6.

Lingua Franca/Sabir: For more on this, see ch 15 and ch 28.

Population 100,000/many races: Pétis p7, p50; Dan; rec, Fisher pp100-1, Spencer p31.

Colour scenes in streets: Reflection of writings of d'Aranda, d'Arvieux,

Lane-Poole etc; see later chapters.

Slaves on Mole; rocks broken; sleds: Pétis, illustration of The Mole; Foss; Cathcart; Sanders; Lane-Poole p245; also rec, Gosse p71, Earle p82.

Harbour origin, slave labour: Pétis p 45, p51; rec, Spencer p25

Leisure walks on Mole; 900ft long: rec, Lewis p168.

4000 died: Vieil Alger

Probably early May: Start of corsair season. Trip north took five to six weeks (return trip June 20-July 28).

Friday or Sunday, holy man, auguries: Lane-Poole p222.

Visit fountain: Near the Marine Gate. Rec, Vieil Alger.

Money invested, syndicates etc: Lane-Poole pp224-5; rec, Spencer pp48-49; Clissold p33.

Most sought-after slaves: More detail in ch 19.

Haedo quotes: Lane-Poole p222.

Iceland 4 years ago: i.e., 1627. See ch 11.

Patron saint: i.e., Sidi Beteka, whose storm saved city from Spanish.

Call and response: Pitts, p313; Lane-Poole p222.

Flag colours: rec, Spencer p39.

Pasha Hussein's 4th term: rec, Vieil Alger.

Janissaries' rise to power, council, Pasha selected etc: Pétis pp88-89; Rycault p16, p75; Lane-Poole passim, esp. ch 15; rec, Spencer p22, Earle p24-26, Lucie-Smith pp56-61.

Taifa Rais: Library of Congress entry Algiers/Privateers; Lane-Poole p186; rec, Wilson p37, Earle p35.

Ali Bichnin: Lane-Poole pp195-9; rec, Wilson pp43-45, Spencer p77.

Status recognised: rec, Wilson p43.

Voyage targeted: Discussed in depth in chs 34-35.

CHAPTER 4
The Spark And The Powderkeg

Overview: My account of John Harrison's exploits are based on his own despatches to London, as follows.

Undercover trek, meeting with Morat, voyage, encounter with Spanish, return to Sallee with guns: PRO SP 71/1 vol xii, fol 129-39, as reproduced in Castries.

Sallee harbour incident: PRO SP 71/1 vol xii, fol. 173-176, as
reproduced in Castries.

1630 episode; white dog; Morat's secret, 'a Christian at heart', offer to
defect to England: PRO SP 71/1 vol xii fol 154-55, as reproduced in
Castries. (Note, Morat's quotes are indirect, but an accurate
reflection of Harrison's memoir.)

Other sources for this chapter are:

Sallee's role as pirate enclave: Brown's intro to Pellow; rec. Wilson,
passim, esp. ch 6.

'An habitation' etc: Samuel Backer's despatch 27/11/37 as reproduced
in Castries.

Harrison background: rec, entry 'John Harrison' in *Oxford Dictionary of
National Biography*.

Morat's position in Sallee: See note to p33 in Castries.

Two men hit it off: Harrison gives glowing tributes in his despatches.

Harrison despised slavery etc: rec, Wilson p165.

Harrison freed 260: rec, *Oxford Dictionary of National Biography*.

Morat a convert; a new generation: see notes below.

'Seated in great pomp': Quote from artist who visited M's home in
1641; rec, *Atlantic Jihad* and Gosse pp57-58.

Morat in late 50s: he was born c1575 (Rootsweb genealogical archive).

Typical clothes: Illustrations in Russell; also Pétis pp61-62; rec,
Spencer p71.

'A great friend to our nation': Harrison's words in despatches.

Hundred isles: Davis poem, line 1.

Storm from S.E.: Donovan p63 and p89.

Swift verse: Donovan p196.

Carew quote/quality of harbour: *Pacata Hibernia*; Genealogy p93;
Donovan p33-34; also rec, Phelan p32.

Traditional imports, exports: Rec, A. F. O'Brien Politics, 'Economy
And Society' in O'Flanagan; smuggling, Donovan p102.

O'Driscoll piracy: Gibson p519; rec, Kingston p24; Lucie-Smith, p79.

Three families: (with O'Malleys, O'Flahertys). rec, *Oxford Companion
To Irish History*.

Throw stone: anecdotal to author.

Former territory, reduced: Pacata Hibernia; Donovan p99; Gibson p519; rec, Healy.

Three forts: Donovan p34 and p102; also rec, Coleman.

Big house: Donovan p20.

Unlucky name: J.E. O'Mahony.

Waterford battles: Genealogy, pp93-95; Donovan pp20-21, pp47-49; Gibson p519+.

Forts rebuilt: Built mid-1500s, rec, Kingston.

Lives of Fineen, Conor O'Driscoll (generally): CSPI; Genealogy Of Corca Laoidhe; Donovan; Coppinger; J.E. O'Mahony; with modern analyses by (rec) Healy, Kingston, Burke, E. O'Mahony, Barnby, Coleman.

Investiture 1573: Genealogy p100+. (Also rec, Burke and Kingston p53.)

Rod: Genealogy p386.

'The Rover': Anecdotal. Also rec, Healy.

Gaelic clothing: Descriptions appear in Spenser; rec, Berleth pp133-136. Also see Chart, D. A. (1907) *The Story Of Dublin* London: J. M. Dent.

Tanistry system: Summary in *Oxford Companion To Irish History*; also Genealogy pp99-100 and p386.

Last: Donovan, p104.

Land grabbers: rec, Berleth pp42-46.

Collaboration better: See below.

Surrender-regrant system: *Oxford Companion To Irish History*; rec, Burke.

Knighted: General Fineen refs in CSPI.

Conor-Fineen clash: CSPI 1601-03, 1602 letter Carew-Cecil; also rec, Kingston.

O'Neill rising: Donovan p46, pp99-100; CSPI 1601-03, numerous refs; rec, Berleth; Battle of Kinsale.

Bridge into England: CSPI 1601-03, p277.

Other chieftains: ibid, p235.

Suit to surrender: CSPI 1571-75, item 122, SP63/39 no 50.

Malicious rebel, overruled by son: Carew-Cecil, 1602, in CSPI 1601-03.

Spanish in Baltimore: Genealogy pp386-7; CSPI 1601-03 p235; rec,

Burke and E. O'Mahony.

Battle a rout: rec, Berleth, Battle of Kinsale.

Conor held out, escaped: rec, Kingston.

Fineen bribed, charmed: Smith, Donovan.

Pardon: Smith.

Penniless: He soon had to borrow money; also rec, Kingston p54.

Signed deed: Genealogy p99, p390; Smith.

Time, place of Fineen's death: Exact date unknown but 1629-1631. Healy says 1630. Rec, Burke, E. O'Mahony, Kingston. (Smith and Donovan mistakenly say early 1600s.)

Lough Hyne: Good description of lough and legends in *West Cork Walks* by Kevin Corcoran (O'Brien Press).

Six decades: i.e.,1573-1630.

Coppinger's life (generally): CSPI entries; Genealogy; Smith; Gibson; Donovan; Coppinger. Career, legal battle in more depth in chs 34-35.

Spain, O'Driscoll émigrés: Donovan p22; rec, Kingston.

Conor a hero: rec, Burke, 'brave warrior … relentless foe'.

Held out, escaped: rec, Kingston, E. O'Mahony.

Rumour drowned: CSPI 1601-03, p518.

Escape details: ibid, p329; rec, Coleman quoting Pacata Hibernia, and E. O'Mahony.

Captain in Spain: rec, Burke. Donovan says he later went to Austria.

Hatching plots in 1617: rec, Burke. (Also see notes on later O'Driscoll plots in chs 34-34.

O'Neill plotting until death in 1616: rec, Battle of Kinsale.

CHAPTER 5
The Warrior Monks

Algiers like sail: D'Arvieux V p219; also Pitts p312.

Algiers white, dazzling: Contemporary paintings; Pétis p48; Pitts p312; Russell p314; rec, Spencer p29 citing Nicholas Nickolay.

'Well guarded city': Cliché in the 1600s. Rec, Vieil Alger; Spencer x.

Gibraltar rituals: Pitts p315.

Radical protest: See discussion in ch 34; rec, Bono (see ch 34, and De Courcy Ireland p140.

Smith quote: Brown intro to Pellow.

Danser: Andrew Barker's (1609) *A True And Certain Report Of Captain Ward* rec, Spencer p124; Lucie-Smith p85; Gosse pp49-50.

Easton: CSPI 1611-14 notes lxv-lxvi; also Richard Whitbourne's *Discourse And Discovery Of Newfoundland*, London 1620; also rec, Senior p35; Lucie-Smith p83; Gosse p129.

Verney: Rec, Senior p35; Lucie-Smith p84; Gosse p130.

Mainwaring: Mainwaring, H. M. (1618) *Discourse On Piracy*; CSPI 1611-14, as above; rec, Senior p13+, Lucie-Smith p83, and Gosse pp117+.

Ward: Andrew Baker as above; rec, Wilson pp51-59, Senior p35; Lucie-Smith p81; Gosse pp134+.

Harbour, strength of fleet: Pétis pp45,51; Shaw p69; also rec, Spencer p126 and Earle p122, p452; cf England, rec, Lucie-Smith pp64-65.

Morat's ship: Report.

Prefer Dutch: rec, Senior p26, De Courcy Ireland p143 and Barnby p114.

Wax, polish: Pitts p313; Lane-Poole p225; rec, De Courcy Ireland p134.

Stock still: Pitts p316.

Janissaries generally: Pétis pp69-70, pp 76-80; D'Arvieux IV, pp3-4 and V pp244-54; Lane-Poole p62; de Busbecq op. cit. (see ref in ch 1); also rec Spencer pp41-49, Earle pp26-31, p36, p62, Fisher p97, Lucie-Smith p62.

Bulls: rec, Spencer p43.

Uniforms, weapons: Pananti p32; Dan; Lane-Poole, p224; rec Earle p62, Spencer p44, Vieil Alger, The Government Of The Regency.

Arrows: Rec, Janissaries in wikipedia; rec, Earle p53.

Ranks: Pétis pp69-70, p80; rec, Spencer p43, Vieil Alger as above.

Share of money: Lane-Poole p225; Dan; Pitts p313; Pétis pp68-9; rec Spencer p49, Earle p72, De Courcy Ireland p141.

Salary, perks: Pitts p447; D'Arvieux V pp244+; rec, Spencer p45.

Kings, untouchable: Pétis p88-9; rec, Spencer p44.

Once celibate, kouloughis: Pétis pp76-7; Pitts p491; rec, Earle p27, Spencer p31.

Origins, child levy: Pétis p70, p76; D'Arvieux V, p244+ and IV pp3-4.

French diplomat: Pétis pp76-78, p88.

Vizier, choose fairest: Eva March Tappan's intro to James L. Ludlow's 'The Tribute Of Children 1493' in Tappan's (1914) *The World's Story* Vol 6, Boston.

Privation, cloistered quarters: Ludlow in Tappan as above.

De Busbecq quotes: De Busbecq op. cit. (see ref in ch 1).

Passing out parade, white face: Ludlow in Tappan as above.

Final refs: See ch 7.

CHAPTER 6
The Wind Dog

Wind dog: Anecdotal to author; also see Dave Thurlew's anecdote about Baltimore in weathernotebook.org. A poem has been written about this phenomenon.

Boyle's letter: The Letter Book of Richard Boyle (19/2/31) Devonshire collection, Chatsworth House. I am grateful to Mark Samuel's article and especially Rev J. Coombes's article in CHASJ for bringing this letter to my attention.

Boyle's background: Gallwey; also rec, *Oxford Dictionary of National Biography*.

£4,200 ransom/pirate encounter: rec, Fitzgerald, Brian, p83 and p61, Coombes op. cit.

CHAPTER 7
'All Was Terror And Dismay'

French ship: Report.

Low profile: Haedo, Lane-Poole 224

Mainwaring quote: Discourse On Piracy, 1618.

Plodding: Dan in Lane-Poole p227.

TS quote: TS 8-10 (TS's book was ghost-written, and possibly incorporated authentic slave memoirs from more than one source.)

'In 1793 … ': Foss.

Morat/Holland: rec, Gosse 56-57, quoting Vrijman, L.C., Kaapvaart en Zeeroverij, Amsterdam 1938.

Brooks: Brooks p5.

Pitts: Pitts p302-3.

D'Aranda: Relation, 7.

'All was terror ... (etc)': Pananti 32ff.

Pinch, pull: Cathcart.

Searches: e.g., Pitts p302, Foss.

Coin swallower: i.e., Jean Foi Vaillant, 1632-1706; rec, Vieil Alger.

Rais confrontation: Foss and Pananti as above.

'All is brought ...' *Present State Of Algiers*.

Morat sank ship: Report.

CHAPTER 8

Desperate Men, Shameless Women

Hooke frustration, hunger, debt: CSPI 1625-32, pp622-625; June 19, July 23, Aug 24 letters.

Motley crew, drunken master, Tanner &c, soldier murder: CSPI 1625-32, p645, p664, p671.

Pressganged: eg CSPI 1642-56,377.

'Ragged beggars': rec, Senior 17.

'Since fourth ...': CSPI 1625-32 p623.

Whelps background: 'A List Of The King's Ships 1633' from Derrick, Charles, *Memoirs ... of the Royal Navy* (London 1806) 54-56; SP Dom 1625-54, 16/98; letter from Sir Guilford Slingsby 23/9/1628; SP Dom 1625-54, 16/173, all quoted in (rec) John Wassell's website on the Lions' Whelps, http://homepages.which.net/~j.wassell/whelps.htm. Also Smith 268. Rec, De Courcy pp145-6 and Fitzgerald, Brian op.cit. p63.

'Hooke complains ... ' : CSPI 1625-32, pp624-5.

Button background: rec, Thrush, Andrew, entry for Button in *Oxford Dictionary Of National Biography*; rec, De Courcy pp 142-4.

'Confederacy': CSPI 1608-10, lxx.

Not as criminals: eg, Easton and Ward 'kings', rec, Wilson p 52; Ward.

Jennings etc: CSPI 1608-10,p277 22/08/09

Four captains: CSPI 1603-06 p386; also CSPI 1611-14 lix-lxxi.

Danvers afraid: CSPI 1608-10 p130 and p100; CSPI 1611-14, lxi.

Easton Bishop, Leamcon fleet: CSPI 1611-14 lxv-lxviii; CSPI 1611-14, p99.

Vicar, jurors: rec, Senior p57.

Hull: CSPI 1625-32 p182; CSPI 1608-10 pp355-6; also rec, Senior p139.

Goods sold: CSPI 1618-25 p560, pp585-6.

Two bases: CSPI 1611-14 p238; CSPI 1611-14 lxix.

Ports razed: CSPI 1611-14 lxx

Estates America: CSPI 1611-14 lxvii; CSPI 1608-10 p278.

Cary plan: CSPI 1618-25, letter to Conwey 18/04/24.

Pirate hangout: CSPI 1611-14 lxix

Piracy not illegal: CSPI 1611-14 lxiii

Effect on Baltimore: rec, Senior p54

Alehouses: Kinsale, letter 6/8/1610; danger there, *Council Book Of Youghal* 1631 p171; rec, Senior p56.

Notting: rec, Senior, citing HCA report 18/8/1609.

King warned ... brawls: Kinsale letter 16/8/10

Prostitutes: Council Book Of Youghal 1630, p154; Mainwaring's Treatise On Pirates; De Courcy p144.

Robinson: rec, Senior p56 citing HCA 13/97/208

Pieces of eight: CSPI 1611-14 p99.

Spanish ship: CSPI 1608-10 p157.

Cheaply victualled: CSPI 1618-25 p480; also rec, Senior p53.

Held out: CSPI 1608-10 p277.

Steal cattle: Mainwaring, op. cit.

Crooke accused, cleared: CSPI 1606-08 p448; CSPI 1608-10 p100; rec, Senior p56.

Captain Williams: 1608-10 pp42-49.

Button's successes: De Courcy Ireland pp142-3.

CHAPTER 9
The Turning of Edward Fawlett

Overview: Morat's activities are based on the Report, with commentary. The Baker/Nutt document is from The Examination Of Hugh Baker, 22/5/1623 in the *Council Book Of Youghal* xlix. Final hours in Baltimore: see overview in ch 2 footnotes for sources behind my re-creation of a typical Sunday.

From Dartmouth: But the CSPI version of Report says Falmouth.

Fawlett's intimate knowledge: Report.

Pirates used local guides: Lane-Poole p202; Wilson p122; also rec, Cordingly's refs to Captain Woodes Rogers.

Torture: e.g., Pitts p 302, p342-3; Pananti p39; also rec, Senior pp16-17, Lucie-Smith p62, and Cordingly, various refs.

Sabbath ban not so strict: See refs in Boyle's diaries and Council Book Of Youghal; rec, 'The Politics Of The Protestants in Munster 1641-49', p1-20 in CHASJ lxxvi, July-Dec 1971.

St Ives: St Ives and Hayle tourist literature.

Typical menu: From menu of 21/8/1625, Southampton.

'Contentment general': Fitzgerald, Brian, p67 citing CSPI 1630.

Events at Old Head: Report.

'It had not … community at Baltimore': Mostly based on CSPI 1635, introductory section on Religious Toleration.

Influential report: i.e., from Francis Annesley, 1/4/1629.

Franciscan Church, nuns, friars: rec, Fitzgerald, Brian, pp 66-69.

'Lewd and … ': *Council Book of Youghal* p5.

Carbery sunset: Donovan pp95-6.

Castlehaven: Report.

CHAPTER 10
The Dreadful Hour

Overview: Main events based on Report.

Difficult entrance: Pacata Hibernia.

Eastern Hole: anecdotal. Also rec, John M. Feehan (1978) *The Secret Places of the West Cork Coast*, Cork: Royal Carbery Books, p94; and rec, Barnby, p116.

Oakum: some versions have '*sarambo*', a muffling cloth.

'Walked around' version: CSPI 1625-32 pp616+.

Circadian rhythm: This time also termed the 'circadian nadir'. For good overview, see www.shiftwork-resources.com

'Dread not death': Murad Rais before battle 1589, cited in Gosse.

'My falcons … ': From John Gillingham (trs) (1942) Die Geschichte von Kerkermeister-Kapitan, in *Acta Orientalia* xix, cited by (rec) Earle p230.

Verse: Davis.

Used noise: eg, Dan; Pananti pp32-33; Foss; Pitts; Lane-Poole p224; also rec, Senior pp21-22.

Scimitars, robes etc: Dan cited in Lane-Poole p224; Pananti p32; also rec, Earle p62.

'Storm them …:' See 'my falcons' above.

Blasphemies/devil: Rec, Cordingly quoting captive Philip Ashton. Also rec, Earle p151-7.

Best time to escape: *The Individual's Guide For Understanding And Surviving Terrorism* (US Marine Corps, Dept of Defence, 1999).

Rowlandson quote: Mary Rowlandson, *The Captivity And Restoration of [MR]* (Cambridge, Mass., 1682).

Loviot quote: Fanny Loviot, *A Lady's Captivity* (London, 1958), p62.

Capture shock: *Individual's Guide*, op. cit.

D'Aranda quote: D'Aranda, Relation, p8.

Carrigan quote: Mary Buce Carrigan, *Captured By Indians* (Minnesota, 1712).

'Anna' with children: List of captives in Report.

Value of slave haul: See discussion in ch 19.

CHAPTER 11
A Wretched Captivity

Overview: This chapter compares the Baltimore raid (source, Report) with Morat's earlier raid on Heimaey. The main sources for the latter are written in Icelandic – Ólafur Eigilsson's (1627) *Litil Saga Umm Herhlaup Tyrkjans* (Reykjavik, 1852) and the saga, *Tyrkjaranio a Islandi* (1627), Sogurit Vol. 4. More accessible is Knut Gjerset's *History Of Iceland* (Unwin, London, 1922), which on pp317-20 describes the Heimaey raid citing the Tyrkjaransaga as source. I also found helpful Katherine Scherman's (1976) *Iceland, Daughter Of Fire* (London: Little Brown), pp42-43, and Terry G. Lacy's (1998) *Ring Of Seasons* (Ann Arbor: University Of Michigan Press), pp 185-7, and I was also helped by modern tourist literature from the Westmann Islands.

'Many towns … ': Haedo cited in Lane-Poole p202.

'Morat was … was over'. Details from Report with comments. For e.g.s of corsairs lured into traps, rec, Earle p167.

Kill, maim etc: Rec, Scherman pp42-43.

Five ships, split up: rec, Lacy pp185-7.

Trio of vessels: rec, Gjerset pp317-20.

110 from Grindavik: rec, Lacy.

Method of landing: Westmann Island accounts.

Three hundred troops: rec, Gjerset.

Rape, mutilation etc: rec, Scherman.

Three assault units: rec, Gjerset.

Cave ordeal: Westmann Island accounts.

Cut in half, snap necks: rec, Scherman; also Eyjolfsson below.

'Anyone ... blood': Klaus Eyjolfsson (1584-1674), eyewitness, writing June 19, 1627.

Flames leaped ... beaten: Eyjolfsson and rec, Gjerset.

Warehouse: rec, Gjerset.

Number seized: rec, Gjerset and Lacy.

Wife and children: rec, Gjerset.

Gudridur: rec, Lacy.

Thirty-six to forty killed/four hundred slaves: Westmann Island accounts.

1898 report: i.e., Nelson Annandale on visit to Haemaey.

Elderly folk: e.g., interviewee on Atlantic Jihad.

Scandalise: rec, Gjerset and Earle.

Gentleman: rec, Gjerset p318.

Haedo quote: Haedo, op. cit.

Torture: For e.g.s of pirate behaviour during land raids, see Alexander Exquemelin's *History Of The Adventurers* (Paris 1686). Also, rec, Senior pp23-24.

Fugitives, Bennett: Report.

Salmon buying cloth: rec, Senior p56.

Carter's letter: Kinsale, 20/6/1631; also CSPI 1625-32 pp621+, 26/6/1631.

Glib: Spenser; rec, Berleth.

Tally of toll: Author's computation based on official list (see Preface notes).

'3-4 pm': Report.

Lords' letter: CSPI 1625-32, 11/2/1632 to English PC.

'Longer than they could … ': Report.

Murad in Lanzarote: Lane-Poole pp192-3; also rec, Gosse.

Sounds of departure: Richard Henry Dana, *Two Years Before The Mast*
London: 1841.

CHAPTER 12
Manifesting The Calamities

Dana quote: Dana, op. cit.

Captivity, The Extreme Circumstance: Navy non-resident training
course (May 2001).

Keenan quote: news conference, Dublin 30/8/1990.

Spratt: Diary; also reproduced in Seymour.

Pananti quote: Pananti p42

Loviot: Loviot op. cit., p83.

'As time passes': US Marine Corps *Guide*, op. cit.

'My thoughts ran … ': Rowlandson op. cit.

Jemison quote: *Narrative Of The Life of Mary Jemison* by James E.
Seaver (1824).

Carrigan: Carrigan op. cit.

'The morning sun … interrogated': Extrapolated from Report.

Panic/refugees: See aftermath correspondence in ch 18.

Sleeping conditions: cf experiences of Icelandic captives (Eigilsson
op. cit.).

Dana: Dana op. cit. pp17-22

Cleanliness … lice: cf Pananti, Foss, Cathcart. Rec, Cordingly.

Loviot: Op. cit., p104.

Pananti plague: p42.

Meanwhile … help itself: Report.

'Our clothes … ': Dana op. cit.

Toilets: Rec, Cordingly.

Hull, St Leger and Hooke letters: CSPI 1625-32, pp616-7.

'But the Turks … ': Report.

CHAPTER 13

A Bed Of Thorns

Fettered: cf. Spratt, Pitts.

Cathcart: James Leander Cathcart (1785), *The Captives* (published 1899).

Foss quote: Foss.

Pananti quotes: pp36, 39 ,42.

Put to work: cf. Foss.

Dana quote: Dana, op. cit.

Hugh Baker: Examination of [HB], 22/5/23, *Council Book Of Youghal* xlix.

Rawlins: Case quoted by Joseph Morgan; also rec, Clissold pp74-75.

Lurting: Thomas Lurting, *The Fighting Sailor* [etc]. London: 1771.

Nutt, Mrs Jones: Baker as above.

Pitts escape bid: Pitts p306.

Avery: Rec, Cordingly, Lucie-Smith.

O'Malley: Legend. Also rec, Anne Chambers *Grainuáile* Dublin: Merlin.

Woman reconciled: Cathcart.

Icelandic birth: The story of the Saengurkonusteinn, Westmann Islands.

Donated shirts: Olafur Eigilsson, op. cit.

Loviot quote: Loviot op. cit., p93.

CHAPTER 14

A Remedy For Grief

Gunter story: From the Letter Book Of Richard Boyle in Chatsworth. Rec, Barnby p124 and Wilson, p135.

Numbers seized at sea: Rec, Michael Oppenheim's *Maritime History Of Devon* (University Of Exeter, 1968). Also see CSPI 1611-14, introduction.

Mount's Bay raid: Rec, Milton p10, citing CSP (Devon) and CSP (Venetian) both 1625-6.

Penzance raid: Rec, Fisher, Appendix H.

Figures reliable?: See Fisher (above) who says State Papers have three conflicting reports of Penzance raid and two local histories don't mention it at all.

Sixty Mount's Bay, eighty Looe: Rec, Milton p10.

'Roguish pirates': Fisher as above.

'Unprecedented': CSPI 1625-32 p621-2, 10/7/1631.

Hull quote: CSPI 1625-32 p616, 21/6/1631.

William Thomas: PRO 71/1 folio 107, Dec 1631.

Boyle quote: Letter to PC, CSPI 1625-32, p645, 11/2/1632.

Beacons: Smith p268 and footnote.

Capt James: 1634. In CSPI 1647-60.

Boyle begged/blockhouse: CSPI 1625-32, p645, 11/2/1632.

Woodstock background: UK tourist literature. For more, rec,
    Oxfordshire Museum.

Tennis courts: Installed c.1630.

'This event ... ': CSPI 1625-32, p621, 10/7/1631.

'The invasion ... ': CSPI 1625-32, p627, 23/8/1631.

Hooke protected/Boyle letter to Dorchester: CSPI 1625-32, pp617-8,
    28/6/1631.

'Captain Hooke complains ... matter': CSPI 1625-32, p622, 14/7/1631.

Hooke's three letters: CSPI 1625-32, pp623-5, 19/7/1631 (x2) and
    23/7/1631.

'Later that summer ... far from over': Based on Hooke's recollection
    of the dialogue in CSPI 1625-32, p628, 24/8/1631. Quotes are
    indirect, but an accurate reflection of the exchange.

'Victualled for a month': As above.

CHAPTER 15
Black Paste And Putrid Water

Dana quote: Dana, op. cit.

Corsair schedule, no sleep: Foss.

D'Aranda: Relation, p8.

'It consisted ... pitcher': Pananti, pp 36 and 43.

Eat heartily: Foss.

'A ration ... obtained': De Busbecq, op. cit.

John Nutt's food: Hugh Baker op. cit.

Hotter/awnings: Rec, Gosse p313.

Livestock: Rec, Cordingly.

Multilingual: D'Aranda, Relation p8; also rec, De Courcy Ireland p141 citing Haedo.

Sabir: See notes in ch 28.

Cheerful inactivity of Janissaries/captain: Pananti p51; also rec Earle pp 28 and 36.

Invited to cabin: Pananti, Cathcart.

Pananti mellowed: p50-51.

Cathcart fruit, tobacco: Cathcart.

Ragged shirt: Foss.

Stockholm Syndrome: Summaries accessible to the layperson appear in the U.S. Marine Corps document *The Individual's Guide...*(op. cit.) and the *U.S. Navy's Captivity...*(op. cit.). For more, rec, Louis West's and Paul Martin's *Pseudo Identity And The Treatment Of Personality Change* (Guildford Press, 1994).

'Sexual' theory: H. H. Cooper, *Close Encounters Of The Unpleasant Kind* (USA 1978).

'Babyhood' theory: M. Symonds, *Victim Response To Terror* (USA, 1982).

Hooke letter: CSPI 1625-32, p628.

Plumleigh: De Courcy Ireland, p146.

CHAPTER 16
The Diamond City

Intro description of Algiers: Based on Pitts p308, Pétis p48, Russell pp314+ and Cathcart; Several contemporary graphics of Algiers from sea (e.g., Pétis) contain detailed explanatory codes.

Fourscore ships: Dan's estimate, 1634.

Put in irons: D'Aranda, Relation pp12-13.

Welcome gunfire: Pitts pp313-4; Lane-Poole p225.

D'Aranda quote: As above.

Throughout the city ... to the harbour: Pitts p307, Lane-Poole p225.

Arrival date: PRO 71/1 folio 157.

CHAPTER 17
Moving Next Door To Hell

Document in introduction: PRO 71/1 folio 157.

Frizell unhappy: PRO 71/1 folio 99.

Six years: He arrived 25/10/1625.

Slave numbers: PRO 71/1 folio 99 (ie, 340 less 109+24 taken by Morat = 207).

Frizell wrote regularly: PRO 71/1 records 1625-30.

Warning to Roe: Lane-Poole p265; rec, Gosse p54.

20,000 slaves: Rec, Spencer p127.

Dan's 25,000: Dan, also cited in Gosse p70.

Bypassed: Lane-Poole p267.

Frizell paid by ...: PRO 71/1 folio 99.

Salary dried up/starving: PRO 71/1 folios 102 and 99.

Ordeals of consuls: Playfair (1884); Lane-Poole p261.

Frizell depression, thraldom, neglected: PRO 71/1 folios 99 and 102.

Up 60 per cent: i.e., 207+133 (Folio 99).

Scenes at harbour: Composite of experiences of eyewitnesses featured in this book; also rec, Spencer p39.

Lowlife contingent: Haedo.

Cornish slave trader: T.S., pp17-18.

Frizell kind-hearted: In Folio 99 (op. cit.) he becomes emotional when he refers to the women and children.

Tallied numbers: PRO 71/1 folios 99 and 157.

Paraded to palace: Most sources report this ritual. D'Arvieux (V,p266) says it was routine.

Murad: Lane-Poole p193.

TS and weights: TS p22.

'We were paraded ...': Rec, Gosse p83.

Pananti quote: Pananti p66.

Past chain gangs: Cathcart, Foss.

La Consulaire: Vieil Alger, Le Port; also rec Lucie Smith p77, Clissold p128.

Alleyways, balconies: Russell p323; rec, Lewis p168 citing D'Arvieux V, pp221-7, Fisher p98, Spencer p35.

Algiers street scenes: Composite of contemporary descriptions; Russell pp322-3; Shaw p69; Pétis pp 46, 48, 66; rec, Spencer p38-39.

Many nationalties: Russell pp322-3; Shaw p69; Pétis pp7, 46-48 and 66.

Died from terror: *White Slaves, Pirate Gold*.
Heads displayed: Pananti p67.

CHAPTER 18
'A Good Prize! Prisoners! Slaves!'
Palace beautiful, descriptions: Pétis p49; TS p33; rec, Vieil Alger.
Wives choose: D'Aranda, *History*, Rn.3.
'His feet …': Joel Barlow, consul to Algiers 1795-97, cited in (rec)
    Spencer p65.
TS experience: TS pp 24-29.
Bichnin ploy: Lane-Poole p199.
Portuguese noble: D'Aranda, History, Rn 8.
Show trials: Pananti pp66-67. Also rec, Lucie-Smith pp76-79.
Pananti hearing: Pananti pp66-67.
Frizell argued: PRO 71/1 folio 141.
17th C. English diplomat: Rycault p16.
'The Pasha was normally …': Lane-Poole p236.
Entitled to 1/8 females: Fr Dan's figure. Although according to
    D'Arvieux (V, p266) and also *The Present State Of Algiers*, it was one
    in five; and TS says one in ten.
Only the best: D'Arvieux's words (above).
Tutsaklar, etc: rec, discussion on this in Spencer p112.
Dragged screaming: Dan pp276-77.
Rich women could avoid: rec, Spencer p113.
'Exultation and contempt': Pananti p68.

CHAPTER 19
The Slave Market
Fr Dan's report: Dan pp276-77.
Trinitarians, substitutes, uniform: Rec, *Encylopaedia Brittanica*, entry
    for Trinitarians; also rec Gosse p87.
Description of Badistan: Dan, Pitts p307, Lane-Poole p236, William
    Okeley: Ebenezer … London: 1675; rec, Gosse p75.
'As soon as … much the same': D'Arvieux V, pp 266-67.
Bon quotes: Bon, p162.

D'Aranda's auction: D'Aranda, Relation, p14.

Auction patter: Pitts p307.

Women privacy: Rec, Spencer p113 and Clissold p40.

Three classes: rec, Vieil Alger, The Slaves.

Ample and quote: Zara, Bassano Luigi da (1545), I Costumi &c

Pale Cornish women: Rec, Linda Colley *The Captives* (2002) London, Random House.

Prices fetched by Joane, Bessie, Ellen: Cason list.

Intimate examinations: Pitts p392; Hill; Nerval, Gerard (1851) *Le Voyage En Orient*, Paris.

'When there is a virgin … ' Bon, p163.

Hill quote: Hill p103.

Pitts on examinations: Pitts p392; Hill.

Nerval: As above.

'The value set …': D'Aranda, *History*, Rn 16, pp152-8.

Craftsman £46: Cason list.

Ransom 5x, 6x that: eg, Spratt.

Irish captive to Boyle: Boyle's Lismore papers, vol 3, p37.

Doctors: D'Aranda as above; Lane-Poole p243; rec, Gosse p71.

Prices of others: D'Aranda as above; Lane-Poole p243; Cason. Rec, Earle p34.

Glut: Lane-Poole p236.

'An Englishman … ': D'Aranda as above.

Currencies: D'Aranda references; rec, Vieil Alger, La Monnaie; and Spencer p111.

Dollar-pound conversion: It varied. I have taken 4s3d as a median between 4 shillings (Seymour) and 4s 6d (Cordingly). Allow for a 5% error margin.

Remarkable price list: i.e., list appended to Cason.

Clergyman £20: rec, Irwin.

Other wages and prices at home: rec, Fitzgerald, Brian, p58, McCarthy Murrogh p183 and Canny pp262-272.

Purchasing power today: Thanks to Economic History Services <http://eh.net/hmit/ppowerbp>

'After slaves are sold … ': *Present State of Algiers*, 1675; also Pitts, p308.

D'Aranda: Relation.

Shareout ratio: According to Fr Dan (rec, Wilson p146). The precise
figures vary. Cf., *Present State of Algiers* and rec, Vieil Alger, Les
Ésclaves; Spencer p49; De Courcy Ireland, p 141; and Earle pp 71-72.

Profits: Say 100 slaves (after Pasha's cut deducted) selling for at least
£27 each = £2700, or c.£250k today, minimum. Probably much
higher.

Mansions: Pétis p55; Shaw p71; rec, Earle pp35 and 259+.

Diplomat's daughter: Elizabeth Broughton (1840) *Six Years' Residence
In Algiers* (London); also rec, Earle p239.

Wild animals: Rec, Lucie-Smith p85; outlets, Lane-Poole p225, and,
rec, Spencer pp83-84.

Frizell petition: PRO 71/1 folio 99.

William Thomas: PRO 71/1 folio 104.

CHAPTER 20
Condemned To The Oar

'Hell': eg, D'Arvieux, see below.

4,000-900 and decline of galleys: Rec, Fisher p104; Spencer p116;
Lucie-Smith p77.

1640s tally: ie, Cason.

Sanders and Fox: works as cited in Bibliography.

Morgan: Joseph Morgan cited in Lane-Poole p215.

Bread etc: Lane-Poole p215; also rec, Gosse pp71-72.

De Bergerac: French slave quoted by Lane-Poole pp214-215.

No needles etc: Sanders, as above.

FitzPen: Memorial in St Mary's Church near Truro, Cornwall.

Slave share etc: Fr Dan; Pitts p313; also rec, Earle p88 and de Courcy
Ireland p141.

Decades at oar: Lane-Poole p215.

Earle case: In 1682. Earle p171.

'Free to walk … ': rec, Gosse, p313.

Fontimama story: D'Aranda, History, Rn. 16, pp152-8.

'Through reason of ill usage …:' Fox, above.

Fox barber: Fox, above.

D'Aranda in Morocco: History, Rn 7.

'The English … to freedom': Sanders and Fox.

CHAPTER 21

'Dog Of A Christian, To Work!'

Overview: My description of the bagnio is an amalgam of eyewitness accounts, particularly those of Pananti, D'Arvieux, D'Aranda, Sanders, Foss and Cathcart.

Circuit/building/gateway: Pananti p36.

Grand Bagnio details: Rec, Fisher p97; Earle p84; Lucie-Smith pp74-75.

Ryder enters ... (etc): Mostly D'Arvieux V, pp228-229.

Pork: Foss.

Pallid spectres: Pananti p68+.

Shaved: The Lamentable Cries ... (see ch 20). Also Capt. John Smith as cited in Charles D. Warner's (1881) *Captain John Smith* (Hartford).

Clothing: Pétis pp61-62; Pananti p88; Foss; Cathcart.

'No sooner ... ': Pananti p88.

Annual reissue: Foss.

'I do assure you ...' : Cason.

Metal ring/chain: Cathcart (who says 16 oz); Lane-Poole p241; D'Aranda Rn 3.

'Terrifying jails': D'Arvieux V, p229.

Bread: Foss.

Three loaves: Lane-Poole p241; Foss.

Guardian, bribery: D'Arvieux V, p229; Sanders; Cathcart; Foss.

Buy a cell place: Foss.

'In the unlikely ... betwixt us': All based on Sanders, op. cit.

Places of horror: D'Arvieux V, p229.

3am start: Cathcart.

Dawn march: Pananti pp74-75; Cathcart.

Slaves stealing: Cathcart.

Job allocations: Lane-Poole pp 241, 245; Foss; Cathcart.

Pepys: *Pepys's Diary* 6/2/1661.

TS: TS pp29-37.

Pulling ploughs: Lane-Poole p241.

Smith: From Warner, op. cit.

Quarry scenes: Foss; Lane-Poole p245; Cathcart.

'Figure …' quote: Cathcart.

Incentive/a third: Okeley, op. cit.; rec, Spencer p113.

Sleep in home: Pitts p360; Lane-Poole p251.

Warm relationships: Pitts p505; Okeley op. cit.; rec, Lewis p124.

Joyce: Anecdotal; also recounted in several Claddagh Ring websites; rec, Wilson p156, quoting J. Hardiman (1820); and Cecily Joyce's (1991) *The Claddagh Ring Story*, Clodóirí Lurgan Teo; also rec, De Courcy Ireland pp146-147.

Pipe of wine: D'Aranda, History, Rn 16 pp152-8.

Okeley: Okeley op. cit.; Lane-Poole p268; Seymour op. cit.; rec, Gosse p76.

French slave: Rec, Lewis p125, citing D'Arvieux IV, pp38-9.

Braithwaite: Told in John Braithwaite's *History Of The Revolutions in … Morocco* (1729). Rec, Milton pp145-6 and Clissold p100.

Cathcart: Cathcart.

Janissary post: D'Aranda as above; Pétis pp49 and 55; rec, Fisher p97.

Baths musician: Mouette, G. (1683) *Travels*; rec, Clissold p46, Lucie-Smith p75.

Sabir quotation: From Haedo, quoted in Sabir by Dr Alan Corré (see notes to ch 30).

Adultery punished: Pitts p360; Lane-Poole; rec, Spencer p83.

Algerian women attractive to slaves (dress, cosmetics etc.): Pitts p360; Russell; Foss; *The Captives*; rec, Spencer p74-75, Fisher p101.

Metal crown: Foss; rec, Spencer, above.

Widows, 'promises': rec, Lewis, p124.

CHAPTER 22
Beyond the Gate of Felicity

Intro: Rycault p32

Overview: Mainly based on the contemporary writers Rycault, Bon and Hill. Topkapi layout: Bon pp1-28, Hill pp168 (Map) and pp148-159; rec, Penzer pp154-61, Croutier p23. Roles and careers of women: Bon ch 4, pp 39-59; rec, Penzer p178, Croutier p33. Concubine selection and bedchamber rituals, Bon ch4 pp39-44, Hill pp 163-7. Careers of Murad, Ibrahim, Kiosem: Rycault pp3-89 (Murad) and pp1-35 (Ibrahim).

Reign of women: Rycault; rec, Croutier p140.

'Mr McDonell's … ': Sir Lambert Playfair; rec, Gosse p68.

Mrs Shaw: Told in John Braithwaite's (1729) *History of … Morocco*; rec, Milton pp230-1.

Brooks quote: Brooks, Barbarian Cruelty p35; rec, Clissold p90.

Expected to replenish: Bon, ch 4, p39

Size of palace: Hill p148.

4000: estimates vary; Bon (p39) says 2,000.

1,000 women/security: rec, BBC *The Ottoman Empire* 1300-1922.

Power structure: Bon ch 4; rec, *Encyclopaedia Britannica*, Penzer pp174-6.

Multinational women: Bon ch4, Hill; rec, Croutier p30.

Career women in harem: rec, BBC as above; rec, Croutier p30, Penzer p187.

Examined: Bon p39-41.

Kiosem: Rycault in Murad and Ibrahim.

Training of concubines: Bon p52; rec, Penzer p178.

Sought after: rec, Croutier p33.

Gesture: Hill p163; rec, Croutier p78.

Horseplay, fountains: Rycault, Ibrahim p13.

'They practise … ': Hill p163.

'When he is prepared … ': Bon pp 42-43.

Joyful: Bon p44.

Murad profile and anecdotes: Rycault.

Bedchamber ritual: Bon p43-44; Hill pp165-7.

Eunuch chorus: Hill p167.

Robes, jewel: Bon p44.

Bon 'nunnery': p40-41.

Hill on matrons etc: pp162-3.

Warm clothes, heaters: rec, Penzer p176.

Exercise: Bon p41, Hill p163.

Dallam quote: Dallam, T. (1599-1600) Early Voyages … London.

Spyglass: Rycault p43-49.

Eunuchs, beatings, sexuality: Bon p47, p74; rec, Croutier p135, p138.

Hammams: Bon ch 4.

Zara quote: Zara, p5.

Harem daily life: Bon pp75+ and pp154+, Hill.

Ibraham career: All Rycault except beard jewels (rec Penzer p189), stallion orgy (rec, TV documentary *The Harem* and rec, Penzer p189 citing Demetrius Cantemir (1734) *History Of The Ottoman Empire* and drownings (rec Croutier p112 and Penzer p186.)

CHAPTER 23
Through The Silk Tunnel

Prize catches: See ch 19.

Playfair: p121 cited in Fisher p257 and Clissold p90.

Glogg: Rec, Mini-Biographies of Scots and Scots Descendants, featured in www.electricScotland.com.

Fisher on two rulers: Fisher p101.

Lalla Sargetta/Mrs Shaw: Rec, The Alawi Dynasty-Genealogy featured in www.4dw.net/royalark/morocco. Mrs Shaw also mentioned in John Braithwaite's *History* ... (London 1729); rec, Milton p230-1; see ch 22.

Dawn Light: Moroccan tourist information services. Also rec, www.AfricanVacationGuide.com. For more on Abou El Hassan, rec, *Encyclopaedia Brittanica*.

Waited faithfully: e.g., mission reports of Fr Garcia. Rec, Clissold p122.

Gudrid's story: rec, Lacy pp185-187; steadfast in faith, rec, Atlantic Jihad; converted to Islam, rec, C. Venn Pilcher (1913) *The Passion Hymns Of Iceland*.

Embroidery skills/Pasha's wife: D'Aranda History, Rn 3.

Female domestics' lives. Rec, Fisher pp101-3.

Wedding rituals/home life: Foss; Pitts pp333-4; rec, Spencer p83; rec, Sharawi, Hudi (1965) *Harem Years*, London: Spring Books.

Nerval: Nerval, Gerard (1851) *Le Voyage En Orient*, Paris.

Balconies touch: Russell, p314, pp322-3; rec, Spencer p35.

Rooftop life: *The Captives*; rec, Spencer p37.

Routine/trips out: Pétis, p61; rec, Spencer p78, p89.

CHAPTER 24

The Children

Fifty: Report, Kinsale; see Appendix and notes to Preface.

Lock of hair: Pitts p392.

No bread, auctioneer's routine, return to Pasha: Pitts p307.

Davis: Sack of Baltimore, op. cit.

Very gallant: Cason.

Prized, accepted as family: eg, Pitts, Pellow.

Pasha's selection: eg, T.S. p29; D'Aranda *History*, Rn 3 (see ch 27); Cathcart.

Icelandic boy: Eigilsson; rec, *Atlantic Jihad*.

Pitts's biog: Pitts pp307-355.

Pellow biog: Pellow.

English diplomat: Brown intro to Pellow.

Paedophiles: Dan; T.S. p29; Pitts p323.

Marry at 13: rec, Spencer p80-83. Earl of Cork daughter: see Gallwey

Concubine training at early age: Hill.

Girl, 12, saved: *Journals of Fr Garcia Navarro*, cited in (rec) Clissold, pp121-2.

Maidservants/investments: See two cases below.

£100: Cason's list.

Montagu on page girls: Montagu, Lady Mary Wortley (1708) *Letters*. London.

Mrs Jones: Playfair; rec, Gosse p310.

Naksh: Life story originally told by 'Madame' de [thought to be Comtesse de] la Ferte Meune (1821) in *Lettres Sur Le Bosphore* ... 1816-1819, Paris; rec, Croutier pp121-3, who suggests that Naksh may have been Aimée Debusq de Ravery. Naksh's story was fictionalised by Barbara Chase-Riboud in the novel *Valide*, New York: William Morrow.

Abdulhamid I: rec, *Encyclopaedia Brittanica*; wikipedia.

CHAPTER 25

Cursed With Iscariot

Back home ... the King: CSPI 1625-32, p646, 27/1/1632.

King Charles ... soon: CSPI 1625-32, p642, 19/1/1632.

February 11 letter: CSPI 1625-32, p645, 11/2/1632.

Friends in high places: See ch 20.

Ship sank: See Capt. Popham's account in SP Dom 16.363.

Button final years: Rec, Andrew Thrush's biog of Button in *Oxford Dictionary Of National Biography*.

Boyle on borrowed time: His dominance was ended by Wentworth two years later; rec, Fitzgerald, Gallwey.

St Leger enemy: Rec, entry for Boyle in *Oxford Dictionary Of National Biography*.

Hackett trial: CSPI 1625-32 11/2/1632.

Hung on cliff: Donovan p22.

Davis quote: 'Sack Of Baltimore', op. cit.

Hawkridge: PRO 71/1, Folio 102, 1/12/1631.

Petition from slaves: PRO 71/1 Folio 104.

CHAPTER 26
The Sweetest Voice

Frizell letter: PRO 71/1 Folio 141.

Frogmartino: Others have written this as a nickname 'Job "Frog" Martino'. Having inspected the original document, I believe it to be a single surname.

Six ways out: Author's analysis; c.f., the five means of exit cited by Fisher, p103.

Wages and ransom examples: See ch 19.

Eleanor Walsh: CSPI 1647-60 p271.

Boyle's riches, dowry, quilt etc: rec, Brian Fitzgerald pp42, 50.

Gerald FitzGerald: Grosart, Lismore 3, p37.

Ransom process: See PRO 71/1 folio 171; rec, Earle pp86-89.

Comfortable house: Cathcart; rec, Spencer p114.

Gunter: Smith pp268+.

Levies, bribes, free card etc: Pitts p447; Spratt; Cason; rec, Vieil Alger.

Quarantine: Rec, Earle p90.

Ti star franco: Pananti pp74-75.

Hard work: eg, Joyce (see notes to ch 21).

'For instance ... Christian captive': Cathcart; Thomas Jefferson's (1790) *Report Concerning Barbary Pirates* citing 2:1 or 6:1 exchange rate; also rec, Earle pp88-90.

D'Aranda freedom: D'Aranda, Relation; rec, Clissold p104.

Relgious orders: Lane-Poole p251; Moore p37; also rec Gosse p87 and entries for Trinitarians and Mercedarians in *Encyclopaedia Brittanica*.

Redemption process: Lane-Poole 253+; rec Spencer p115. See also De Courcy Ireland p147.

1624 collection: rec, Gosse p85.

Kenelm Digby: See *Somerset Notes And Queries* vol 9, 1904-05, p203.

Charity list: Treasurer's Books in Rochester Cathedral 1541-1994.

Peace treaties: Lane-Poole pp257-8.

Gain edge over rivals: Lane-Poole p256.

Move along coast: eg, Algiers to Tripoli after USA deal 1798-1805.

Commons: Lane-Poole p267; rec, Gosse p85.

'Supplication': Somerset and Dorset Notes, above.

1633 document: PRO 71/1 Folio 100.

For two centuries: ie, until Exmouth's victory in 1816; Lane-Poole p259.

CHAPTER 27

Apostasy Now

'Divers' etc: Cason.

Per force: Frizell in PRO 71/1 Folio 141.

Pictures of scenes: eg, in Dan and d'Aranda.

Haedo 3 reasons: Haedo; rec, Earle p92.

Rawlins and Sandys: Rec, Nabil Matar's (1999) *Islam in Britain 1558-1685* Cambridge: Un. Press.

Pellow: Pellow.

Pitts beaten, not common: p393.

300 blows: D'Aranda History Rn 3.

Cathcart trickery: Cathcart.

Voluntary converts, migrants: 5000 in Algiers alone; rec, Wilson's book on renegadoes; and discussion in Lucie-Smith.

Bichnin: Lane-Poole; rec, Wilson pp44-45 and Spencer p88.

Nelson, Bishop: Rec, Matar above.

Myths, infamous: Pitts p457.

Pasha and boy: D'Aranda *History* Rn 3.

Sanders/Frenchman: Sanders.

Greatest corsairs renegadoes: Dan; eg, Ward, Easton, Danser, Morat.

Could become successful soldiers: eg, Pellow, Pitts.

'What I love...': Interviewed by Fiona Ryan in *Irish Times* 5/5/2001.

No property rights: rec, Fisher p102.

Religious tolerance: rec, Fisher.

'It is true ... too much': D'Arvieux V, 3-4.

Metal hooks: D'Arvieux V 273-5; Pétis p47.

Visitor, hooks: i.e., Joseph Morgan.

Geronimo: Haedo; rec, *Encyclopaedia Brittanica*.

CHAPTER 28
Fleeing The Pirates' Nest

Overview: Spratt's experiences are based on his own diary (Spratt) and
the book by his friend Okeley. Also rec, Seymour (pp9-12) and
Courtenay; and see Lane-Poole p266. Okeley's own escape story is
also featured in (rec) Gosse pp77-78.

Holy Trinity: Courtenay; also rec, *Encyclopaedia Brittanica*.

Calming mantra: This fascinating 'slave lullaby' from Haedo (1610) is
drawn from Prof. Alan D. Corré's website on Lingua Franca (Sabir)
at www.uwm.edu/~corre/franca.go.html; highly recommended.

Spratt's marriages/baptisms: Lane-Poole p266.

Okeley in earlier chapter: ie, ch 21.

Mitchelstown: He was rector in St George's Parish Church at Brigstown.
Also rec, Bill Power's (2004) *Evensong* (Mount Cashell Books).

Pananti on escape: Pananti p356.

John Smith: in Charles D. Warner (see notes to ch 21).

Portuguese: Playfair; rec, Clissold p81.

McDonell escape: Rec, *Encyclopaedia Brittanica*; also rec, Gosse p 67.

Rudders: Pitts p313; Lane-Poole p225.

Galley hijack: Lane-Poole pp268-9.

Roots, snails: e.g., Thomas Phelps (1685) *Account of Captivity*, London.

Mule, punishments: Pitts p507.

Cervantes: rec, Cervantes digital library
www.csdl.tamu.edu/Cervantes; Lane-Poole p246-8; also Gosse p82.

CHAPTER 29
Bagnio Days, Bagnio Nights
Overview: All the D'Aranda references from *History*, Rn 16, pp152-8.

Universities for life: D'Aranda.

Pork sausage: eg, Foss.

Transition call: Cathcart.

'The main bagnios ... make deals': D'Arvieux IV pp3-4.

Guardian Bachi, chapel: D'Arvieux V p229.

Private bagnio/vines: Lane-Poole p195.

Bichnin feast: Lane-Poole pp195-6.

Refused to feed: D'Aranda; Lane-Poole p196.

Blows of a stick: Rec, Lewis p168.

Diamond: Lane-Poole p196.

Thieving slaves: D'Arvieux V p229+; D'Aranda.

Fontimama's scam: D'Aranda.

Bribe guardian: e.g., Foss, Cathcart.

Okeley tobacco: Okeley.

Taverns: Cathcart.

Sausages: Foss.

CHAPTER 30
Habituated To Bondage
Frizell 1634 petition: PRO 71/1, Folio 141.

1637 petition: PRO 71/1, Folio 99.

'Yet according to ...': ie, Cason.

'So habituated ...': Okeley.

Mini-Constantinople: Rec, Spencer p28.

'The city of Algiers ...': *The Captives* (1804).

City layout: Pétis pp45-48; Shaw pp68-69; also rec, Spencer p29+; Fisher p97.

Narrow: Russell p320-2; rec, Spencer p35, Fisher p98.

Healthy, clean, water: Pétis p46-8; Shaw p72; Cathcart; also rec Spencer pp28-32, Fisher p98.

Foolish conceit: ie, Grammaye, cited in Fisher p98.

Medicine: Rec, Ibrahim B. Syed's 'Islamic Medicine, 1000 Years Ahead Of Its Time' in www.islam.usa.com

Smallpox: Lady Mary Wortley Montagu (1689-1762) brought the
   practice of vaccination back to England. See her Letters, London,
   1837.

Crops: Pétis p55; also rec Fisher pp98-99, Spencer pp98-100.

Climate: Foss.

Healthier, longer lived: Rec, Fisher p98 and p101.

Sneers: Quote from The Captives (1804).

Menu: Pétis p61.

Time off: Pitts p443 and p360; Lane-Poole; rec, Fisher p103.

Visit bathhouses etc: Pétis p50; rec, Fisher p99.

Music: rec, Spencer pp85-86.

Sabir: Rec, Alan Corré website, see ch 28.

Alcohol common: Pitts p322.

Opium story: D'Aranda History.

Licensed brothels: Rec Spencer, p95.

'Two whores': From journals of Thomas Baker 1677-85; rec, C. R.
   Pennell's (ed) (1989) *Piracy And Diplomacy*, Associated University
   Press.

Justice, penalties: Pétis pp 47-8; Pitts p306, p360,p507; rec, Spencer
   92-96.

Life in Algiers ... eight governors: Rec, Vieil Alger, History;
   Lucie-Smith p77; Lane-Poole p194; Rycault.

Feast days: Pitts p445; rec Spencer p87.

Amusements: Pitts p443, p445; D'Aranda History p152-8; also rec
   Spencer p87 and Lewis p161-2, citing D'Arvieux V p157.

Women's life: Pétis p61; rec, Spencer p78, Fisher p99.

September 1646: See ch 31.

CHAPTERS 31-32
The Redemption of Captives & Homeward Bound

Most of these chapters are directly drawn from Cason.

Waite quote: ABC tv interview 3/11/86.

'Hearts were joy': Foss.

Rowlandson quote: Rowlandson op. cit.

Entebbe: Rec, Operation Entebbe in wikipedia.

Shoving,in Divan: Rycault (first quote), p75, Murad; Francis Knight (second quote), cited in Wilson p36.

Note on Joane Broadbrook: We know for certain that a Mrs Broadbrook, pregnant wife of Stephen and mother of two little children, was abducted by Morat. 'Joane Broadbrook of Baltamore' is listed among the captives redeemed by Cason. In my opinion, the unusual name and the specific location makes it certain that this was the same woman. It has been suggested that the ransomed person could have been a daughter of Mrs Broadbrook (which is assuming her children were girls), but, in my view, the sale price rules out this possibility: female children were in high demand and would have fetched a much higher sum (see Cason). Besides, someone who had been raised from childhood to adulthood in the culture of Algiers would hardly have been interested in returning, alone, to an Ireland she hardly remembered after fifteen years.

Parent goes, child remains: eg, Gudrid (see ch 23).

'Mary's' ransom: PRO 71/1 Folio 135.

Healthy place: Rec, Fisher p98; also rec, *Encyclopaedia Brittanica*.

Average lifespan: Actually fifty-nine years. Rec discussion on seventeenth-century life expectancy in 'Did They All Die Young?' in www.plimoth.org

Many embraced Islam: PRO 71/1 Folio 135.

De Courcy Ireland: p146.

Barnby: p129.

Stockholm Syndrome: See discussion in ch 15 and ch 32.

List of factors: *Individual's Guide For Understanding And Surviving Terrorism* (see notes to ch 10).

Thomas Shirley: rec, Matar op. cit. (see ch 27).

'No notice ...': Cathcart.

Pseudo ID: Louis West and Paul R. Martin, op. cit. (see ch notes in ch 15 and 32)

Aid captors: eg, Patty Hearst cited in West and Martin above.

'The devil ...': Pitts P505.

Two women 'transfer': Rec, Earle p91.

Mary Jemison: Jemison, op. cit. (see ch 12.)

'Poor slaves', shackles heavier: *Treasurer's Book*, Rochester; rec Clissold p116.

Lady Mary quote: Lady Mary Montagu (1837) Letters, London.

CHAPTER 33
The Legacy of Baltimore

De Courcy Ireland story: I have heard several versions of this. (One appeared in the *Irish Times*.) J.D.C.I himself refers to the red-hair phenomenon in (rec) De Courcy Ireland p146.

Morat, autumn 1631: PRO SP Foreign and Barbary States vol xiii, 29/11/31, cited in Castries.

Morat capture: Dan; rec, Gosse pp57-58.

Morat's retirement home: *A Brief Relation* etc (1638) cited in Castries pp 485-6.

Lysbeth: Rec, Gosse pp57-8; 'great pomp' quote from touring artist who accompanied Lysbeth in 1641, rec, *Atlantic Jihad* and Gosse p58.

'End very bad': Rec, Gosse p58.

Morat's American descendants: My main source was 'The Van Salee Family', an article by genealogist and researcher Mario de Valdes y Cocom arising out of his Frontline TV documentary on the Public Broadcasting Service (www.pbs.org). Also recommended reading is the lively correspondence among Van Sallee descendants on www.genealogy.com. Sheer distance, and my lack of expertise in the minutiae of genealogical research has prevented me from following up this intriguing topic as it deserves. But articles recommended to me were: Hershkowitz, Leo, 'The Troublesome Turk' [ie, Anthony V.S.] in *The Quarterly Journal of the New York Historical Association* Vol XLVI no 4, Oct 1965; and 'Early Southards Of New York And New Jersey' in the *New York Genealogical And Biographical Record* Vol 103, p16. I would be interested in further information.

Smith quote on Baltimore: Smith p268+.

Miserable collection: rec, O'Flanagan, 'Town And Village Life' in O'Flanagan, p413.

No house could pay tax: Rec, O'Flanagan as above, p426.

Rotten borough: Donovan p23

Increasing rapidly in 1837: *Lewis's Topographical Dictionary*.

Famine ships etc: Rec, Patrick Hickey, 'Famine In West Cork', in
O'Flanagan, p907.

Reuter, 'Baltimore never recovered ...:' Donovan p23.

'Agony ...:' J. E. O'Mahony.

Fishing, shipbuilding: rec, Seamus Fitzgerald.

Property hunters: *Sunday Times* (24/8/2003) 'Cork's Holiday Homes
Romance Turns Sour'.

US Declaration influenced?: rec, discussion in Muslim Spain
(21/11/02) in BBC Radio 4 history series *In Our Time*.

Stubbe, Robert Boyle: rec, Matar op. cit. (see ch 27).

Ship money (general): rec, *Encyclopaedia Brittanica* entries for Ship
Money and Hampden.

Influence of Baltimore raid: rec, Kingston p58.

CHAPTER 34

The Three Knights

Liam Irwin quote from Politics, Religion etc

'The allegation ...' From tourist website www.Baltimore-ireland.com

'As the pirates ...' From website
www.12travel.co.uk/ie/corkkerry/Baltimore.html.

'Some believe ...' *The AA Guide To Ireland*.

Gray/Edinburgh: From notes by Robert Brown to Pellow.

Bono refs: rec, Salvatore Bono, *I Corsari Barbareschi* (Torino, 1964).
Also rec Earle p62 and p282.

None saints: e.g., rec, Healy, 'none were angels'.

Spenser quote: Spenser.

World shifting, etc: rec, O'Flanagan p173, Berleth.

Waterford disputes: Genealogy pp93-95; Donovan, pp47-49; Gibson
p519.

Rebuilt: rec, Kingston, who says castles built mid-1500s.

Carraghs: Genealogy; 1608-09 Inquisition; rec, Kingston pp47-48
Burke, Healy (who says Carragh's claim to superiority was correct).

Fishing levies: Genealogy pp99-100; Donovan p102; rec, Phelan p33.

English entrepreneurs: rec, E. O'Mahony, quoting CSPI 1509-73,
p523.

Asked Perrot: CSPI 1571-75, item 471, SP 63/69 no 50.

Perrot's comment: ibid, item 721.

Fineen's next petition: ibid, item 699.

Neutral stance: Yet he received a general pardon (rec, Kingston p24, E. O'Mahony).

Enthusiastic loyalty: Numerous refs in CSPI 1586-88; rec, E. O'Mahony, who cites cases.

Invited to Parliament/took his lands: *Annals Of Four Masters*; Genealogy, Note in Herald College; rec, Coleman.

Tight English clothing: D.A. Chart (1907), *The Story Of Dublin* London: J. M. Dent.

Fenton: 1586 survey by Geoffrey Fenton.

Sheriff: rec, Healy, Burke.

Conor clash: See ch 4.

'Ancient civil …': CSPI 1601-03, p235

'The poor old …': Ibid, Carew to Cecil 1602.

Generous host/silver well: Smith; Genealogy p390; Donovan p101-2; rec, Kingston p54, Healy.

'All kind and mild …': *Pacata Hibernia* in Genealogy p390.

'Never in the course …': ibid p387.

'Very odious': ibid p390.

Pardon, invitation to London: ibid p390; Smith; Donovan p102; rec, Healy.

Penniless: He soon had to borrow; also rec, Kingston p54.

Servant intruded: Smith; Genealogy p390; Donovan p102.

Russian nobleman/yardarm/dungeon: Donovan pp210-11; also rec, Kingston p56.

Jeanette Grant: Case dated 1630 in CSPI 1647-60, p168.

Ellen ni Driscoll: ibid.

Viking stock: Copinger.

Eight mayors: rec, Brady, p100.

Page to Raleigh: rec, Kingston p50.

Servants in gold: rec, documentary *Elizabeth's Pirates* (Channel 4, 2001).

Page to Fineen: Donovan p208.

Made a fortune: Donovan pp208-9; Kingston p54.

Confusion over loans: e.g., McCarthy Oldcourt dispute (Copinger) and

Fineen mortgage dispute (Smith, Copinger); rec also Kingston p51. (Further complicated because a mortgage meant different things in Irish/English laws).

Cloughane: Copinger; rec, Kingston p50.

Church fine: CSPI 1606-08, xciii.

Assisted English: He guided Percy to Kilcoe Castle, 1600.

East India episode: CSPI 1611-14 p369+; rec, McCarthy Morrogh p179, de Courcy Ireland, pp128-9.

Rowry project: Copinger; Donovan.

Ships built: rec, De Courcy Ireland, p129.

Descendents insurgents: Family tree in Copinger.

Bishop quote on Crooke: CSPI 1608-10, p100.

Fellow leaders: CSPI 1618-25, p190.

Third motive: Various commentators, e.g., rec, E. O'Mahony.

Crooke cleared: See later notes.

Influential testimony: CSPI 1608-10, p29.

Zero to £200: CSPI 1647-60, p81.

Clive Senior refs: rec, Senior, pp 56-7.

Remainder of this chapter: CSPI 1608-10, pp42-43, p100.

CHAPTER 35
Endgame

Beginning quote: Copinger, 1608 deed.

1600 lease: Genealogy. Produced at an inquisition in 1608. Also rec, Kingston p47.

Voided agreement: Donovan p22.

Few Irish: CSPI 1606-08, p571.

Conditional letting: Genealogy; rec, Kingston pp46-47, Coleman.

Regrant to Crooke: rec, Kingston p46.

Dispute with Carraghs/rulings/Coppinger role: Genealogy, pp99-100, 1608 inquisition; Donovan p102; rec, Kingston p48, Burke.

Coppinger-Carragh pact: Copinger, 1608 deed; rec, Healy, Kingston p51 (but my interpretation).

Contrasting clothes: rec, McCarthy Morrogh, p188.

Quote from deed: Copinger, 1608 deed.

'Coppinger was on familiar ...' &c: CSPI 1615-25,pp190-1; Copinger.

'After a complex ...' &c: Copinger; rec, Kingston p51.

£2000: Smith; Genealogy p390.

Improvements: Smith p268+; CSPI 1615-25, pp190-1; changes also shown on Map.

Improving tenant: rec, Canny in O'Flanagan, pp265-70.

'Breaking the rocks ...' 1641 depositions, Hull at Leamcon (TCD); also rec CHASJ LII pp55-68.

Smith quote/new houses etc.: Smith p268.

Borough: Kinsale.

'Despite the twenty-one-year ...' &c: Copinger; CSPI 1615-25, pp190-91; also rec, Kingston p52.

Plea to King: CSPI 1647-60, p81; CSPI 1608-10, p100.

Fineen borrowing: Copinger.

Conor and exiles: see notes to ch 4.

Fishing: Smith vol 2 pp310-11; rec, Arthur Went in CHASJ vol 51 1946.

Value and scope of fishing markets: Depositions of Sir William Hull at Leamcon, 1641; CSPI 1634, introduction; also rec, Canny op. cit., p262, O'Flanagan p398; De Courcy Ireland pp125-6; CHASJ LII pp55-68.

Coppinger backs Fineen: Smith.

Eviction: Donovan p22.

Nature of loan, ruling, agreement: Smith; Copinger; rec, Kingston p53, Samuel.

'Meanwhile ... matters among themselves': Smith p268+; Copinger; Donovan p103 and p209; rec, J.E. O'Mahony.

Verse: Donovan p104.

Earl's quote 'It appears ...': CSPI 1625-32, Boyle letter 11/2/31.

Shoals vanished: rec, O'Flanagan p398+.

Leased castle: rec, Kingston p53 (ironically, he leased it to a planter).

Wealthy: Donovan p208.

Hired muscle: e.g., Dundaniel.

Kingston on tales of wealth: rec, Kingston p57.

Wilson: rec, Wilson p122.

Offered to renounce: See ch 4.

Tit for tat: rec, Lucie Smith p79.

List of ancient deeds: i.e., Genealogy.

Mansfield revenge: rec, Peter Earle (1981) *The Sack Of Panama* New York: Viking.

Crucial date: Genealogy. While I have seen no reference to this coincidence of dates in the course of my research, I would be surprised if it has escaped notice. I would be happy to acknowledge any previous reference.

APPENDIX *The Taken*

List From Kinsale.

Picture Credits

The Sultan's Grand Seraglio and harem from the sea: From Hill, pp146-147. Reproduced with the kind permission of the Governors and Guardians of Archbishop Marsh's Library, Dublin.

Barbary slave galley: Reproduced from website www.algerie.info. Thanks to Frederic Messud.

'Alger', picture map of 1600s Algiers with reference key to fortresses and gates: From Pétis de La Croix, p45. Reproduced with the kind permission of the Governors and Guardians of Archbishop Marsh's Library, Dublin.

The Mole at Algiers harbour in the 1600s: From Pétis de La Croix, p51. Reproduced with the kind permission of the Governors and Guardians of Archbishop Marsh's Library, Dublin.

Admiral's galley: From Furttenbach, J. (1629) *Architectura Navellis*, Ulm.

Plan of Sultan's Seraglio: From Hill, p168. Reproduced with the kind permission of the Governors and Guardians of Archbishop Marsh's Library, Dublin.

Street in Algiers: From Russell, p324. Reproduced with the kind permission of the Governors and Guardians of Archbishop Marsh's Library, Dublin.

Front cover:

Main image: *An Action off the Barbary Coast with Galleys and English Ships* by Willem van de Welde the Younger / Yale Center for British Art, Paul Mellon Collection, United States / The Bridgeman Art Library International. Tile border: i Stockphoto.

Back cover:

Baltimore Picture Map, see Picture Section Credits. Tile border: i Stockphoto.

Every effort has been made to contact copyright holders; if, however, any infringement has inadvertently occurred we request the owners of such copyright to contact the publishers.